OUR BOYS IN BLUE AND GOLD

OUR BOYS IN BLUE AND GOLD

A CHRONICLE OF ZIPS FOOTBALL

EDITED BY TARA KALOZ

Ringtaw Books
Akron, Ohio

13 12 11 10 09 5 4 3 2 1

LIBRARY OF CONGRESS CATALOGING-IN-PUBLICATION DATA
Our boys in blue and gold : a chronicle of Zips football / edited by Tara Kaloz.

p. cm.

ISBN 978-1-931968-64-5 (pbk. : alk. paper)

1. University of Akron—Football—History. 2. Akron Zips (Football team)—History. I. Kaloz, Tara.

GV958.U516094 2009

796.332'630977136--DC22

2009028389

The paper used in this publication meets the minimum requirements of American National Standard for Information Sciences—Permanence of Paper for Printed Library Materials, ANSI Z39.48–1984. ∞

All material reproduced in this book, unless otherwise noted, is property of *The Buchtelite* and used with permission.

Cover design by Dave Lam.

Cover images courtesy of The University of Akron Department of Intercollegiate Athletics. Back cover photos by Bob Wilkey, courtesy of The University of Akron Department of Intercollegiate Athletics. Frontispiece top photo courtesy of The University of Akron Department of Intercollegiate Athletics, bottom photo by Bob Wilkey, courtesy of The University of Akron Department of Intercollegiate Athletics. Table of contents photo courtesy of The University of Akron Department of Intercollegiate Athletics. Chapters 1–4 opening photos from the Library of Congress, public domain. Chapters 5–11 opening photos from *Tel-Buch*, courtesy of Archival Services, University Libraries, The University of Akron. Chapter 12 opening photo courtesy of The University of Akron Department of Intercollegiate Athletics. Appendix opening photo by the University of Akron Press, courtesy of Archival Services, University Libraries, The University of Akron.

The interior was designed and typeset by Amy Freels, with help from Amanda Gilliland. The type was set in Bembo and Optima, with Bank Gothic display. The book was printed and bound by BookMasters of Ashland, Ohio.

Disclaimer: Every effort has been made to verify all facts and data. The stories have been reproduced as they originally appeared. Over the course of decades, spelling, grammar, punctuation, and style have changed. We chose to make minimal alterations and adjust content only when absolutely necessary.

CONTENTS

Alma Mater

Close beside Cuyahoga's waters, Stream of amber hue,
O'er old Buchtel, Summit's glory, Waves the gold and blue.
Hail we Akron! Sound her praises, Speed them on the gale;
Ever stand our Alma Mater, Akron, hail, all hail!

Akron Blue and Gold

(The University of Akron Fight Song)

We cheer the Akron Blue and Gold,
We cheer as the colors unfold,
We pledge anew we're all for you,
As the team goes crashing through,
FIGHT! FIGHT!

We cheer the Akron warriors bold,
For a fight that's a sight to behold,
So we stand up, and cheer and shout
For the Akron Blue and Gold.
Zzzip! Zip go the Zippers!
Zzzip! Zip go the Zippers!
Akron U Gold and Blue,
All for you and the Zippers too!

ACKNOWLEDGMENTS

Throughout the course of the book's compilation, I relied on the help of many people and departments at The University of Akron, without which this book would not have been possible. I cannot say how much I appreciate all of the assistance and support that has been given and would especially like to thank:

The University of Akron Archives and its staff for their extensive hours of assistance as well as the permission to use their multiple and varied resources. All copies of *The Buchtelite* and *Tel-Buch* used as well as many of the photographs herein were located in the Archives. Thank you to the Archives employees and students who assisted with this project, especially Vic Fleischer, Craig Holbert, Mark Bloom, and Amanda Blackford.

The University of Akron Department of Intercollegiate Athletics, especially Mike Cawood, for their assistance and the use of information from their annual media guides, websites, files, and photographic resources.

The Buchtelite and Bruce Zake for the use of all articles and images reproduced from newspaper.

All photographers, including Bob Wilkey, Russell D. Sibert, Tobias Studio, Jeff Harwell, and John Ashley for the reproduction of their works.

Jim Tressel for graciously providing the wonderful foreword to this book.

Robert D. Jorgensen, Director of University Bands, for providing the history of the marching band.

Akron Magazine for the use of the article on John Heisman and the article about Zippy, the 2007 Capital One Mascot Challenge champion.

The Departments of Institutional Marketing and Student Affairs for their assistance.

The current head coach of The University of Akron Zips, J.D. Brookhart, for his assistance and support.

Of course, the University of Akron Press for their countless hours of assistance, guidance, and support, especially Thomas Bacher, Paul Evans, Amy Freels, Amanda Gilliland, Shurice Gross, Carol Slatter, Kaitlin Trushel, Daniel Von Holten, and Myles Wallace.

PREFACE

This project began, as all worthwhile projects, with an idea: outline the history of The University of Akron's football team from 1891 to the present. I hoped to discover the authentic pieces of a gridiron chronology. Akron initially competed as Buchtel College (1891–1913) before playing as The University of Akron for the first time in 1914. Through the 1973 season, the team competed in the NCAA College Division. In 1974, The University of Akron moved to Division II and then, in 1980, became a Division I-AA program. Gerry Faust coached Akron's first season as a Division I-A school in 1987. In 1992, the team joined the Mid-American Conference.

My journey was one of trekking to the University's Archives over the course of several months. The Archives contained nearly all of the articles except for the ones provided by the Athletics department. Throughout my countless hours of research, I tried to find stories about games both remarkable and ordinary, wins and losses. A true story depicts triumphs as well as obstacles young athletes face along the way.

Reading the articles certainly gave me a sense of pride in the University and its football team, and also provided a valuable case study in how newspapers have changed over time. The older *Buchtelites* were packed with articles, cartoons from all over the map, witticisms and jokes, ads for various items, services, and even smokes. It was especially interesting to note the differences in language and word choice, which you will discover just as I did. There is more tradition imbued in the Akron Blue and Gold than I had ever realized. Akron's team has survived war, handed out its fair share of upsets, been upset, but always showed up the following Saturday. There is truly no such thing as defeat for the Akron team. They are the Zips; they were "our boys," and they always will be.

As any true follower of the sport knows, a team is also shaped by its fans, its rivals, and its coaches. There were many trips to distant cities in neighboring states for the sake of the game. Over time, the uniforms changed; leather helmets evolved into engineered headgear; the size and shape of the football varied over time; rules were evaluated and modified; and the opinions of the sport became more accepting.

Within these pages, you'll find games featuring prominent names from recent years such as Charlie Frye and Jason Taylor, as well as those of the past—John Heisman played quarterback during his brief time here in Akron. There are rivalries with Wooster, Kent State, and Western Reserve; notable Bowl opponents like Louisiana Tech, quarterbacked by future hall-of-famer, Terry Bradshaw; traditions such as the Cowbell, Wagon Wheel, and Acme-Zip games. Relive the final seconds and close calls with nationally-ranked opponents. Find out the origin of "The Zips" and how Zippy turned into a champion among mascots. Learn about the marching band and cheerleading. Follow the team from Buchtel Field to the Rubber Bowl, from natural grass and muddy quagmires to synthetic surfaces.

The new home of the Zips, InfoCision Stadium-Summa Field, provides a fresh beginning for the team, another chance for the football program to reinvent itself, to add to the legacy that began over a century ago. The location of the new stadium brings the program back to the heart of campus. One fact is certain, more landmark games and memorable moments are in store for our boys in blue and gold and more pages will be added to their history.

FOREWORD

It is with great humility and emotion that I attempt to contribute the foreword to this publication of Zip football history.

I have lived through and observed the extraordinary growth of Akron football. As a youngster watching my Dad's B-W teams compete in the OAC versus the Zips, and then having the privilege of coaching at UA under the tutelage of the legendary mentors, Gordon Larson and Jim Dennison, as they moved the Zips from "small college football" into Division II then Division I-AA.

I have so many vivid memories of four of the most formative years of my coaching career. Living in Buchtel Field House as a Graduate Assistant. The thrill of coaching my first collegiate game in the Acme Zip game versus Marshall, enduring the tragedy and sadness of the death of Chris Angeloff in that very same game. Our last minute victory over Temple on a third down TD pass from Tom Kot to Glenn Evans. Play-off victories over UNLV and Northern Michigan, followed by a trip to the National Championship game in the Pioneer Bowl. There is no question that the years I spent at Akron set the stage for every opportunity that would follow.

Then competing against the Gerry Faust teams as they entered the Division I ranks, and admiring the progress that Lee Owens and his staff made at the turn of this century. J.D. Brookhart has taken the Zips to the MAC championship and our first ever bowl game . . . now the new stadium! Wow, from John Heisman to the present, what a success story that every Zip needs to read!

Jim Tressel
Head Coach, The Ohio State University

THE BUCHTELITE.

A WEEKLY NEWSPAPER.—ESTABLISHED 1889

. V. BUCHTEL COLLEGE, AKRON, O., NOVEMBER 21, 1893.

WORTH NOTICING.

is a significant fact that of our ty-three Seniors, ten wear ses, and only one of this number e them upon entering college.

t least twelve different states are esented in the attendance at ite!, the most western being Col- o and the most eastern Vermont.

he smallest class that ever grad- d from the college was that of ; which had only one member; largest, those of '87 and '93, h had nineteen members each.

uchtel has graduated more law- than any other professional men. chers are almost as plentiful, and in order, though far inferior in ber, come manufacturers, clergy- and doctors.

it be true that you can find the x to a man's character in the s he reads, there may be food reflection in the fact that the *ing* is the best read magazine in ibrary. After the daily papers, *per's Weekly* is the favorite news- er.

uchtel College can claim the dis- ion of having for one of her ents Albert C. White, who was youngest soldier in the Union y. Mr. White enlisted as drum- boy at the age of nine. He en- d Buchtel in '73 and is now a gyman preaching in Massa- etts.

he list of the alumni of Buchtel ege shows the names of exactly e as many men as women. ut one-third of the women who e been graduated have never ried. In connection with this, it teresting to note that there are resent six more girls than boys ne collegiate department.

A Plea for Examinations.

ome years ago a great outcry was ed against term examinations. y were denounced as worse than ess and the warfare has resulted eir abolition in the majority of ools and colleges. If we are tly informed, most of the pro- onal schools adhere to the ex- nation system.

he writer, for one, has no faith e educational advantages of the grading system. Under this *me* the student is subjected to ergarten methods. He is re- sible for every hour of recita- in the term. At the end of this od he is not asked what do you ember, but how many hours did attend invitations.

o matter what occurs or how he , he must be in the class-room ake up the day's recitation in a al manner, so that the tyranni- rade-book may be satisfied.

he comes to recitations when posed he derives little benefit than the class-room work. Whether right or wrong, the fact remains that their attention is engrossed. Now this often gives rise to a great temptation to dash through a lesson in order to have time for "accessories;" because even the most cursory perusal of a lesson will float one through a single day.

Again, one does not systematize his work when he knows that when a portion is once recited he will not be called to account for it again. The lessons may be apparently well learned, but an examination a few months later would reveal an appalling ignorance.

The new system makes a time-server not only of the student, but the disease may also affect the faculty. The professor has outside demands on his time just as his pupils and, as in them, that universal failing, "indisposition to work" may have gained a foothold; so, just as there is incoherence in learning lessons, there may be a lack of system in teaching, because neither instructor nor instructed look forward to any summing up or calling to account.

It must also be a damper upon the teacher's enthusiasm if compelled to stop ever and anon and put down a "grade" or make a mental note of what per cent. of the lesson a student seems to have at his command.

By the time a student enters college he should be past that tender age when the excitement and worry of examinations is too great a strain for the little over-worked brain.

As to stuffing for examination, we have only to say that the student who will cram for examinations finds an easy way of slipping through under the new order of things. He peeps in his book, writes on his cuffs, or glances over the leading points just as he enters the class-room so that the impressions will not fade away before he can make use of them. The daily-grade dispensation furnishes one perpetual holiday for the superficial student and the laggard, but gives no thorough training whatsoever.

We think that the most earnest student will admit that some spurring on to systematizing and classifying one's knowledge and an incentive to develop the powers of the memory are helpful to even the most diligent.

Hence we would say, make the student self-reliant and self-responsible. Say to him, pass your examinations and you can receive your degree; but without this, no matter what your daily recitations may be, you cannot be passed.

Let the teacher, by lecture or recitation, review the field of work frequently, recapitulate and classify the leading points to serve as pegs

STUDENTS' ORGANIZATIONS.

How Far is the Student Bound to Support Them?

DISCUSSED BY A STUDENT.

Every college is infested, if I may use the word, with many different organizations. There are athletic clubs, oratorical associations, literary societies, reading clubs, etc., and in a small college it becomes a question of importance to the student to determine how much time he can devote to each one. Shall he support all, none, or merely a few? If the latter, with which shall he identify himself?

Doubtless the inclination of nearly every student, on entering college, is to "go in" for everything. He longs to grow into the life of the college and to aid every enterprise which promises renown for himself or for his college. However, it often happens that he cannot do this. Very often his purse is so limited that he is compelled to have no part in many things which really interest him. Quite as often, perhaps, he finds his college duties so arduous that he has no time for the extra amount of work these organizations entail and is for that reason compelled to be a mere spectator.

Thus it can be seen that in all probability a large majority of the students cannot, for various reasons, support everything connected with the college, and, indeed, it may be questioned whether any *can*, though there are always some who try. A choice must be made, and in the making of the choice the student decides upon the course he is to follow while in college. If he chooses athletics, he will be so known throughout his college course and he will be popular or otherwise, as athletics are successful or not.

The first thing for the college man to consider is his own peculiar fitness for this or that; his own adaptability to this or that line of work. He should associate himself with those organizations whose purposes harmonize with his own tastes and inclinations. He should become a member of that organization which he can do the most good and which in turn can render the greatest service to him. He has come to college primarially for self-improvement, and first and foremost he should seek that end.

In the next place his college should be considered. Every organization in college reflects more or less credit upon the college. Therefore, of two, choose the one which will do the most good for the college. Why? For two reasons. First, you owe your allegiance to the college which you have chosen for your *Alma Mater;* and, second, it is for your own interest. After graduation your

stands out by itself clear and distinct; it is disconnected from all associations; it acknowledges neither superior nor inferior, for it spurns both.

College days come into the life of the young man as something foreign to himself. For years he has looked forward to his college work and associations; he has dreamed about it and built stately and grand castles in the air. In his mind he has gone over the whole four years many times and planned his entire policy. He imagines that he knows all about it, for he has talked with his friends who have been in college, and have they not given him "pointers" on every subject imaginable? Thus he enters college with a preconceived idea of it, carrying with him the grandest of air castles. How lucky he is if they are not tumbled down about his ears!

At first a tumult of new ideas and new combinations of ideas strives to impress itself upon his mind, and as a consequence he goes about for a time in a dazed condition, groping blindly, as through a mist, for the truth. But at length the mist clears away and he begins to see things in their true relations. Perhaps that which impresses itself most forcibly upon his mind is the absolute democracy of college life. He observes with wonder and astonishment that not wealth nor position, social standing or even brains, are sufficient to bring a man prestige among his fellows. As time passes he notes with increasing satisfaction that *worth* is the measure among college men. He sees that those of his classmates who are popular, are deservedly so; that those who occupy positions of honor and trust have won them by hard, earnest and conscientious work and by manly actions at all times. He sees that the Freshman who entered college under such auspicious circumstances and who created so much excitement at that time, has been left far in the rear by the slow plodder, who, while he never put himself forward, was discovered to be far the superior of the former in mental and moral qualities.

The influence of these facts on the man after he leaves college can hardly be overestimated. They shape and mould his whole life and tend ever to make him a better citizen. He sees more clearly any evils existing in the state and is prompt in applying the proper remedy. He respects his neighbor for his character and his conduct, and not for the dollars he may have accumulated. He can never become a mere hero worshipper; but, on the other hand, he can never deny to each man his just dues. He is a better citizen because he recognizes the worth of other men.

LOCALS.

What beautiful weather

Mr. Martin is *now* a tendant at social.

Buchtel students are ju Oberlin's defeat by Case.

Adelbert defeated Ke day by a score of 21 to 0.

The time for the Thanksgiving box is near

W. A. Putt has alread some reputation as a crimi

There should have been ple in attendance at game.

The Sophomore girls w in the college parlors n evening.

The class of '94 alm social in the college pa evening.

The Thanksgiving danc postponed until the w Thanksgiving.

A number of students preparations to eat Th turkey at home.

The mechanics class ru other day. A pair of sh were brought into class tion.

The local Oratorical has decided upon the thi day in January as the d local contest. There wi teresting contest.

The college council is g no more. The question would punish students for If no one has authority things could be made very students were so inclined.

Miss Garrigues has o reading club, composed o of the Junior class, which purpose the reading of s and current literature. every Monday evening.

Buchtel vs. O. W. U.,

The Buchtel College Wesleyan University tea Saturday at the former The O. W. U. men were er and stronger than th nents but were not in th all. The O. W. U. men to secure one touchdown not have had that one. up a fine game, the best son.

The teams lined up as

BUCHTEL.	POSITION.
Webster, Capt.	left end.
Yerrick,	left tackle.
C. Taylor,	left guard.
Putt,	center.
McKnight,	right guard.
D. Taylor,	right tackle.
Loudenbeck.	right end.
Clark,	quarter back.
Calmer,	left half back.
Heisman,	right half back.
Fisher,	full back.
	SUBSTITUTES.
Donovan,	
Mitchell,	
Green.	

Buchtel carried the bal line in two minutes, scori

CHAPTER 1
1891–1899

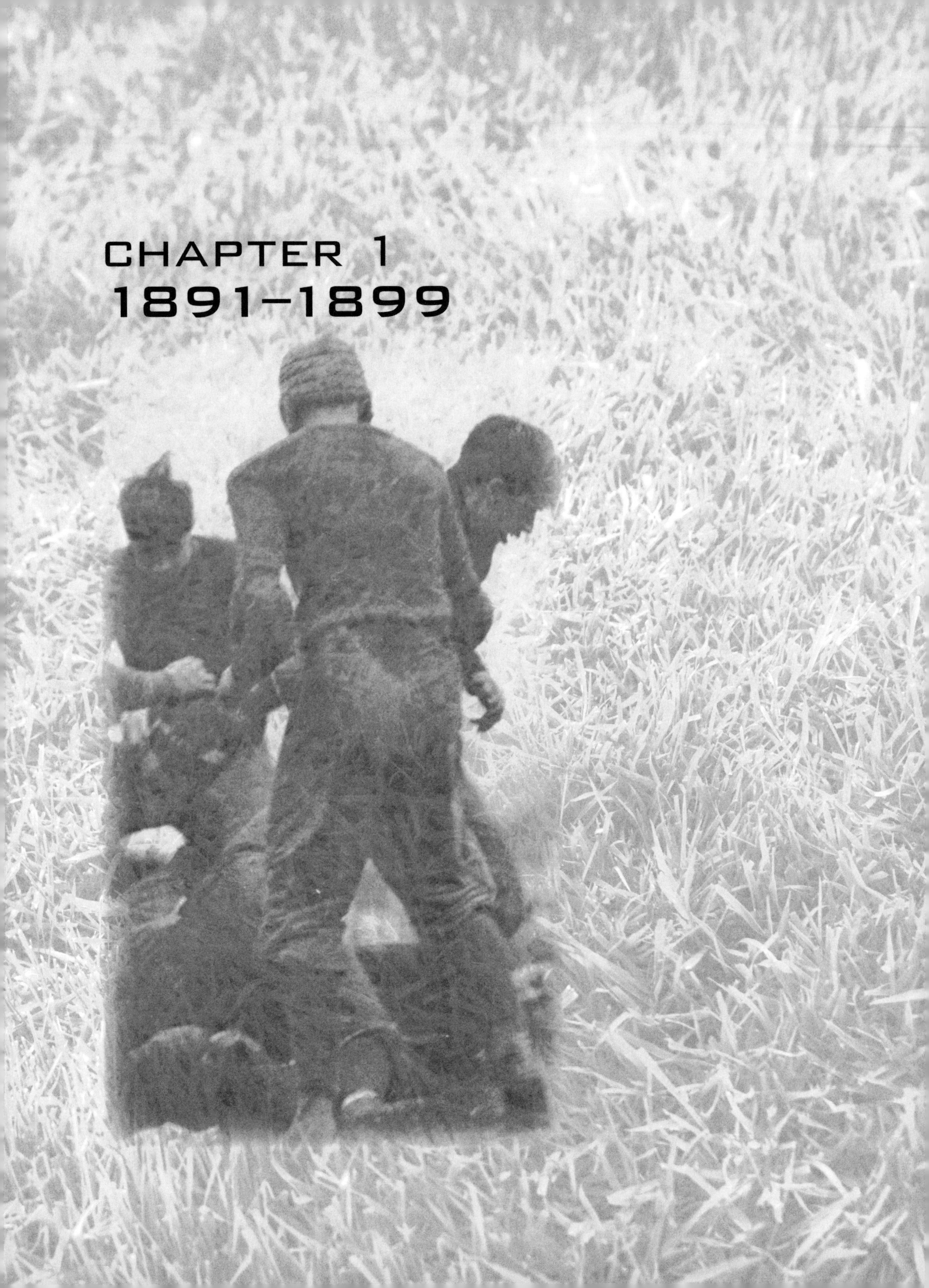

1891, The First Football Team. Seated: Eli Hardin, John Eddy. Front row: Alvin McKnight, Charles Meade, Carlos Webster, Charles Weeks (captain), Robert Osbourne, Wilson Putt, Walter Coe. Standing: Benjamin Kingsbury, Bryant Campbell, Charles Mignin, Johnson McLean, Harry Clark. Courtesy of The University of Akron Department of Intercollegiate Athletics.

November 5, 1891

Buchtel vs. Western Reserve

The manager of the foot-ball team procured tickets for twenty-three to Hudson last Monday. The boys were in good spirits but not very confident. It was to be a contest to find out their weak points and what stuff was in the eleven.

If they got beat they could excuse themselves with the fact that it was their first game, and if they really did win it would be because the team was composed of good foot-ball players.

The Hudson boys met them at the train. Part of the crowd was sent to the hotel and the rest took dinner with the boys. After a hearty dinner the crowd began to collect on the field. Buchtel's team looked rather rusty in their motley suits compared to the appearance of the Reserve boys in their new canvas jackets.

Referee Tuttle called the game at a little after two, Hudson getting the toss and the ball. Buchtel took the wind and the down hill side. Their opponents started with a "V" and rushed so well that things looked rather dubious for Buchtel. The twenty-five yard line was reached, Hudson gaining. Then twenty, then fifteen. Buchtel's crowd became frightened, but the mad career of Hudson was checked at last. The ball went to Buchtel. By strong shoving, quick passes and hard runs she slowly gained ground. Now she was back to the twenty-five yard line. Next on the center line and next—ah! Mac has the ball. He jumps by the end, dodges the half and goes tearing down the line, the entire 'leven at his heels.

Will they catch him? The end is right upon him. Mac feels the Indian's hot breath on his neck. He thinks his time has come. He makes a last effort, crosses the goal line and is safe. The crowd cheered. The boy whirled his razzle dazzle, his friend blowed the horn and when the ball went sailing over the pole the game was almost won. The Reserves rushed the ball again but the half closed just after Buchtel had made another touch down.

The score was 10 to 0.

The next half Buchtel had the ball and easily made a down, and a goal. The score stood 16 to 0.

Hudson then took the ball and slowly but surely beat the Buchtels back by attacking their rush line. The Buchtels gave ground slowly and stubbornly but surely nevertheless. The only really bad play on Buchtel's part took place here. Fry got the ball by some unaccountably quick work, but became confused and started in the wrong direction.

He soon saw his mistake however but it was too late. Hudson was upon him. They pushed the boys right across the goal line. A goal was kicked and the score stood 16 to 6.

The ball was started off again and Hudson's shoving was just as effective as before. She was slowly gaining and approaching the twenty-five yard line when MacLean made another of his famous runs. He got within three yards of the line when he slipped and fell, and the Indian was upon him. The boys lined up again and at last Mac, with the assistance of Clark, crawled right through in under both teams, stretched out his hands and crossed the line with the ball. It was the finest play of the whole day. Time was called after the goal was kicked leaving the score 22 to 6.

The team were as follows, Clark taking Welsh's place the second half, Welsh having been hurt:

Weeks, r.e.	Osborne, l.t.
Meade, r.t.	Fry, l.e.
Coe, r.g.	Eddy, q.b.
McKnight, c.	Mclean, Kingsbury, h.b.
Putt, l.g.	Welsh, Clark, f.b.

October 10, 1893

For the past week the work done in practice has been decidedly encouraging. Still not enough men turn out for practice to satisfy the very reasonable demands of Mr. Heisman. Mr. Heisman says that he has never had better material to work with and that he is willing to promise anything in the way of results if a second eleven will only come out to practice. Surely the students owe this much to the College and to Mr. Heisman. The best material in the world cannot be moulded into an efficient team without practice, and if our team is to have the necessary practice we must get out a second eleven every day.

Another thing which is not only discouraging but surprising, is the fact that there are men in College who will deliberately pledge their word to come out and practice, and then never go near the field except at rare intervals. If approached on the subject they will say, "Oh well, you knew when I promised that I didn't intend to come every day." Pledges kept in this way do not reflect much credit on the men who give them. We give below a list of those who have agreed to work every day regardless of success, in making the team. Most of them have fulfilled their pledges: C.G. Webster, H.H. Hollenbeck, W.C. Green, Frank Fisher, D.S. Taylor, J.L. Donovan, A.C. McKnight, H.C. Loudenback, Chas. C. Taylor, J. Ed Dougherty, C.M. Chapman, R.H. Hamlin, C.E. Petty, H.E. Calmer, Hal J. Thrasher.

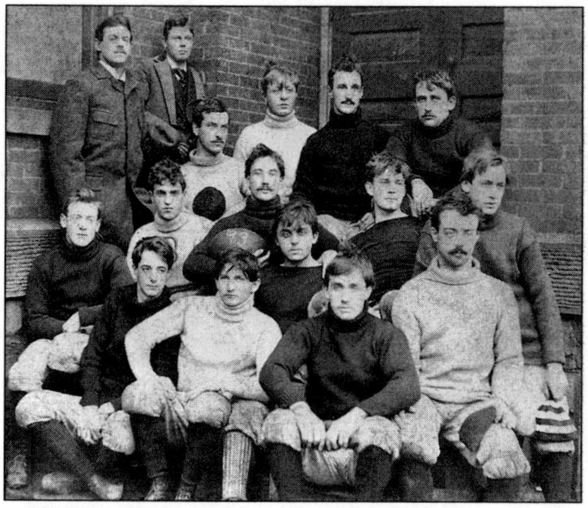

John Heisman with the 1893 Buchtel College team. Courtesy of The University of Akron Department of Intercollegiate Athletics.

October 24, 1893

Hiram vs. Buchtel

Hiram met Buchtel on the football field yesterday and suffered defeat with a score against them of 54 to 2. The score should have been 80 to 0, but the Buchtel men failed to play their usual game. No one seemed to know just what the trouble was, but each man seemed to play as if he were the only one on the field. The interference, especially in the first half, was exceedingly poor, and the men running with the ball showed very poor judgment. In the last half a different game was played and we caught a glimpse of what the team could really do. Gardner and Calmer both made beautiful end runs in this half. There were several bad holes in the line and the guards and tackles failed to hold their men as they should. However, it was only the first game of the season and the men will not be nearly so nervous another time. Several of the men were in the game for the first time and it was not to be expected that they would show the coolness of veterans.

The Hiram team played a very ragged game, though they are heavy men and plucky players. They have material for a first-class team, but lack training.

The teams lined up as follows:

Buchtel		*Hiram*
Webster, Capt.	left end	E. Dyson
Yerrick	left tackle	Vincent
Wise	left guard	Harvey
C. Taylor		
Putt	center	Bogrand
McKnight	right guard	Metcalf
D. Taylor	right tackle	Wheeler

Buchtel		*Hiram*
Heisman		Slocum
Loudenback	right end	Wood
Clark	quarter back	Ewing, Capt.
Calmer	right half back	Blair
Donovan		
Gardner	left half back	Ross
		Ayers
Fisher	full back	H. Dyson
	Substitutes	
Calmer		Ross
C. Taylor		Wheeler
Cassidy		Parker
Mitchell		
Green		
Heisman		

Referee and time-keeper-Hiram, G.R. Miller; Buchtel, T. Cassidy.

Case plays Buchtel at Akron next Saturday. This will be an interesting game and every student should make an effort to see it. Case has a good team and last Saturday defeated Adelbert 32 to 0, so we may expect to see a close and exciting game. Let everyone come.

October 31, 1893

Buchtel vs. Case

Last Saturday Buchtel suffered almost as great a defeat as she administered to Hiram the week before. Case defeated Buchtel by a score of 36 to 0. Nevertheless, the spectators and the team were better satisfied than they were after the Hiram game. Buchtel played a stronger game and the men played steadier and evener than before. Case owes her victory to the fact that her team is heavier than Buchtel's and at the same time more experienced. Case's heavy men repeatedly broke through Buchtel's line and also made large gains by end runs, at which times her interference was especially noticeable. Buchtel's defeat was not due to poor playing on the part of any man—each one did his part—but it was simply the inevitable result under the existing conditions.

The teams lined up as follows:

Buchtel		*Case*
Webster, Capt.	left end	Reiley
Yerrick	left tackle	Repp
Wise	left guard	Abbey
Putt	center	Bragg
McKnight	right guard	Hill
D. Taylor	right tackle	Carter
Loudenback	right end	Brown
Clark	quarter back	Smith, Capt.
Gardner	left half back	Holdy
Donovan	right half back	Gleason
Calmer		Davidson
Fisher	full back	Lovely
		Donovan
	Substitutes	
Calmer		Shaw
C. Taylor		Gaylord
Cassidy		Gallegher
Green		Williams

November 21, 1893

Buchtel vs. O.W.U., 46 to 4

The Buchtel College and Ohio Wesleyan University teams played Saturday at the former's grounds. The O.W.U. men were much larger and stronger than their opponents but were not in the game at all. The O.W.U. men managed to secure one touchdown but should not have had that one. Buchtel put up a fine game, the best of the season.

The teams lined up as follows:

Buchtel		*O.W.U.*
Webster, Capt.	left end	Hall
Yerrick	left tackle	Hough
C. Taylor	left guard	Crawford
Putt	center	Shaw
McKnight	right guard	Conklin

Buchtel		*O.W.U.*
D. Taylor	right tackle	Prentiss
Loudenback	right end	Colburn
Clark	quarter back	Jones
Calmer	left half back	Priddy, Capt.
Heisman	right half back	Spencer
Fisher	full back	Welsh
	Substitutes	
Donovan		Beacom
Mitchell		Flannegan
Green		

Buchtel carried the ball over the line in two minutes, scoring the first touchdown. O.W.U. scored their only touchdown in the first half when Spencer broke through Buchtel's line, but Prentiss failed to kick a goal. Buchtel's big gains were made by long runs of which Calmer had his share.

In the last half Donovan was substituted for D. Taylor at guard, where he played a good game.

The halves were 30 minutes long and the score stood 46 to 4 in favor of Buchtel.

The game Saturday was an interesting one and well played, especially by the Buchtel eleven. It was a pleasure to witness it, as it was nearly free from exhibitions of slugging. The O.W.U. team contains some good men, but it was evident that they had had but little training and practice.

Speaking of Saturday's game, where were all the college students? After Buchtel had made the first touchdown one of her players asked a bystander if there were any college people present. And no wonder. Think of it! A touchdown made against a team from as large a college as O.W.U. in less than four minutes, and not a cheer from one of Buchtel's supporters! Such support is enough to take the nerve out of any team. What was the trouble? Were there no college students present? Very few, indeed, were there, and those who were there could not be kept in one place long enough to make any noise.

We believe it to be the duty of every student to attend the best games if it is possible—but perhaps we have preached this enough, at any rate further talk would be useless.

There will be no more games here until Thanksgiving Day. Buchtel plays with Mt. Union then, and it is hoped that a good crowd will be in attendance. The game will be a good one, and many town people will doubtless profit by the opportunity to see the teams play.

Saturday the Buchtel boys go to Mt. Union to play the eleven of that college. May good luck go with them!

December 12, 1893

The Thanksgiving game has been played and it was a decided success, both as an exhibition of fine playing and, what is, if possible, more agreeable to hear, a big success financially. The players, freed from the restraint of training, are now enjoying themselves hugely. They revel in oysters, lemonade, candy, and all those delicacies for which they longed so ardently before the season closed. One of the players said, a day or two before Thanksgiving, that as soon as the last game was played he should "go down town, buy a pound of chocolate, go off into a corner and eat them all."

September 25, 1894

Buchtel vs. O.S.U (The Latter Defeated by a Score of 12 to 6)

"We have met the enemy and they are ours." Buchtel College has for three successive years maintained a foot ball team in the field and once during each of those years has she received a drubbing at the hands of Ohio State University. Of course we claimed that the defeat of Buchtel in the first game played with O.S.U., which took place on the West Hill grounds in the fall of '91 and in which we were beaten by a score of 4 to 0, was merely an accident and was not due to superior men or team work. Not so, however, in the games of '92 and '93. We were clearly beaten by our own lack of practice and team work.

This year our highest ambition has been realized and O.S.U. has gone down before us. In the game at Columbus we had no better individual players than in former years, but our devotion to the principles of training and the faithful daily practice in which our boys indulged, won the game.

On Tuesday, Sept. 4, our boys went to Columbus with the determination to trail O.S.U.'s banner in the dust, and how well they succeeded is told by the score. The boys had trained faithfully for two weeks at Silver Lake and each man was in prime condition.

The 1894 Buchtel College team, John Heisman at far right. The Buchtel squad, featuring Heisman at quarterback, was the first Akron team to beat OSU. Courtesy of The University of Akron Department of Intercollegiate Athletics.

A large crowd assembled on Wednesday, Sept. 5, to witness the contest. The grounds had been arranged within the enclosure of the race track at the State Fair grounds and every precaution had been taken by the Fair managers to keep the crowd from in any way interfering with the game. O.S.U. had many friends and sympathizers in the crowd, who continually cheered the University boys, while Buchtel received little encouragement at the hands of the spectators.

Mr. M.C. Lilley, jr., sub-quarterback for Princeton, refereed a faultless game, not one of his decisions being questioned by either side. Kent P. Johnson also umpired a good game. To mention the individual work of the players would require a mention of each player on the team, for all played a practically faultless game. The work of Captain Fisher as full back, Loudenbeck at right end, Johnson at left half, Stewart at right half, Heisman at quarter, and Cook at left tackle, was especially good.

Only twice during the entire game was the ball in Buchtel's territory, while Loudenbeck's runs around the end during the first half were irresistible.

The following rather fair account of the game is taken from the *O.S.U. Lantern:*

The way Buchtel forced their way over Snedeker's guarding meant defeat for O.S.U. from the start.

It was clearly noticeable that O.S.U. as a team did not play their usual good game, but individually they were doing well.

Buchtel opened and Fisher gained three yards. Advancing the ball about twenty yards they gave it to O.S.U. on downs. O.S.U. lost the ball on downs in short order. Fisher goes through center, fights hard, and breaks away, making a touchdown in thirty yards. Goal, Buchtel 6, O.S.U. 0. Time 7 minutes.

Then O.S.U. scores a touchdown in two minutes. Smith kicks ball, Fisher returns kick and Smith again secures it. Carson gains ten yards. Dunlap goes around for thirteen yards and Smith breaks through center and scores in eighteen yards. Goal, Buchtel 6, O.S.U. 6.

Eleven minutes were then spent in sharp skirmishing with the ball in O.S.U.'s end of the field. No score. Buchtel 6, O.S.U. 6.

The second half was hard fought. At one time Buchtel brought the ball within two feet of goal and lost it on a fumble to Nagel. Time was called and no score. The special rule requires the game to be played out and Buchtel succeeds in scoring in a long twenty minutes. Goal, Buchtel 12, O.S.U. 6.

The men lined in the following order:

Buchtel		*O.S.U.*
Webster	left end	Dunlap
Cooke	left tackle	Walsh
D. Taylor	left guard	Snedeker
C Taylor	center	Mathers
McKnight	right guard	Gibbs
Wise	right tackle	Carson
Loudenbeck	right end	Nagel and French
Heisman	quarter	Wood (Capt.)
Jounson	left half	Gill and Potter
Stewart	right half	Smith and Nagel
Fisher (Capt.)	full back	Howard
	Substitutes	
Carter		Wilson
Putt,		Knauss
Chapman		Westwater
Donovan		Potter

Buchtel	*O.S.U.*
Substitutes	
	Calkins
	French

Summary touchdowns, Buchtel-Fisher 2. O.S.U., Howard.

Notes: Buchtel Boys made "Rome howl" on the way from the field of victory to the hotel. A number of Akron people were on the grounds and cheered lustily for our boys. The scores for the remainder of the tournament were as follows: Thursday—Miami 6, Dennison 0. Friday—Wittenberg 6, O.S.U. 0. Buchtel won suites all around by beating O.S.U. She also won ten foot balls for scoring the greatest number of points during the tournament.

EXTRA POINT

Buchtel College: The Early Years

Since 1882, Buchtel College students had clamored for the administration to sanction football. In 1891, BC fielded its first intercollegiate football team.

As a member of the Ohio Intercollegiate Athletic Association (a forerunner of the Ohio Conference), BC participated in baseball, track, and oratorical contests. On June 5, 1891, at the annual meeting of the association, a proposal was made and passed that the colleges in the association must field football teams or be dropped from the group. Rather than drop, Buchtel College decided to form a team. That summer, a committee headed by freshman Wilson Putt journeyed from Buchtel to the University of Pennsylvania campus to find out the intricacies of this relatively new game.

On Monday, Oct. 26, BC traveled to Hudson, Ohio and defeated Western Reserve Academy, 22-6. Johnson McLean scored all 22 points in the victory. The first intercollegiate game was played the following week against Kenyon on an area that eventually became Buchtel Field.

Football in those days was a far cry from the present day. Halves were 45 minutes, the field was 110 yards long and scoring went as follows: TD-4 points, field goal-5 points, extra point kick and safety-2 points.

The most successful season in those early years came in 1910 when team captain Lee Jackson led BC to a record of 7-2.

Courtesy of The University of Akron Department of Intercollegiate Athletics

THE BUCHTELITE

A Bi-weekly Newspaper—Established 1889.

VOL. XIV. BUCHTEL COLLEGE, AKRON, OHIO, OCT. 2, 1902 N

NEW YEAR AT BUCHTEL.

An Auspicious Opening.

The new college year for 1902 d 1903 has opened with a good tendance and very auspicious cir- mstances for a highly successful nter term. With the exception less than a half dozen outside of e class graduated last June, all of e former students have returned take up anew their college duties, lled with renewed enthusiasm and ew resolutions as a result of their mmer vacation.

In addition to the old students, s a result of the efforts of Presi- ent Church, and the other college uthorities, Buchtel has added to er roll a larger number of new ames than has been added to the ollege proper for some time. This ear's Freshman class numbers hirty seven members, which is the argest class for a number of years.

The Academy has added a num- ber of new students, and while its roll is not now so large as last year, new students are coming in daily and in the course of a few weeks Principal Olin expects to have one hundred pupils, as last year. A majority of the twenty-three gradu- ated from the academy last June haved proved their loyalty by entering the college this fall.

The music school is prospering, and while the total enrollment is not yet known, there will undoubt- edly be more than last year. The Art school, has also opened with an increase of students.

The total enrollment for Buchtel will slightly exceed that of last year, but the encouraging feature

ANNUAL INITIATION.

Freshies Submissive.

The annual Freshman initiation was administered to a large class of submissive victims on Friday eve, the twenty-sixth, that the entire program was a success cannot be doubted, and while the Freshmen were treated to all the tortures known to college enthusiasts, as a means of ushering them into the wiles and depths of college life, still they departed felling glad that they had come.

The Freshies met at the home of Miss Amy Saunders, near the campus, and marched to the gym- nasum in a crowd. This was done however with a feeling of fear on the part of a few of the largest men in the crowd, lest the upperclass- men should take it as a sign of re- sistance. Jolly and noisy, they received at the gym doors and were immediately locked in the locker rooms, awaiting their fate.

With eyes blindfolded and hands tied behind their backs, the entire aggregation of Freshmen Braves, and also the Freshman Belles, ap- peared on the gym floor ready for action. A complete program of events had been prepared, thro' which every man was rushed amid the shouts of amusement from the upperclassmen and their invited guests.

After enjoying a good roll over the floor, they were treated to an abundance of limberger cheese as a nerve stimulus to support them thro' the evening. After this they were put thro' the foot bath, which often resulted in partial suffocation, and at times in a complete shower bath. In rapid succession they ... to the very top of the

it was over, curly locks, straight locks, black hair and brown was strewn promiscuously about the floor. Each man had been branded with a pair of hair clippers so that dur- ing the next few weeks the Fresh- men wise men might not be mis- taken for upper classmen. In order to further insure their identity, each was branded on his right cheek with an iodine cross. The young ladies also received the iodine brand, and with flowing hair, and painted faces, they looked charm- ing indeed.

After the uppers were entirely satisfied that their victims were scared into meek submission. Band- ages were removed, ropes cut, shoes and hose were hunted, and in a short time dancing and general merriment was indulged in by Freshies and Uppers alike over the "bug inhabited," and "cheese be- smeared" floor.

Appropriate refreshments con- sisting of bread and milk, were served by the gallon.

This year's Freshman class is a large one, and contains much good material for the making of loyal Buchtelites. The following mem- bers were initiated:

MINA L. ADAMS,	Akron, O.
CLARA F. BROUSE,	Akron, O.
ALBERT BROWN,	Mt. Gilead, O.
HENRY K. BUTLER,	Akron, O.
RUTH CARNAHAN,	Akron, O.
ETHEL M. CARNS,	Akron, O.
HOMER W. CASTER,	Everett, O.
HAGEL I. CLARK,	Pittsburgh, Pa.
MATILDA CLARK,	Chicago Jct., O.
FANNY FERBSTEIN,	Akron, O.
JACOB J. GAYER, (Not Present.)	Akron, O.
ESTHER GREENWOOD,	Akron, O.
EDITH HEACOCK,	Chicago jct., O.
LUCRETIA HEMINGTON,	Akron, O.
BESSIE L. COOK,	Kent, O.
HAL KNIGHT,	Akron, O.
MAURICE KNIGHT,	Akron, O.
BYRON T. MOTTINGER,	Akron, O.
G. BENJAMIN MOTZ,	Akron, O.
GLEN E. MYERS,	Barberton, O.
BLANCHE M. OLIN,	Akron, O.
EDWARD PARSHALL,	Akron, O.
PAUL R. PITKIN,	Akron, O.
AMY L. SAUNDERS,	Akron, O.
BESSIE M. SELDEN,	Akron, O.
HOWARD SPANGLER,	Akron, O.
... T. ...TZGER,	Kent, O.

Two or three of the me initiated are not full-fledged man, but it was tho't best to ate them, as their preparatory will soon be completed.

RECEPTION OF STUDENT

The annual reception to th students, and this year, to th professors as well, was he Buchtel Hall on the Friday e following the opening of col

The Reception Committe sisted of Pres. and Mrs. Church, Prof. and Mrs. Brookover, Dr. Joseph C. R Dr. C. F. Kolbe, Princip Mrs. O. E. Olin, Prof. and I. Spanton, and two membe each of the upper classes.

A committee of intro made everyone feel acquaint up in the natural science lab a refreshment committee se freshments consisting of an ance of ices and cake.

The reception was free f formality, and was one of cial events in Buchtel's colle enjoyed by everyone presen

ATHLETICS.

The long sought end of the tuition fee of each stu clude one dollar each year benefit of athletics was acco last year, and with a nice remaining in the treasury f year athletics have been p excellent financial basis the new year.

The foot-ball team has for practice nearly every since the opening of coll while there is some good it is evidnet to those intere three or more good str

CHAPTER 2
1900–1909

NOVEMBER 6, 1902

Allegheny 23 Buchtel 6

On Saturday Oct. 25, the college team went to Meadville, Pa., and played the Allegheny College team there. Although the men had worked hard preparing for the game, they were defeated 23–6. The Allegheny team was somewhat heavier than the Buchtel boys, but their strong point was in the swiftness of their line-up and their close formation plays. Buchtel made her only score in the first half, when Weary got the ball on a fumble and ran one hundred yards for a touch-down. Weary also kicked goal. By the end of the first half the Buchtel men were well tired out. The second half was not so well played on the part of Buchtel, as the men seemed overworked, and were unable to put the necessary speed into their plays to make any gains. Buchtel's failing seemed to be in high tackling and slow formation.

Buchtel 11 Bethany 6

Following the defeat at Meadville, Coach Firestone put the men through a week of hard practice, and as a result the team lined up against the strong team from Bethany College, in the best of condition. Swanson was unable to play because of injuries received at Allegheny, but Brown filled his place well.

Buchtel kicked off to Bethany and Parshall immediately got the ball on a fumble, Pitkin made twenty yards around left end but the ball went to Bethany on a fumble. Bethany lined up and the ball was again fumbled and Parshall ran forty yards for a touch-down. Two of the Bethany men were in hot pursuit, but were unable to catch Buchtel's swift right half. Weary kicked goal, and the score stood 6–0 in just three minutes of play.

Bethany kicked off and Pitkin made twenty yards, then four, and Weary five. The ball was again fumbled but Bethany failed to gain a yard in three downs and Parshall made a twenty-yard run, and Weary made form. Parshall gained five and Pitkin ten, then Parshall thirteen in two downs and Pitkin twelve in one down. Parshall again circled the end twice for nine yards, and Pitkin did as well in one run. Bethany then took a brace, held for three downs, and then punted the ball thirty-five yards and downed Weary in his tracks. Pitkin made three then failed, and Buchtel punted back thirty yards. Bethany again resorted to punting in the first line-up, and Weary bro't the ball back fifteen yards. Parshall kicked three yards and Weary four, and time was called just as the signal had been given for a place kick from Bethany's ten yard line. If the half had continued one minute longer Buchtel would have easily scored.

In the second half Bethany kicked off to Buchtel and downed Weary after he had carried the ball back ten yards. Parshall gained ten yards in two bucks, then Weary made two and Pitkin three. Parshall gained two but the ball went to Bethany on a fumble. Bethany made ten yards in two downs and was penalized five yards for a forward pass. Their full-back was injured and forced to retire. Buchtel then held for downs. Parshall and Weary then made twenty yards in six downs, Pitkin failed to gain and Buchtel punted thirty yards. Bethany was forced to do the same, and the ball went back twenty yards. Pitkin easily made ten, Parshall twenty-five, Weary five, and then Parshall went over the line in a ten yard run. Weary failed goal.

Buchtel should have had two more touchdowns, but Bethany suddenly woke up and by a series of bucks and end runs, usually good for five yards, they finally rushed the ball across Buchtel's line by a twenty yard run by Stucky, and kicked goal, making the score 11–6 in Buchtel's favor.

The rest of the half the ball was in Bethany's territory, and in Buchtel's possession. On Bethany's fifteen yard line, Doyle tried a place kick. The line held and it seemed that the kick would be successful, but the ball hit the cross-bar of the goal posts. A Bethany man missed the ball as it re-bounded and Gayer fell on it. After Doyle had kicked for fifteen yards, Bethany kicked vigorously for fifteen minutes, and in order to settle the kick the ball was given Bethany, who fumbled and Pitkin fell on the ball. Time was called with the ball very near Bethany's goal, and a touchdown would have resulted in a minute's more play.

The team is greatly encouraged over its victory as Bethany had played five games without being scored upon before coming to Buchtel. The score here should have been 23–0. A tackling machine has been purchased, and the men are being given some hard practice in tackling. None of the players were seriously injured, altho' several were badly bruised.

Wooster—Next Saturday

Buchtel plays Wooster University here next Saturday, and considering the fact that Wooster defeated Mt. Union last Saturday to the tune of 28–0, it seems that Buchtel has a hard game coming. The team has greatly improved since the Mt. Union game, and expects to hold its own against Wooster.

October 22, 1903

First Foot Ball Game

The first foot ball game of the season at Alliance, October 10, resulted in a defeat for Buchtel at the hands of Mt. Union, by the score of 10–0. The game was a close one and was hard fought at every point. Mt. Union kicked off to Buchtel, and in the first down Parshall was injured and compelled to leave the game. Not only was the team greatly weakened by this piece of hard luck, since Parshall was the mainstay of the team in the half back line, but the effect upon the team was disastrous. There was no sub half to take Parshall's place, and Crist who had practiced for an end position was put in.

Mt. Union made her first score early in the game, but was unable to score again till the very last of the second half. The score was made just as the whistle blew. The feature of the game was a 70 yard run by Brown, assisted by Swanson and Thomas. Swanson opened a big hole, and Thomas and Brown plunged through. Thomas did some excellent work in interference while Brown sped down the field for a splendid gain. Buchtel was then held for downs and was unable to score.

Coach Place expressed himself as highly pleased with the work of the team, and held that victory would have gone to Buchtel had not Parshall been injured. The game was a disastrous one for Buchtel in the way of accidents. Parshall is suffering with a sprained ankle, and will not be able to walk without crutches for at least a month. Captain Thomas received a broken nose, a black eye, and a badly scratched face. In spite of the fact that Thomas's nose was broken in the first part of the game, he played a great game to the finish. Hal Knight got off with a sprained ankle which laid him up for a week. Brown, Thomas and Swanson did the star work for Buchtel.

Instead of being discouraged, the members of the team had good reasons, under the circumstances, to feel proud of their work. The failing of the team this year is a lack of men. With the assistance of Coach Place, the prospects for a winning team would be bright, if there was more available material. As it is, it is not definitely decided whether the entire schedule will be played or not. Hiram, at Hiram is scheduled for Saturday, October 24.

All last year some form of Jonah or hoodoo seemed hovering about all of the Buchtel teams. Here is a chance for some hero to do the Beowulf vs. Grendel act, and thereby win everlasting laurels.

October 1908

Pittsburg Lyceum Game

Pittsburg Lyceum defeated us at Pittsburg on October 3rd. It takes more than a little grit for a green team to choose a heavy professional team like this for its second game.

Outweighed over 50 pounds to the man, Buchtel could do nothing but play on the defensive and yet they played the best kind of football against the professionals, a brand of football that brought forth words of praise from Pittsburg papers.

The Pittsburg team was composed in part of former Massillon and Canton players, the men who took part in the games for the world's professional championship. Eddie Murphy, who was manager of the Canton ball club last spring and who formerly played with the Canton football team, played left guard for Pittsburg. Sweeney, another former Canton player, was at left tackle. Shiring, McChesney and "Bullet" Reilly, all former Massillon players, were with Pittsburg.

An idea of the difference in weight between the teams can be gleaned from the center position. Gulick, 145 pounds, was pitted against Shiring, who tips the scales at 250 pounds. The Pittsburg Press speaks as follows of Buchtel's work:

Heralded as one of the most aggressive football aggregations in Ohio, the Buchtel College eleven appeared on the bluff grounds yesterday afternoon and gave the Pittsburg Lyceum one of the toughest battles they have fought in many years. The score ended 36 to 0 in favor of the maroon and white team, but the visitors showed their quality at every stage and the playing was much closer than the score indicates.

A feature of the game was the defensive playing of the Buckeye team. Though light, they were able to hold the local eleven on more than one occasion when a few yards meant a touchdown. During the first part of the fray the Ohioans seemed to be afraid to let themselves out, the result being that the maroon and white team got a good start, which they managed to maintain until the end of the game.

Line-up and summary:

Buchtel		*Lyceum*
McGarry	left end	Dillon
Read	left tackle	Sweeney
Costigan	left guard	Murphy
Gulick	center	Shiring
Conrad	right guard	Timmins
Fuchs	right tackle	McChesney
Kelly	right end	Blair
Cruickshank	quarter back	McInerney
Reese	left half back	Campbell
Belden	right half back	Kelly
Williams	full back	Brassell

Substitutes-Moore for Costigan, Nelman for Dillon, Dillon for Sweeney, Reilly for McChesney, Moorehead for Kelly. Touchdowns-Campbell 2, McChesney 2, McInerney, Sweeney. Goals from touchdown-McChesney 6. Referee-Waddill. Umpire-Dunn. Head linesman-Jahant. Time of halves-20 minutes.

December 1908

Buchtel vs. Findlay

Friday afternoon, Nov. 27th, Buchtel ended its football season by defeating Findlay College, 6–5. The game was played at Nolan's field.

The Findlay aggregation missed their train Friday morning and did not arrive at the field until 4 p.m., when the game was to have been called at 2:30. The crowd of about three hundred stuck loyally, however, and gave the visitors a rousing reception when they did come.

The 1908 Buchtel College squad. Front row: unknown, Fred Fuchs, "Pudgie" Konrad, Robert Gulick, unknown, Verne Read, Charles Jahant. Second row: Thomas Reese, Russell Dobson, Charles Williams, Russell Belden. Back row: D. Harrison Slaybaugh, Myrl Tremelin, unknown, Sleeter Bull, unknown, Bob Dutt, unknown, James Cruickshank, unknown, unknown, Herman Pfaff, Harold Thomas, Herman Jones, unknown, unknown, Dr. Bradley (coach). Courtesy of The University of Akron Department of Intercollegiate Athletics.

The game started off with a rush and five minutes after play began, Findlay, in possession of the ball on their 30 yard line, tried a double pass; Jordan was tackled for a loss and fumbled, Sandy Read grabbed the ball and ahead of interference ran 30 yards for a touchdown. Fuchs kicked goal. After the second kick-off Buchtel struck her gait. First came an exchange of punts, Findlay having the advantage, as they used a short punt, which was successful, their ends getting down and recovering the ball. Buchtel then started line bucks and short end runs; the Buchtel formations went through the Findlay line in great form and four plays by Fuchs, Cruickshank, Reese and Williams carried the ball 40 yards. It looked like another touchdown, when a penalty and a fumble lost the chance. Time of first half—20 minutes.

Buchtel started fast in the second, carrying the ball 30 yards in two plays. Buchtel tried a forward pass, lost the ball and Findlay punted and recovered it on Buchtel's 40 yard line; another recovered punt and Chelsey ran down the sideline for a touchdown. Manchester missed goal. Time—5 minutes.

After the kick-off a series of flukes and penalties carried the ball into Buchtel's territory. The Buchtel line held, however, and the ball worked back and forth. The growing darkness made the play inaccurate and when time was called the Buchtel line was breaking up play after play. Time of second half—15 minutes.

On account of the injury of Jahant's knee, Sandy Read was shifted from tackle to end. He played a splendid game, spilling everything that came his way. Moore filled Read's position at tackle and worked well, stopping several plays. The other men playing their regular positions showed great improvement, although the darkness of the second half made it impossible to avoid errors.

The visitors were a good game bunch of players and were sportsmanlike throughout. They played hard and fast, Chelsey and Manchester starring for them. Jordan and Nier were fast and did great work getting down under punts.

Buchtel		*Findlay*
V. Read	left end	Ulrich
Moore	left tackle	Orwick
Costigan	left guard	Mitchell
Costigan	center	Demmy
Conrad	right guard	Edington
Fuchs (c)	right tackle	Cole
Reese	right end	Neff
Cruickshank-Dobson	quarter back	Manchester
Belden	left half back	Nier
Kelley	full back	Jordan
Williams	right half back	Chelsey

Touchdowns-Read, Chelsey. Goal-Fuchs. Referee and umpire-Van Horn, Stevens. Field judge-Jackson. Time of halves-20–15 minutes.

November 1909

Buchtel Spirit

This last fall, at the football games, the Buchtel yell was scarcely given often enough and loud enough for a Freshman to learn it. The few who attended the games seemed afraid to let out their voices, and the subs brought with the opposing team could completely drown out our rooters.

The editor of this paper had the opportunity of attending one of the High School games on a day when there was no Buchtel game. He came away feeling that if our rooters had one-half the energy and spirit shown by those High School enthusiasts, our team would have won every game this year and would have been looking for more to conquer. Why, six or seven of those fellows would bunch together, and let out a yell that would make what we call our "rooting" sound like the sigh of a sick zephyr! What's the matter with our throats, anyway? We surely have as good lungs as any school around the country. Why not use them?

The basketball and baseball seasons are coming. We want to win as many of the games we play as possible. And any player will tell you that good, systematic rooting from the crowd is as good as a tonic to any team. Let's root! You who can't play, come to the games, open up your throats, and—let 'er go! Teach the Freshman the yells. Get some new ones. Review the old ones. But whether the yell be old or new, get out and help give it! That's the spirit our teams expect, it's the spirit we ought to have. It will win games, it will increase scores, it will overcome all kinds of difficulties. So come on, be a rooter; in the none too elegant, but very appropriate words of the excited old Irishman, "Root, you son-of-a-gun! Root!"

Buchtel 6—Findlay 0

Saturday, Nov. 6, the Buchtel College football team played the Findlay College team and were successful in winning the game by a score of 6 to 0. It seemed impossible to keep the crowd off the field, and the Buchtel boys thought that if conditions had been otherwise they might have scored several touchdowns. The first touchdown of the game was made by Moore, who succeeded in blocking a forward pass, caught the fumbled ball and carried it over the line. But this touchdown was not allowed on account of alleged slugging by a Buchtel man.

The next touchdown was made also by Moore, and Grimm kicked goal, giving a final score of 6 to 0.

Buchtel 8—Hiram 10

The Buchtel team journeyed over to Hiram, Wednesday, November 17, and after driving from Ravenna to Hiram through a heavy snowstorm, met with defeat by a score of 10 to 8. Hiram thus made things even for its defeat here, October 23.

Hiram made a touchdown during the first five minutes. No scoring was done again until the last of the second half, when a Hiram man broke through the line for another touchdown. By this time Buchtel had commenced to warm up and played a hard game. Fleming succeeded in getting around the end for a touchdown, Jackson kicking goal.

Buchtel kicked off to Hiram and forced them to punt. There were about two seconds of play left when Buchtel kicked for a goal. The pigskin shot over the bar, making two additional points.

The grounds were wet and sloppy, making it difficult to play. Our team played excellently considering the obstacles in the way of a good game.

The following is the lineup:

Buchtel		*Hiram*
Read	left end	Spencer
Moore	left tackle	Peden
Costigan	left guard	Cook
Gulick	center	Hennessey
Conrad	right guard	Robinette
Brainard	right tackle	Beyers
Dutt-Fleming	right end	Foltz
Boone-Grimm	quarter back	Craig
Zimmerman	right half back	Meikel
Belden	left half back	Harris-Hall
Jackson	full back	Bradshaw

Buchtel 24—Bethany 0

The Buchtel football team ended the season by defeating Bethany on Thanksgiving by a score of 24 to 0. Buchtel played one of the best games of the season. Their line was impregnable, and the backs were like chained lightning.

Bethany were powerless throughout the game, and were unable to get near a touchdown. Buchtel's goal was not in danger any time during the game.

The touchdowns were made by Zimmerman, Jackson, Fleming and Belden.

The following is the lineup and summary:

Buchtel		*Bethany*
Read	left end	Bevens
Moore	left tackle	Watson
Costigan	left guard	Bristol
Gulick	center	Chapman
Conrad	right guard	Sonderson
Brainard	right tackle	Aiken
Fleming	right end	Shettleworth
Zimmerman	right half back	Corwin
Belden	left half back	Dailey

Buchtel		*Bethany*
Jackson	full back	Kemp
Grimm-Boone	quarter back	Unkenhower

Touchdowns-Belden, Fleming, Jackson, Zimmerman. Goals from touchdowns-Jackson 4. Referee-Carter of Akron. Umpire-Bill Laub of Akron.

This game closed the season of 1909. The team has done excellent work all year, and has raised Buchtel's football standard considerably. Coach Weed, in expressing his opinion on the season, seemed very well satisfied with the work done, and prophesies a victorious team for 1910.

EXTRA POINT

THE CHANGES IN FOOTBALL RULES

The football guide for this year shows very little change in rules. Perhaps the most important is that of the field goal, which this year will count but three points instead of four. Thus two field goals will not count more than a hard earned touchdown and a goal. The change is evidently intended to protect good teams from weaker teams with good kickers.

The forward pass is about as it was last year, except that a man must be at least one yard back or at the end of the scrimmage line before he can take part in the play.

October 1909 Buchtelite

TIME-OUT

THE WAGON WHEEL

According to legend, the 'Wagon Wheel' came into being in the spring of 1870 when John R. Buchtel, an Akron industrialist, at the insistence of Rev. Andrew Wilson of the Kent Universalist Church, set out for Kent in search of a site for a proposed college. However, his wagon became bogged down in the mud where Kent State University is currently located, the horses broke away and left bits and pieces of the carriage scattered, including one of the wheels, which remained wedged in the mud.

Buchtel eventually found his way back to Akron, where he settled on a site for Buchtel College, the forerunner of the present University of Akron.

During construction of a pipeline along the Western Reserve Trail in 1902, the wheel was discovered and eventually became the property of Dr. Raymond Manchester, who in 1945 as the Kent State Dean of Men, suggested the wheel be set up as an award to the winner of the annual Akron-Kent State football game.

Manchester had the wheel painted blue and gold, the school colors of both schools, and it has been a prized trophy ever since. Each spoke bears a plaque verifying the score of each game.

In 1946, Kent defeated the Zips, 13–6, to capture the Wagon Wheel Trophy. After a Kent win in 1954, the series between the two schools went into hibernation. Not until Sept. 9, 1972, was the series revived. In that game, played at the Rubber Bowl, 25,131 saw UA grab a 13–0 lead, but KSU battled back to score 13 fourth-quarter points, and the contest ended in a tie. Akron was then awarded custodial rights for a two-year period for its first possession of the prized trophy since its inception. However, in 1979, UA earned the honor of possessing the Wagon Wheel when it edged the Flashes, 15–13. Since then, the two adversaries have traded the trophy back and forth.

The Zips have outscored Kent by a 392–258 margin in the last twelve seasons and won the Wheel in ten of those twelve meetings. UA leads the all-time series, 29–20–2.

Courtesy of The University of Akron Department of Intercollegiate Athletics

The Wagon Wheel. Courtesy of The University of Akron Department of Intercollegiate Athletics.

The Buchtelite

OL. XXVI — THE BUCHTELITE, NOVEMBER 2, 1914 — N

ADY NICOTINE TO PROMENADE CAMPUS

udents Circulate Petition to Secure Right to Smoke on the Campus—Many Signers

Should smoking be allowed on e campus? This question is daily rcing itself more and more upon e attention of the faculty. That should be allowed seems to be e belief of the majority of the ale students of the college. Cerin ones of those who are in favor the change have gone to the ouble of drawing up a petition the faculty. They have already cured 135 signers among the ys. So far, only two have reused to sign, while many of those ho have signed are non-smokers. he proposition, therefore, seems be a popular one with the stuents.

The arguments of those who are ttempting to get this new rule re mainly: That under the prest rule preventing smoking on the ampus, the students make a busiess of congregating in groups ust off the campus for the purose of smoking and that this ooks worse than if they smoked n the campus itself; that many f the larger colleges, many of hem co-ed, allow smoking on the ampus; that there is no real reaon why smoking should not be alowed.

The contention of some that moking on the campus would be howing a certain lack of respect or the young ladies of the college s refuted on the grounds that it vould be showing no less respect han smoking in their presence on he street. Those in favor of the uling feel the idea that the habit of smoking is a particularly bad ne and should be hidden, is gradually dying out, and that the attiude of the faculty toward it is hanging.

ORCHESTRA PLANS CONCERT

Plans are being formulated by the orchestra for a concert to be given the second Friday before Christmas.

Since the ruling has come into effect that members of the orchestra shall receive certain credits for their services, much time has been spent in studying some of the world's masterpieces. At present the players are studying Tschaikowsky's Barcarolle "June," Schubert's "Unfinished Symphony," and von Weber's "L'Invitation a la Valse."

There is also a possibility of a trip during the Easter vacation to cover territory of a hundred-mile radius in and about Akron.

AKRON TROUNCES KENYON 13-0

"Akron will shine to-night."

And she did by trouncing Kenyon in a fast contest by a score of 13 to 0. Also the varsity got a firmer hold on the top-rung of the Ohio conference.

After playing a strong game during the first half, the light Kenyon team weakened, and in the last half, "Slops" scored two touchdowns. The 6-14 ...

THE COLLEGE CALENDAR

Nov. 3.—Business meeting of the Y. W. C. A.; business meeting of the Woman's League; Lone Star will entertain their alumni at the fraternity house.

Nov. 5.—Orchestral rehearsal in Crouse gym. at 7 p. m.

Nov. 6.—Rushing party of Kappa Kappa Gamma.

Nov. 7.—Wittenberg game at 2:15 Buchtel field.

Nov. 12.—Orchestra rehearsal in Crouse gym. at 7 p. m.

Nov. 13.—Delta Gamma rushing party.

Nov. 15.—Reserve game at Buchtel field.

PHILIP MUSSER '17 CALLED BY DEATH

Succumbs to Second Attack of Typhoid After Friends Think He is About to Recover

Philip Musser, a graduate of Buchtel academy and a member of the class of '17, died at his home, at 231 Ash st., Saturday afternoon, October 25, of typhoid fever.

He had been held up in his studies once before by typhoid fever while in the academy. This made it necessary for him to attend summer school at Cornell last summer before coming back to Akron again this fall and be in full class standing. Having completed his work at Cornell he was about to register for the coming term at Buchtel when he was taken with the old trouble. He was sick for over a month, when he seemed to have recovered, but complications set in and the end came at 3:30 in the afternoon of the 25th. The funeral was held Sunday. Rev. H. W. Lowry officiated. The body was sent to the old home in Aaronsville, Pa., for interment.

At chapel on Tuesday morning of October 27, Prof. Olin, in a few words of respect for his memory, spoke of him as a young man with a promising future and many bright prospects suddenly shut out by death. The professor then requested the assembly to arise while he delivered a prayer in commemoration of our lost comrade.

WHERE ARE ALL OUR YELLOW FRESHMEN HATS?

"By their hats ye shall know them," doesn't apply on the campus this year. The freshies have either refused or neglected to wear their customary carrot-topped wigs during the first semester, and trouble looms grim ahead.

You see, it's this way. Last fall a crowd of high-thinking freshmen got together and decided they ought to do something for the school. So they decided to brighten things up in a few respects. They began by painting red the big time-honored rock that sleeps under the flagstaff, and then to infuse a little more color into the landscape, they bedecked their heads with green and yellow hats. Then, pleased with the success of their efforts, they decided to make it a custom of the college. So one night they met in solemn conclave and decided that, whereas they had subjected themselves to scorn and ridicule and all sorts of contumacious remarks from upper classmen because of their yellow and green garniture, be it resolved

ROSS FEATURES AGGIE GAME WITH SPECTACULAR 60-YD. RUN

AKRON OUTPLAYS FARMERS IN HEAD WORK AND OPEN PLAYS, BUT LOSES, 75 TO 6, BECAUSE OF BRUTE STRENGTH TACTICS OF OPPONENTS—"BILL" SMITH SCORES BLUE AND GOLD'S ONLY TOUCHDOWN.

Battling every moment, and even after they were sure of defeat pulling off plays which sent thrills through an enormous crowd of spectators, Akron university, outweighed and battered by the old army style of football tactics, went down to defeat at the hands of the Michigan Aggies, Saturday at Lansing by a score of 75 to 6.

But, however ignominious as this score may look to a casual glance, it does not tell the story of the game. Although beaten and with no chance of winning, the plucky Gold and Blue footballers began the third quarter with such a spurt that took the Aggies clear off their feet. They held them doggedly and even at the brute strength methods of line bucks were their equals. In this period the farmers could score but one touchdown, and Akron using head work and skill, in which departments they were conceded to be superior throughout the game, scored their one touchdown. The whole crowd of rooters rose to their feet and cheered in admiration of their plucky fighting spirit.

To Tony Ross belongs the honor and the credit of the third period of the game, and in individual feats his spectacular 60-yard run in this third period was the feature of the game. Intercepting a forward pass, he zigzaged across the field with the whole farmer aggregation in pursuit.

To Palmer and Smith also is due a glad hand on their work. Palmer was there with his forward pass work and made the Aggies open their eyes with his skill in this respect. Bill Smith gave him excellent support in receiving passes. To Bill belongs the credit of making the one touchdown. Immediately after Ross' 60-yard run, which placed the ball on Michigan's 10-yard line, Palmer made a perfect heave to Smith, who fell over the line.

The farmers gave up all attempts at forward passes after the first period because Akron was always there when it came to intercepting them.

Out of twelve attempts at forward passes the Aggies were successful with but two. Akron completed every pass attempted and netted gains.

The line-up and summary:

M. A. C.		Akron.
Blake Miller	L. E.	Foltz
Smith	L. T.	Crisp (capt.)
Straight	L. G.	Yackee
Vaughan	C.	Sours
Vandervoort	R. G.	Graham
Blacklock	R. T.	Driesbach
Chaddock	R. E.	Wilson, Smith
Dutch Miller	Q. B.	C. Palmer
Hamill	L. H.	Standefield
Julian	F. B.	Weeks
Deprato	R. H.	Ross

Score first quarter, M. A. C. 21, Akron 0; second quarter, M. A. C. 21, Akron 0; third quarter, M. A. C. 7, Akron 6; fourth quarter, M. A. C. 26, Akron 0; totals, M. A. C. 75, Akron 6. Substitutes—M. A. C., Oviatt for Blake Miller, Childs for Oviatt, Dutch Miller for Childs, Hutton for Smith, Loveland for Straight, White for Loveland, Reynolds for White, Loveland for Vandervoort, Coryell for Blacklock, Henning for Chaddock, Fick for Dutch Miller, Hewitt Miller for Hamill, O'Callaghan for Julian, Cobb for Deprato; Akron, Johnson for Foltz, Foltz for Yackee, Yackee for Sours, Auer for Graham, Knowlton for W. Smith, Brunner for Stansfield, Kuentz for Ross. Touchdowns—M. A. C., Julian 7, Deprato, Hamill, Fick, G. Smith; Akron, W. Smith. Time of quarters—15 min. Officials: Referee, Haines, Yale; umpire, Lynch, Brown; head linesman, Cox, Ohio State.

GRADES OF FRESHIES IMPROVE THIS MONTH

The first month's grades are now on file at the dean's office. A study of them reveals several interesting points. The freshmen grades are better this year than they were last year at the same time.

From the entire freshmen only two failed in every subject in contrast to the large number that failed last year. Three subjects, Rhetoric, Chemistry and Mathematics, seem to prove most difficult for the freshmen.

A number of students failed in six or more hours. They were notified by the dean of their condition. To aid them, conferences were formed which students may attend in order to receive special help.

A large number of students failed in one subject the first month.

PLAN ENGLISH CLUB TO TALK PROBLEMS

English teachers of Summit county met Wednesday night, October 28, in the library for the purpose of organizing a club.

The main aim of the club is to discuss all problems relating to English teaching. Many social affairs are also planned.

RANNEY LANDS JOBS FOR MANY STUDENTS

Seventy per cent. of the students in the school at the present time who are working secured their positions from Arthur Ranney, the manager of the Students' Employment bureau.

Ranney has made personal calls on 166 employers. Out of these calls he secured 58 positions of various kinds.

At the present time, 34 students

AKRON IS NOW MEMBER OF INTERCOLLEGIATE ATHLETIC ASSOCIATION

University of Akron has recently been admitted to the National Collegiate Athletic Association, organized to control intercollegiate athletics.

This association recommends faculty control of athletics, believing that the man in charge of physical education should be a member of the faculty. He should also have a thorough knowledge of athletic sports, and should be able to teach the difference between a clean played game and a game of brutality.

AKRON WILL HAVE FAST B. B. QUINTET

Palmer and Foltz Only Veterans Available—Good Material for Freshman Team

Four more weeks and we will have reached the second lap in the annual athletic journey. Prospects for a winning basketball team are as bright as ever. Though Foltz and Palmer are the only two men back from last year's 'varsity, Coach Haggerty will have last year's subs and men of last year's freshman team from whom to pick.

The most promising are Smith, Shea, Taylor, Knowlton and Stansfield. From these Coach Haggerty should be able to put another winning quintet into the field.

Owing to the fact that we are now in the conference, which does not permit freshmen to play on the 'varsity, a freshman team will be organized. From the material, there is no doubt but what a good freshman team will be put into the field.

The most likely looking candidates for this team are Bevington and Jackson, stars on last year's Central High team; and Thompson, captain of last year's South High team. There are also many other good candidates.

No schedule has as yet been arranged.

BACKS SEATS ARE AT A PREMIUM

Grand Rush for the Rear in Senorite Rines' Class in Spanish—Girls Are Driven to the Front!

Have you ever lined up down at the Colonial for some good show and waited for two hours to get a front seat in the "coop"?

Very likely you have. But if you have not, and wish to experience the varied joys of such an experience, just join the breathless throng that awaits the opening of the Spanish class.

For ten minutes before class time students congregate before aforesaid class room door. Then when the five-minute bell rings, with a mad pushing and shoving, they rush headlong into the room.

Now, don't get the idea that this is done because of any particular love for Spanish. Far be it from such! The reason is much simpler. Senorita Rines, the Spanish teacher, with great goodness of heart, did not assign seats for the class. For some strange reason or other, the students, especially the masculine ones, have a particular fondness for the back seats.

Hence, with ungodly haste, the

STUDENTS FORM ENGINEERS' CL

Officers Elected at Smoker F Saturday Night—All Engineers Eligible

For the purpose of organi an Engineering club, 25 stud of the Engineering departmen the university held a supper smoker Saturday evening, Oct 24, at the Savoy restaurant, on Market st.

The following officers elected: President, E. Glick; president, J. Kennedy; secre and treasurer, C. Soderlund. fessors Ayer and Mathewson, are interested in the movem were of much assistance to the dents in the preliminary wor organization.

A committee was also appoi to draft a constitution and to about making plans for the fut If it is possible a house somew in the vicinity of the school be procured, where meetings be held or where the members go at any time to talk over t work in the different factori the city.

According to the present p of the club, all those who are ing the course in Co-operative gineering will be eligible for n bership. The purpose of the will be to promote college s and to give future students o school a good chance to get quainted.

According to the present rangement, the students of school are divided into two tions. Naturally, those in one tion never come in contact those of the other section. I club is started, however, the n bers of the two classes will be to mingle and get ideas from another.

PICK KOLBE TO HEAD WORK FOR FAMILY X

Dr. Parke R. Kolbe, preside the University of Akron, has named by the chamber of merce as chairman of the co tee which will arrange Ak community Christmas celebr

Kolbe is to appoint other bers of the committee. He ex to have full membership by Thursday night when a me will be held to outline first for the celebration.

The chamber's thought in se ing Dr. Kolbe as chairman that as head of Akron's muni university he would best repr the idea back of a communi municipal Christmas.

Notices of Thursday ni meeting were sent out Satu by Dr. Kolbe to most of Ak civic organizations. Kolbe w able to announce his comm and further details early week, he said.

PALMER'S 45-YARD KICK TIES SC

"Slops" Robs Allegheny of tory and Saves Akron Scalp with 3-3 Score

Palmer's toe saved Akron defeat in the game with Alleg Dropping back and shaking mud from his shoe, he gav ball a mighty boot and sent it ing forty-five yards throug goal posts. The three point

CHAPTER 3
1910–1919

The 1910 Buchtel College team. Courtesy of The University of Akron Department of Intercollegiate Athletics.

November 1911

Outlucked

The game between the Varsity and Hiram was the best exhibition of football that has been seen upon the local gridiron this year. The loss of the game was due to the fact that Dame Fortune smiled upon Hiram with her most benevolent smile. The team never played harder than in the Hiram game, and four times was the ball within easy striking distance of Hiram's goal and a touchdown for us seemed almost inevitable, but it was at such critical points as this that luck broke against the team and a costly fumble recovered by a Hiram man lost for us every opportunity of placing the ball behind the goal line.

Hiram kicked off and we returned the ball about fifteen yards. Then a steady march up the field by line plunges and short forward passes, Jackson to Criss, until the ball was lost on a fumble. Hiram, unable to gain consistently, resorted to the boot of Leach, whose punts covered more distance than those of Zimmerman. The ball see-sawed back and forth, Buchtel rushing it up the field only to lose it on a fumble or on a final down, while Hiram would keep their goal line out of danger by punting. The greater part of the playing was done in Hiram territory.

In the second period, Buchtel clearly outclassed Hiram in line plunges, and the quick, short passes from Johnson to Criss was indeed a revelation to the crowd. These passes were pulled off so rapidly that the large band of loyal rooters stood with wide-open mouths and were so deeply interested then that they never gave a yell to cheer the team on. A fumble or a blocked punt was usually the cause for Buchtel losing the ball. Hiram seemed to be very fortunate in blocking our punts and then recovering the ball. This period passed without any scoring by either team.

During the third quarter the ball was in Buchtel's possession in Hiram's territory practically all the time. After having advanced the ball to within about 20 yards of Hiram's line Zimmerman tried a drop kick, the ball sailing straight for the crossbar but falling short by about ten feet. Alterdorfer immediately punted the ball out of danger for Hiram. Neither team was able to score during this quarter.

The play in the last period was in Buchtel's territory most of the time. The blocking of punts by Hiram was the chief reason for this. Also the fast work of Foltz, Hiram's fast right end, prevented us from running punts back very far. Upson attempting to punt upon our twenty-yard line Hiram blocked the punt and recovered the ball and by line plunges advanced it to the ten-yard line. Here we held them for two downs without them gaining any ground and on the third down with only about five minutes more of play left, Alterdorfer placed a drop kick between the uprights, scoring three points for Hiram. Darkness had begun to settle over the field and it made playing difficult. Hiram kicked to Buchtel and recovered the ball which they lost after a couple of downs on a fumble. A forward pass, Grimm to Criss, allowed Criss to get away for about fifty yards and a touchdown seemed within our grasp once more when the whistle sounded.

The work of Jackson and Criss with forward passes was great to see. The playing of Costigan, Zimmerman and Adams stood out prominently. Sidnell at half-back looks like a season veteran and his running mate Bethel was responsible for many long gains. Vittel was in the game all the time and bears evidence of it. Hochenschmidt upon going into the game prevented Hiram's right guard from grabbing Adams before he could get the ball to the other back field men. Johnson and Waldsmith both played an aggressive game.

December 1911

Reserve 0–Buchtel 0

Buchtel came back strong after the Ohio game and held the strong Western Reserve team scoreless through four periods before the largest crowd that ever witnessed a Buchtel football game. Reserve used all kinds of plays, but was unable to penetrate the varsity line. Both teams resorted to punting all through the game, the lines being solid on defense. Hoagland, who did the kicking for Reserve, had a little something on Zimmerman in this department of the game. In spite of Reserve's heavy line, the blue and gold played them to a stand-still. For Buchtel, Jackson was easily the star. On defense, offense and tackling he was "Johnny on the spot." Costigan also played a brilliant defense game. The entire struggle was hard fought. In the last quarter, Buchtel advanced within the shadow of the Reserve goal posts, through a series of finely executed forward passes by Jackson and Adams to Criss and Grimm. Here our last chance to score was lost by a bad pass to Zimmerman. For Reserve, Snider, Stroup and Hollinger, former Buchtelite, played a strong game. The varsity gained (3) first downs to Reserve's (1).

Lineup and summary:

Buchtel		*Reserve*
Grimm	left end	Geraci-Jewett
Costigan	left tackle	Barnes-Harsh
Vittel	left guard	Portman
Waldsmith	center	Evans
Hockenschmidt	right guard	Hoagland
Zimmerman	right tackle	Schulman
Criss	right end	Alleman-Knight
Adams	quarter back	Stroup
Bethel	left half back	Hollinger
Sidnell	right half back	Spurney

Buchtel		*Reserve*
Jackson	full back	Snider (c)

Referee-Connors (Bates). Umpire-Newcomb (Reserve). Field Judge-Jones (O.S.U.). Head linesman-Knight (Buchtel).

Case 5–Buchtel 0

After three-quarters of hard playing on a field which reminded one of an enlarged country road in early spring, Case sneaked over a touchdown, which proved to be the winning score. That five to nothing, however, does not give any record of just what the game was like. Coach Haggerty sent in the same lineup as was used against Reserve the previous Saturday. The condition of the field made fast playing impossible, and fumbles frequent. For three quarters Buchtel played rings around the Brown and White. In the first session, after downing a fumble on Case's 20 yard line, a drop was tried, missing by only a narrow margin. During the second and third quarters, Jackson tore off several gains. Roby punted frequently for the longest punts seen here, the wind being with him. Case became dangerous once, but was held on the 15 yard line. In the last period Case got their only touchdown on a fluke. A costly fumble of a punt on the 7 yard line gave Case the chance to push the ball over. There seems to have been some question as to whether the ball was not dead before it was finally carried over the line. Roby failed goal. This ended the scoring. Few trick plays were resorted to, punting and straight football being used almost exclusively. Roby punted great distances. The defense of both teams was good to see. For Buchtel, Grimm, Jackson, Criss, Costigan and Adams played great ball, while Roby, Weiler and Kenyon starred for Case. Contrary to many reports, let it be said that as to weight, matters were about even; that Case did not make 11 first downs to Buchtel's 1; and finally that the substitution of fresh men by Case seemed quite necessary in the opinion of Coach Scott. In view of these facts we feel as did many of the members of the Case team, who said "that they were lucky to have won." It was luck, but it was a football game.

Lineup and summary:

Buchtel		*Case*
Criss	left end	Kipka
Costigan	left tackle	Glaser-Randall
Hochenschmidt	left guard	Parsons
Waldsmith	center	Whelan
Vittel	right guard	Weiler
Zimmerman	right tackle	Hyland
Grimm	right end	Francy-Boley
Adams	quarter back	Roby

The 1911 Buchtel College team. Photo from the Tel-Buch, *courtesy of Archival Services, University Libraries, The University of Akron.*

Buchtel		*Case*
Bethel	left half back	Slater-Goss
Sidnell	right half back	Kenyon-Young-McAfee
Jackson	full back	Marsh

Touchdown-Roby. Referee-Durfee. Umpire-Newcomb. Field judge-Merrill. Periods, 15 minutes.

Heidelberg-Buchtel

The game was cancelled, owing to the sloppy condition of East End field, making play impossible and putting the kibosh on even a fair attendance. Might have added another scalp to the string.

December 1913

Buchtel Wins Marietta Game in Second Half

On November 15 Buchtel had the pleasure of trouncing Marietta to the tune of 23 to 0. Although held scoreless in the first half, the Blue and Gold opened things up in the second half and showed what it could do.

Palmer started the music when at the beginning of the second half he took the ball from the kick-off and carried it through the entire Marietta team for the first touchdown. Sidnell soon followed suit by taking the ball over from the 10-yard line, and, in a few minutes more he drop-kicked a goal over the bar, which brought the score to 16. In the last quarter Ross carried one over for the final score of the game, 23–0.

The entire team did excellent work, both on offense and defense. As things were going pretty smoothly in the last half, the second-string men were put in. They also gave a classy exhibition of football.

Line-up and summary:

Buchtel		*Marietta*
Johnson	left end	Martin
Crisp	left tackle	Humphrey
Foltz	left guard	Miller
Waldsmith	center	Baum
Yackee	right guard	Herlihy
Driesbach	right tackle	Aumend
Eberhardt	right end	Meister
Palmer	quarter back	Freshour
Ranney	left half	Kelly
Ross	right half	Rowland
Swinehart	full back	White

Touchdowns-Palmer, Sidnell, Ross. Goals from touchdown-Crisp 2. Goals from field-Sidnell. Substitutions-First quarter: Weeks for Ranney. Second quarter: Picket for Rowland; Rowland for Meister. Third quarter: Sidnell for Weeks; Thomas for Johnson; Sours for Foltz; Smith for Eberhardt; Stansfield for Sidnell; Crawford for Ross. Fourth quarter: Watters for Yackee; Ross for Stansfield; Sidnell for Swinehart; Johnson for Thomas; Eberhardt for Smith; Ranney for Crawford; Reed for Sours; Musser for Yackee; Swinehart for Sidnell; Weeks for Ranney; Sours for Waldsmith; Thomas for Johnson. Officials-Kinney of Yale, referee-Newcomb of Reserve, umpire-Knight of Buchtel, head linesman. Times of quarters-15 m. and 12 ½ m.

November 2, 1914

Football Not as Dangerous Now

"Better knowledge of the game has lessened the dangers of football more than the changing of the rules," Coach Haggerty believes. As coaches become more familiar with the game, and are better able to teach the fundamentals of the sport, the dangers to the player are lessened.

As the player, also, becomes more familiar with the plays, he knows better how to act to avoid injury.

A great many changes, tending to lessen danger, have been made in the rules since 1906, and coaches and players have been able to become familiar with the rules.

One revision this year that has not lessened the danger of the player is the one where the words "running into the fullback after a kick," have been changed to "roughing" the kicker. Last year a player breaking through the line to block a kick was not allowed to run into the kicker; this year he is permitted to run against the kicker. The player charging through the line may in some way injure the kicker; the referee, however, is to decide whether the foul was committed on purpose or not.

Another revision this year which has attracted more attention and more criticism than any other is the amendment which prohibits the head coach from walking up and down the side lines. In the past, coaches like Yost, by following their teams as the battle ebbed and flowed between the two goals, more easily could see what play or plays were proving effective and where the opponents were gaining. Thus they were able to send instructions to the quarterback and captain as to both offense and defense.

Another important change, and one that has done away with a troublesome technicality in the rules, is the revision prohibiting the "grounding of a forward pass." Last year, and even before that, the forward passer, if caught yards behind the line of pass, would toss it to the ground before being tackled, thereby creating an incomplete forward pass. Instead of losing the distance he was pushed back and merely lost the down, the ball going back whence it was put in play. This time, however, the ball goes into play where the passer was tackled under such conditions.

In order to prevent the roughing of the passer, which frequently took place last year, and which surely would result with the prohibition of grounding the pass when endangered, a penalty of five yards has been established for roughing a forward passer. This will do away with many attempts to put a star with a long hurl out of the game.

A forward pass is incomplete if any part of the body of the passer or the player who receives the pass is over the side line or line of the end zone.

The touchback no longer will be followed with a kickout, as in the past, but with the new rules the ball, after touchbacks, will be put in play on the 20-yard line.

This change, with the addition of the field judge, to the list of officials, in cases where a field judge is desired by both coaches, completes the list of revisions.

Akron Trounces Kenyon 13–0

"Akron will shine to-night."

And she did by trouncing Kenyon in a fast contest by a score of 13 to 0. Also the varsity got a firmer hold on the top-rung of the Ohio conference.

After playing a strong game during the first half, the light Kenyon team weakened, and in the last half, "Slops" scored two touchdowns. The field was dry and fast and the visitors appeared to advantage in the early stages of the game, but Akron's experience and weight soon began to tell.

For Akron, Crisp, Palmer and Smith shone, while Stout, Kenyon's red-haired end, starred for the visitors. In the second quarter, Ranney, considered by many to be Akron's best linesman, suffered an injury to his leg, so serious that he was compelled to leave the game.

In the fourth quarter, Palmer received a punt on Kenyon's 40-yard line, and with Bruner for interference ran through the entire Kenyon team for a touchdown. By his playing in the last two contests, Palmer deserves a place on the "All-Ohio Conference" football team.

The line-up:

Akron		Kenyon
Ranney	left end	Kinder
Crisp	left tackle	McGormley
Foltz	left guard	Axtell
Sours	center	Sayer
Johnson	right guard	Zeaman
Driesbach	right tackle	VanVorhies
Smith	right end	Stout
Palmer	quarter back	Schaefer
Stansfield	left half back	Vance
Ross	right half back	Engle
Weeks	full back	Hallwood

December 1, 1914

Football

Being an Exposition of the Horrors and Brutalities of Football as Practiced in Our Colleges

By Reginald Aloysus Van Ransaelaer

FOOTBALL! How that single word strikes me with a sickening sense of horror. And to think that our American colleges and universities allow it to be played and even foster it.

When I think of a football game (and I never wish to witness another) before my mind's eye comes the scene of the crowded amphitheatre like the barbarous arena of Roman days. Out on the gridiron (a warmer place than the name implies) the rival teams, composed of the best developed young men the college produces, are struggling in strenuous strife. How they charge each other, features drawn, disheveled and distorted, their tense, rigid forms come cruelly clashing into each other. Onslaught after onslaught, they try, and if they are held by their ruthless, unrelenting rivals, they kick the ball (an inflated leather missile) high into the air only to renew the strife as it falls to earth. At times the field is strewn with maimed and incapacitated members who are urged back into the fray by a brutal bloodthirsty bunch of spectators. For a whole hour this horrible fray continues with only several pauses for the recovery of their fleeting vitality.

O you, Grant Hague and other eugenic writers, do not attack war as the destroyer of the nation's best, but direct your energies against this terrible Gorgon which is annually maiming, killing and disabling our American youths. If we must have contests, let them be in studying of the classics. But (using the thought of Emerson), football! football! What brutal, bruising, brawl is that to develop the animal tendencies of Nature's greatest work, college students.

November 23, 1917

Akron U. Beats Camp Sherman

When Soldier Lads Missed their Guess and Slated Seftonites as Easy Money. A.U. Team Shows Fine Form and Training.

The local University, strengthened by Coach Sefton and Ollie Driesbach, showed how team work may overcome individual stars. The Chillicothe team was composed of ex-college stars, including men from some of the well known colleges throughout the country. The team which came to Akron was the second team from Sherman, the first team going to Cincinnati. It would seem from the results that it would have been a good idea to send the first team to Akron. The score was a surprise to most people for the Army men were in good shape and every man on the team was an experienced football player of note.

About two thousand people saw the game, which was exciting from beginning to end. The game was preceded by a prize drill by two hundred of the Chillicothe men, who came to Akron for the game. Jack Knowlton, of U. of A. fame, played with the Army.

Akron started the game by kicking to the Army men. The Army failed to gain and punted. Haley and Welker gained, Haley through the line and Welker around the end. Haley gained on a 10-yard pass from Tomkinson. Akron made first down when Haley made a 15-yard pass to Bierce, placing the ball on the Army 4-yard line. Tomkinson made the first touchdown. Haley missed goal. Akron again kicked. The Army team failed to gain, and Meredith made a 30-yard punt to the Army's 25-yard line. Tomkinson gained two yards and lost one yard, netting one yard. On fourth down, Haley made a 30-yard pass to Bierce back to the goal line, making another touchdown for Akron. Haley kicked goal.

The Army kicked to Sefton, who carried the ball to Akron's 40-yard line. Haley fumbled, but Vogt recovered the ball. Haley made a 10-yard pass to Bierce. Akron then failed to gain and Haley punted to the Army's 20-yard line. The quarter ended.

The Army punted to Akron. The ball was put in play on the Army's 40-yard line. Haley and Bierce gained, then Akron lost the ball on incomplete passes. Army punt-

The 1915 team. Photo from the Tel-Buch, *courtesy of Archival Services, University Libraries, The University of Akron.*

ed to Haley, who carried the ball to Army's 45-yard line. Haley and Welker gained, making first down on Army's 35-yard line. The Army intercepted Akron's pass, but fumbled and the ball belonged again to Akron. Getz intercepted a pass and made a 40-yard run. Englehart made a touchdown. Conant kicked goal. The Army kicked to Akron's 2-yard line and Welker carried the ball to Akron's 30-yard line, where Akron lost the ball on a fumble. The half ended, 13 to 7 in favor of Akron.

The Army punted to Haley. Akron failed to gain and Haley punted. The Army did not gain and punted to Sefton. Haley gained five yards and Welker four yards. Haley then made a 30-yard run, placing the ball on the Army's 10-yard line. Tomkinson gained five yards. Welker passed to Tomkinson, who made a touchdown. Haley missed goal. Akron kicked to the Army. Denaple made a 15-yard run, making first down. The quarter ended with the ball on Akron's 20-yard line.

The Army lost the ball. Welker made ten yards and Haley eight yards on end runs. Haley punted to the Army. Rogers broke through the Army's line and tackled Denaple for a loss. Sefton broke up a pass and Fish grabbed the ball. Haley made a 30-yard run for a touchdown.

Haley missed goal. The Army kicked to Sefton. Welker gained three yards and Haley thirty yards. Haley punted to the Army's 20-yard line. Bierce intercepted a forward pass. Haley made a 10-yard pass to Miller. The game ended. Final score, 25–7 in favor of Akron U.

Getz and Denaple starred for the Army, while Haley and Bierce starred for Akron. Englehart played a fine game for the Army. Sefton's powerful defensive work was an aid to Akron.

The 1916 team. Photo from the Tel-Buch, *courtesy of Archival Services, University Libraries, The University of Akron.*

Lineup and summary follow:

Akron U		*Camp Sherman*
Sefton	left end	Zeemans
Driesbach	left tackle	Meredith
Vogt	left guard	Harsh (Capt.)
Avery	center	Falcon
Pfahl	right guard	Conant
Rogers	right tackle	Turnbull
Bierce	right end	Knowlton
Tomkinson (Capt.)	quarter back	Getz
Welker	left half back	Denaple
Haley	right half back	Whinnery
Miller	full back	Englehart

Touchdowns-Tomkinson (2), Haley, Bierce, Englehart. Goals after touchdowns-Haley, Conant. Substitutes-Boedicker for Pfahl, Fish for Vogt, Shamp for Zeeman, Ablee for Shamp, Selzer for Ablee. Referee-Waldsmith, Akron. Umpire-Costigan, Akron. Head linesman-Stewart, Colgate.

November 14, 1919

Wooster Blasts Akron's Conference Hopes

Akron Team Unable to Play Brand of Ball Which Has Won Former Games. Bole's Team Pile Up a 19–0 Score. First Quarter Disastrous to Sefton's Squad.

Last Saturday Akron again bowed before the football team of Wooster College and incidentally lost their chance for a clean slate and the State title. Akron's championship hopes were dashed upon the rocks in the first quarter, when Wooster scored two touchdowns. Boles' team displayed a variety of attack and a burst of speed that swept the Akron team off its feet. When Sefton's boys awoke and realized that they were playing football they faced a 13 to 0 score. Akron was successful in threatening Wooster's goal several times, but lacked the necessary punch to put the ball over. Again Akron's line held several times when Wooster couldn't deliver the punch. Akron played good ball throughout, but the breaks were not with Sefton's gridders. It was again the same old story of the Wooster hoodoo, which seems to follow Sefton whenever he plays Boles' football teams. Three times have the Wooster boys beaten Akron when the defeat meant the ruining of an Akron championship. Perhaps Sefton and Akron can some day beat Wooster, but it will be after the jinx has been overcome.

The score of the game does not tell the true story of the battle. During the second and third quarters Akron played a great brand of football, and the results show that Akron and Wooster each made 16 first downs. Wooster's, however, were bunched and the breaks favored them. Akron's line between the ends was outweighed fifteen pounds to the man and, although they played to the best of their ability, they were unable to cope with the attack of their hefty opponents.

Four hundred Akron supporters were in the stands, and in cheering easily outclassed the Wooster cohorts. Although beaten, the rooters showed a characteristic Akron spirit of good losers and sports.

Haley, Daum and Bierce star for Akron, while Snyder was Wooster's best.

Daum and Bierce, next to Haley, were the shining lights of Akron's team. Between the ends, outside of center, Akron's line was clearly outplayed. Wentz put up a wonderful game at center, blocking a punt and playing a good defensive game. Red Daum and Scotty Bierce, however, were the real line stars. These men put up a wonderful game and continually spilled the runners for losses. Due to the inability of Akron's tackler's to break through and spill the interference, Wooster's back would fly around the ends with four and five men interference.

Daum and Bierce were equal to the occasion, however, and often spilled the interference and the man also. Daum threw Roderick and Snyder for five and ten yard losses time and again. Scotty was in every play and pulled the runner down from behind several times. In the backfield Haley was easily the star. Swigart and Whalen played well, but were not able to gain consistently. Haley was easily the best man on the field. His gains were even the more remarkable because of the fact that he was alone in his efforts. Wooster's line broke through and broke up Akron's interference before Haley started. As a result Haley made all his gains with no interference. Time and again Akron's star shook off four or five men before he was downed. For Wooster Snyder and Roderick in the back and Walker, Hague and Billingsley on the line played best. Snyder was easily Wooster's star. While Capt. Roderick saw to it that he was the one to score, it was Snyder who always placed the ball in a position to score. Snyder's work of returning punts was also of high class. Wooster's tackles, Walker and Billingsley played fine ball, breaking through and worrying Haley on passes.

Akron's best chance to score came in the second period. When Wentz blocked Roderick's punt and recovered it the ball nestled on Wooster's six-yard line. Akron, however, lost the ball and Roderick punted out of danger. Although beaten, the Akron team was not disgraced and will enter tomorrow's game with a grim determination.

Summary

First Quarter

Billingsley returned the kickoff to Wooster's 20-yard line. Snyder went through right tackle for 22 yards. Fulton, Atkinson, Snyder and Roderick carried the ball for two first downs. Roderick circled left end for 15 yards. Atkinson went through for four yards, and Roderick carried it the last ten yards for a touchdown. He missed the goal. The score was made in four and a half minutes.

Wooster kicked. Haley returned the ball to Akron's 30-yard line. Haley made three yards and Swigart made a first down. A forward pass to Swigart netted 15 yards. Wooster received the ball on downs on her own 40-yard line. Fulton made three yards and Akron was penalized five yards for offside. Roderick made three, Atkinson ten. Fulton made another first down, and Wooster was penalized 15 yards for holding. Roderick took the ball around right end for 30 yards and a touchdown. He also kicked the goal. The second score was made in 12 minutes.

Wooster kicked and Haley was thrown on his own eight-yard line. Haley punted out of bounds of Akron's 25-yard line. Atkinson made 5 and Roderick a first down. Snyder and Roderick made another first down, and the quarter ended with the ball on Akron's one-yard line.

Second Quarter

Wooster was penalized five yards for offside on the first play. A forward pass failed. Akron received the ball on her own 20-yard line. Whalen made five. Swigart gained 15 through the line. Haley made three, and Swigart made 10 more. Wooster's line held, and Haley tried a forward pass unsuccessfully, though the ball was in midfield. Wooster received the ball. Roderick and Snyder made a first down. Atkinson made five. Wooster was penalized five yards. Fulton lost five more, and Roderick went back another five. Roderick punted to Akron's 10-yard line and Haley made a first down. Two slight gains were made through the line, and Wooster drew a five-yard penalty, giving Akron another first down. A forward pass to Bierce netted another first down. Haley and Pfahl made another first down. Akron was then in striking distance of the Wooster goal. A forward pass was tried, with Atkinson snatching it from the air an inch or two ahead of Daum's ready fingers. Atkinson was under his own goal at the time and gained 15 yards before he was thrown. The half ended with this play.

Third Quarter

Akron received the kickoff and Whalen returned the ball 20 yards. Haley tried a forward when the line held and Wooster received the ball on Akron's 25-yard line. Roderick lost eight yards, Daum breaking through and throwing him. Snyder regained the ground. Roderick attempted a drop kick, but the ball went nowhere near the goal. Haley caught the kick and returned it 10 yards. He was forced to punt and kicked to Wooster's 10-yard line. Daum broke through again and hurled Roderick for a big loss on Wooster's five-yard line. Wooster gained on a fake kick, but couldn't make a first down, and Roderick dropped back to kick. The punt was blocked and Whalen fell on the ball on Wooster's 22-yard line. Whalen made 10 yards on the next play, and Haley made five, taking the ball to Wooster's seven-yard line. Swigart lost five yards. A forward pass was tried, but failed, and the ball went to Wooster on her own 12-yard line. Roderick made a first down, and Atkinson made another. Roderick tried another punt, which was blocked. Murray, however, recovered the ball for Wooster on Akron's 45-yard line. Snyder made 17 yards through the line. Roderick was tackled hard by Daum before he got started, and fumbled, Bierce recovering. Haley made a first down. Haley tried six forwards in succession, one to Swigart gaining 10 yards, others failed and Wooster received the ball on downs. Roderick was twice thrown for a loss, once by Daum and once by Bierce. Wooster also suffered a 15-yard penalty as quarter closed, the ball being on her own 20-yard line.

Fourth Quarter

Roderick punted to midfield. Two forwards failed, and Haley punted 15 yards. Fulton caught the ball and returned it past the line from which Haley had punted. He made a first down on the next play. The first attempt at an over-the-line pass failed, but Roderick went through right tackle for a first down. On the next play he broke away from the field and went over for his third touchdown. He missed the goal.

When Wooster kicked off, Uncle Sam's gray-clad mail man came into prominence through his blunder, which robbed Wooster of another touchdown. The ball went in play on Akron's 20-yard line. Haley punted, and in two plays the ball was worked back to the 20-yard line. A forward pass was incomplete and Akron received the ball. Haley was forced to punt again, and when Akron's line held Roderick punted to Akron's 10-yard line. Haley tore off a run around right end for 30 yards, and then started passing. One to Swigart made 10 yards, another to Daum made 20. A second to Daum gained nine. Daum was forced to leave his feet in a headlong dive to catch the ball and, though tackled as he touched it, managed to hang fast to the pigskin. The ball was then on Wooster's 15-yard line. Another pass was tried and, for the second time in the game, it was snatched from Daum's fingers by a Wooster man on his own goal line. Fulton caught this one. Here in the shadow of her goal posts the game ended.

The lineup and summary:

Akron		*Wooster*
Daum	left end	Stiffler
Tisdale	left tackle	Walker
W. Pfahl	left guard	Hague
Wentz	center	Williams
Boedicker	right guard	Laporte
Eckert	right tackle	Billingsley
Bierce	right end	Murria
Haley	quarter back	Snyder
Swigart	left half back	Atkinson
Whalen	right half back	Fulton
C. Pfahl	full back	Roderick

Touchdowns-Roderick, 3. Goal from touchdown-Roderick. Substitutions-Wooster: Dunbar for Atkinson, Hess for Williams, Masi for Fulton, Potts for Stiffler, Watkins for Dunbar, White for Billingsley, Hopkins for Hague, Mitchell for Laporte. Akron: Swinehart for C. Pfahl, Post for Whalen, Knowlton for Tisdale. Time of quarters-15 minutes. Penalties-Akron, 5 yards; Wooster, 45 yards. Referee-Evans, Ohio Wesleyan. Umpire-Tyler, Reserve. Head linesman-Gray, Wisconsin.

At Wooster last Saturday, Bierce and Daum, together with Haley, stood out head and shoulders above every man on the field. "Scotty" and "Red" played their opponents off their feet. Time and time again this pair of ends smashed in and threw the Wooster backs for 5 and 10 yard losses. Wooster could gain around them only with the best of interference, and even then they would stop them. The Wooster crowd thought them the best pair of ends ever seen on Severence Field.

Sidelights on the Game

Akron fans wore out a lot of shoe leather walking back from Wooster. Tough luck, better luck tomorrow.

Whalen and Swigart made some nice gains during the first quarter.

Wooster started so fast that they had the game won before Akron woke up.

Akron completed some great passes, but also lost a few.

Wooster men said after the game that Daum and Bierce were some players.

Although Roderick scored all the points, he was easily outplayed by his own teammate Snyder.

Wentz played a fine game at center.

Wooster had wonderful interference both on end runs and center bucks. Akron was dolefully weak in this respect.

It took the Akron crowd little time to show Wooster how to yell.

The Wooster line was at least ten pounds heavier to the man than Akron's.

Akron students are a little down in the pocketbook this week.

Are We Downhearted? No.

Perhaps the most pleasing thing about last Saturday's fracas was the spirit shown by Akron rooters after defeat. We've all seen the yellow dog before starting a fight with a Tomcat. He approaches, all bark and bristles, with lots of outward signs of courage. But it doesn't last long; one good swipe from the cat's paw and the cur puts his tail between his legs and starts yelping away. Last Saturday Akron showed the opposite quality. Realizing the game was lost, Akron rooters not only encouraged their own team, but also congratulated their rivals. This is real school spirit and commands respect, but it does not stop there. What about tomorrow and next Saturday? Are we downhearted? Are we going to give up and lie down or run away like the yellow cur? We will say emphatically "No." Akron spirit is not made of such stuff. Our school spirit goes deeper than mere physical demonstration. We believe in our team and our school, and are out to fight to the end and through victory or defeat. Let's show the real school spirit of our school by getting out at Buchtel Field, as we did down at Wooster. Let's show that we are good losers as well as good winners.

Reserve and Case are two of the highest games on Akron's schedule. Akron would much rather be defeated by Wooster than by Case or Reserve. Both teams are strong and demand the support of every Akron booster. Do your part; support your team; help beat Reserve.

R AIM
ARGER
BETTER
TELITE

The Buchtelite

OUR
CIRCULATIO
IS
1,200

XXXV, No. 9 The Municipal University of Akron, Ohio November 21, 1

MATIC STUDY UB SPONSORS VALKER THEATER

aneau Production of Three Plays Is To Be Given on Friday

first attraction on this year's n of the dramatic study depart- f the University will be Stuart 's Portmanteau Theater plays shown in Perkins Auditorium evening.

Valker will bring an entire the- hich can be taken apart and in ten boxes, unpacked and set in within three hours. When an entire theater is revealed, ng a stage proscenium, curtains hting scheme. It is so arranged while the interlude is being on the front stage the inner is being arranged for the next A regular professional stage ccompanies the Portmanteau.

A Unique Theater

Portmanteau is the only port- heater in the United States. Mr. r's theater has been known as heater that comes to you," since be set up anywhere. Perkins rium has been selected because niversity chapel has inadequate arrangement for such an

plicity is the keynote of the anteau plays. Various drops are ed so that a different back- is used for each scene. he framework remains the same, olors predominate the stationary r—black, white, blue and gold. single unessential is used that throw off the action of the play. alker believes that the theaters ay are in a stage of realism so e that the audience can hardly hether they are in a neighbor's or in the theater. He has ed his stage of all items that clutter up the performance, re- on color, line effects and light- vices to achieve variety.

Three Shows To Be Given

shows include "The Trimplet," Medicine Show" and "Never- s." A fourth play, "The Gods of ountain," may be added.

Carita E. McEbright, who has of the sale of all the student s, has urged everyone in all her s to take advantage of the op- ity to see something so worth It is her wish that everyone can possibly attend on Friday g would see her for reserved in the balcony, which are the seats in the audiorium. The of these seats is one dollar. side reservations can also be through Mr. Fletcher, of the e Book Store.

NCH CLUB PRESENTS LUEBEARD PANTOMIME

the second meeting of LeCercle cais, held Wednesday, Novem- 14th, in the Woman's League s, the feature of the evening pantomime acted out by the

R. L. S. QUILL CLUB HONORS INITIATES WITH BANQUET

The R. L. S. Quill Club held initia- tion services for three new members in the Woman's League rooms at 6:15 last evening. After the initiation, a ban- quet was held at the University Club.

The initiation services were in charge of Wallace L. MacKinnon (A-4), Chan- cellor of the club. At the end of the services the R. L. S. song, the words and music of which were written by Dr. Raymond B. Fease, was sung. The admission of these three new mem- bers, Margaret Spanton (A-2), Eugene Denning (A-2), and Robert P. Hall (A 4), brings the membership of the club to its quota of twenty members.

The initiates were guests of honor at the banquet at the University Club. Dr. Fease, Dean Albert I. Spanton, and Dorothy Shreve responded to calls for toasts by Wallace MacKinnon, toast- master. Kathleen Masterson read a portion of her novel, "Jerry," for the club.

AMENDMENT TO BE VOTED IN CHAPEL

Will Vote To Reinstate Coach Sefton as Member of the Athletic Board

A vote will be taken in chapel Friday to include Coach Fred Sef- ton in the Athletic Board of Con- trol. The membership of the Board now includes three students, the faculty representatives to the Con- ference, the graduate manager of athletics, the treasurer of the Uni- versity and the president of the "A" Association.

Formerly Coach Sefton was grad- uate manager of athletics, but when W. A. Moore took over the work he was automatically dropped from the Athletic Association. To rein- state him to his rightful position a vote of the student body is to be taken.

The question to be voted on is: Proposed to amend the Constitution of the Athletic Association to in- clude as one of its officers the head of the Department of Physical Training."

BAND TO PARADE FOR LAST TIME

Appearance at Wesleyan Game Will Be Last During Foot- ball Season

The University band will appear for the last time during the football sea- son at the Wesleyan game Saturday.

"We expect to have everything in good shape for the game Saturday," said Mr. James Weber, musical direc- tor of the University band. "The band will march out on the field and play one of the Wesleyan songs in front of their bleachers, and then return to the Akron side and play the Alma Mater."

"We are holding regular rehearsals on Tuesdays and Thursdays," Mr. Weber stated. "The last rehearsal was held out-of-doors and we practiced some formations. Every one must be out to the final rehearsal tomorrow;

UNIVERSITY CLUB GRANTED CHAPTER OF MASONIC FRAT

Installation of Square and Com- pass Will Take Place During December

The Square and Compass, national Masonic fraternity, has granted a char- ter to the Akron University Masonic Club.

The installation ceremonies will take place in December, and will be in charge of the national oficers. A ban- quet will be held following the instal- lation and initiation.

Membership in the Square and Compass is limited to Master Masons and is on the same basis as in all other Masonic organizations. How- ever, members of Greek Letter frater- nities are eligible to membership if they meet the necessary Masonic qual- ifications.

Charter members are: Dr George L. Hayes, Dr. R Pease, Prof. H. V. Eg- bert, Carl Leffler (1922), Pearl Vanica (E-4), George L. Harding (U). Wm. J. Irwin (U), Elmer Houck (U), Wm. Holsinger (1922), Emory C. Auten (U) and Jack Evans (A-3).

The Square and Compass was founded at Washington and Lee. At the present time it has about thirty- five squares (the chapters are called squares). This is the first square to be established in Ohio. It is already established in such schools as the Uni- versity of Illinois, the University of Wisconsin, Tulane University, Colum- bia University, Vanderbilt University, Louisiana State and Brown University.

ALUMNI OFFERS GENEROUS PRIZE

Person Who Writes Best Words For New Alma Mater to Receive Award

A prize of $25 has been offered by the Alumni Association for the best words for a new University of Akron song to replace the present Alma Mater.

The contest is open to all under- graduates of both the day and night schools, alumni, former students and faculty. The music will be written later.

The offer is called forth by various complaints regarding the fitness of the present song in a multiple school Uni- versity as well as its common usage among other schools

The judges of the winning words will be President Parke R. Kolbe ('01), Dean A. I. Spanton ('99) and Francesco B. DeLeone, instructor in music.

Entries must be handed in to the office of the Alumni Secretary, Buch- tel Hall, on or before December 31.

The winning verses will be read at the Founder's Day chapel exercises Friday, January 18th, and also at the Founder's Day ball at the Armory the same evening.

ILLNESS FORCES POET TO CANCEL ENGAGEMENT

John J. Neihardt, Nebraska Poet Laureate, and writer of what is called the greatest American Epic, has been forced to discontinue a tour which would have brought him to Akron to night. Mr. Neihardt was to give read- ings from his own poems at the Little Theater, and was to have been brought here under the auspices of the Summit County English Club, of which Dr. R. B. Pease, professor of English, is president. No details of the illness which caused the cancella- tion have been received by Dr. Pease, but a letter from Mr. Neihardt's man- ager indicated a nervous breakdown. Members of the Literature Club had been given an opportunity to hear the readings, admission to which was to have been by invitation only.

GLEE CLUBS PLAN JANUARY CONCERT

Men's Organizations Divided On The Question of What To Wear

Prof. Francesco B. DeLeone, di- rector of music, stated that the work on the operatic concert is pro- gressing. The plan is to give the concert at the Akron Armory; seats will sell for fom $1 to $2.50. Ar- rangements have not yet been made to obtain the Armory and no date has been set. Prof. DeLeone said that when he thought enough pro- gress had been made to justify an appearance in public he would go ahead with his plans, and not until then.

The question now before the Men's Glee Club is whether to make its subsequent appearance in tux- edos or in full dress. It has been decided to hold the operatic concert next January at the Armory.

In a vote taken on the tux vs. full dress question at the last glee club meeting the result was 10 to 9 in favor of the tuxedos. There are, however, some men who purchased full dress suits for the glee club last year and who are now faced with the problem of selling them or hav- ing the glee club. Other men in school who have tuxedoes would have tried out for the glee club at the beginning of the term if announce- ment had been made to the effect that tuxedoes would be used

GIRLS SHOW PEP IN RIFLE WORK

Over Fifty Girls Have Begun Actual Sighting and Aiming Practice

Actual work in sighting and aiming began for the women's rifle team this week.

Last week the girls were given gen- eral talks on the purposes of the course. Capt. W. L. Tydings started the girls in their real work last Mon- day afternoon He was assisted by Lieut. K. P. Cooley and Master Serg. H. Metzger.

BLUE AND GOLD HERE SATURDAY LAST GAME OF YE

Conference Leaders Have Sl Edge Over Akron in Com ing Battle

Coach Sefton's gridders finish 1923 season next Saturday, pl Ohio Wesleyan at Buchtel field.

Wesleyan is now tied with Wo for the Conference leadership, according to reports the Dela team is improving with every ga

The Methodists have a line wh supposed to average between 17 180 pounds, though their backfie slightly lighter than Wooster's.

The Wesleyan backfield is around "Ten" Turney, a husky back, who smashes the line with mendous force and with speed n ually seen in a man of his size.

Pearce, another heavy back, fl into prominence when Wes played Ohio State. Since the has been shining in all the gam has started.

Sacksteder, Staten and Winter three more backfield men of the water.

Dope For Wesleyan

While the dope of comparative ings gives Wesleyan the edge ove Seftonites this week, several fa discount this handicap to a con able degree.

In the first place, Staten is o hospital list and some other ball on the team are pretty well brise so that they are not in the form that they were in a few weeks a

In spite of this Wesleyan is sa be tremendously confident of me ing Akron. One of their own pl is reported to have said after the leyan-Colgate game that the M ists should be able to trim Akr at least five touchdowns.

Coach Sefton is glad to hear words. As a matter of fact, he i ing that the whole Wesleyan comes here "cocky" of its chanc walking away from the Buchtelit

Nothing would help Akron to half so much as to have the C ence leaders so sure of them that they would play a careless g

Cripples Coming Back

Akron's crippled backfield m ready to start Saturday. Hayes kins has been resting his leg f hopes that the pulled ligamen round into shape.

Jean Smith is also taking good of a wrenched knee, and it is pro that he can appear by taping t jured member tightly

Stump's ankle is weak, but t take a hard blow to put it out o mission.

Spessard held down Brown's position with plenty of credit a ami, so the line looms stronger fo game than it has been at any tin year.

WOMAN'S LEAGUE HAS GOOD PA

Senior Stunt Consisting of

CHAPTER 4
1920–1929

The 1929 team. Photo from Tel-Buch, *courtesy of Archival Services, University Libraries, The University of Akron.*

November 4, 1921

By Defeating Mount, Akron Climbs in Conference

Wise Stops Speeding Visitor Seven Yards from the Goal Line

"They say that Old Akron ain't got no style!"

They may say it, but "she's got style all the while!" The latter fact was well demonstrated last Saturday afternoon when the Blue and Gold walked away with a 28 to 14 victory over Mt. Union.

Playing their best game of the season, the Blue and Gold stacked up against Mount with rather doubtful hopes, but landed on the safe side with the victory clutched firmly within their arms.

The first period was one in which the hopes of the Akron followers were below par, but when the second quarter rolled into place, and Mount had scored the first touchdown of the game, the fans began to realize that there was going to be a football game staged within their very sight. It did not take long to prove it, for in the second period it was staged almost entirely in midfield, with honors about even.

In the third period everything pointed to an Akron victory, for the men came out from a session with Coaches Sefton and Sayger with a new brand of fight. Early in the period they broke loose for a touchdown, and before the end of the quarter Akron was leading 14 to 7. However, Casey's men came back strong and tied the count as the period ended. In the final quarter Akron again proved the superior, hopping off to a touchdown soon after the play began, and near the end of the game they went over for a fourth touchdown, sending Mount down under a 28 to 14 score.

The entire Akron eleven played a cooperative game, working together throughout the entire 48 minutes of play. All of the men deserve credit for the victory, but in the eyes of the spectators flashed the forms of the two Akron ends, Kregenow and Daum. "Skeet" Wise, halfback and "Ching" Bliley quarterback to whom a great part of the honor should go.

But not only should the honor go to those who are visibly heroes, for under the struggling piles of humanity, hardly visible work that should not pass without the proper credit. In this work should be motioned the names of all the men who played on the Akron line for to them is due much of the praise for Akron's victory over Mount. Captain Eckert, Newson and Ellis, tackles; Schachner and Whalen, guards; and Barnes and Olson, centers were the men who held the line when the visitors were threatening to break through for gains, and made it possible for the visible stars to show up so well.

The team developed by Eddie Casey also played a hard game. Their forward passing game baffled the Blue and Gold at times, and their line work proved effective. On the defensive the visitors proved superior when in a tight place, holding Akron backs almost gainless. Captain Wagner, Marsh, and Zimmerman starred for the visitors.

Line-up and summary:

Akron		*Mount*
Daum	left end	Harris
Eckert, C.	left tackle	Bean
Whalen	left guard	Robinson
Barnes	center	Moore
Schachner	right guard	Zimmerman
Newson	right tackle	Cady
Kregenow	right end	Whitman
Bliley	quarter back	Marsh
Wise	left half back	Myers
Hess	right half back	Wagner, C.
Miller	full back	Thompson

The 1923 team. Front row: unknown, Harold "Buss" Thomas, Bill Firick, Carl Stump, unknown, unknown, Oscar "Tiny" Limbach, Hayes "Squirt" Jenkins, Edwin L. "Red" Kregenow, Hazen Kniffin, Kenneth S. Denison, Gene Denning, unknown, Dwight Spessard, Eldrid "Buss" Willyard, Paul Stevens, Kenneth "Weeds" Mason, Francis "Fritz" Wagner, Earl "Pie" Pfeifle, Jean Smith. Back row: Fred S.

October 12, 1923

Second Team Runs Up Big Score: Regulars Add in Final Quarter

Jean Smith Crosses Opponents' Goal Line for Three of Five Touchdowns; Squad is Weak in Several Departments

The Blue and Gold second team received a good workout last Saturday afternoon when the Kent Normal College eleven was defeated in the first game on the Varsity schedule. The "doggies" walked through the visitors for more than three periods, scoring 25 points, and then the first team was sent in for three minutes, during which time they added another touchdown to the count, and made the final score 32–0. The game was the first to be played before the new Alumni Memorial Stadium at Buchtel Field.

Coach Herman Sayger, who was in charge of the Blue and Gold squad, gave every man a chance to get in the scrimmage and to show his possibilities of making the varsity team later in the season. The opposition, however, was not of such quality as would give Coach Sayger any definite idea of the first team, because at the time when the regulars were sent into the battle the visitors were worn down and several substitutions had been made. This allowed the varsity to make first down on every attempt to carry the ball, and to score another touchdown in the final minute.

In the opening period Jean Smith kicked off to McDermott, Kent halfback, who returned a few yards before being tackled by Smith.

Sefton (coach), Harold Barnes, unknown, Joseph "Zep" Schoch, Harold "Slats" Miller, unknown, Cecil Cunningham, unknown, Earl Triplett, unknown, unknown, Harold Minnich, Ralph Brown, unknown, Ross Wilson, unknown, Verlin Jenkins, Ray Shaffer, unknown, Herman E. Sayger (assistant coach), Ted Eberhard (manager). Courtesy of The University of Akron Department of Intercollegiate Athletics.

Throughout the entire period the visitors were forced to play in their own territory, and when the Blue and Gold took the ball a drive was made down the field for a touchdown. Jean Smith went over the line for the necessary three yards, and the first score of the season. Verlin Jenkins drop-kicked for the extra point.

Smith Again Scores

Opening the second quarter with a powerful backfield attack through the line and around the ends, the Varsity eleven again smashed its way to the visitors' goal line. From the ten-yard line Pfeifle heaved a forward pass to Jean Smith, who was five yards over the white mark. Jenkins missed an attempted drop-kick for the extra point.

Immediately after the touchdown Coach Sayger substituted six men in the Akron lineup and Harsh sent one new player in the scrimmage for the Normalites. The remaining time during the first period was passed without scoring, although a forward pass over the line to Firick grounded, and Kent was given the ball on the 20-yard line.

With several more substitutes in the Blue and Gold lineup in the third period, the visitors held firmly whenever their dangerous territory was approached, and did not allow Sayger's men to score. During that period the only punt resorted to by Blue and Gold was made by Schoch, who scooted the sphere about forty yards down the lot.

Score Two More

Kent weakened in the final round, and the Blue and Gold again went on a scoring mission. After forcing the Normal eleven back to the five-yard line early in the period Jean Smith then carried the ball over for the third counter. Smith missed on a drop-kick for the extra point. From the two-yard line, after another fast advance, Verlin Jenkins broke through the line for the fourth score. He failed to drop-kick.

With three minutes to play, Coach Sayger sent the entire first team into action against the visitors. After making five first downs in a row, the Akron backs took the ball up to the five-yard line, from where Hayes Jenkins circled right end for the final touchdown. He also drop-kicked from the 20-yard line for the extra point.

Regulars Go In Game

The entire group of Blue and Gold backfield men displayed good judgment in picking holes, and also gave perfect interference in most cases. The work of Jean Smith, Verlin Jenkins, Stump, Schoch and Hayes Jenkins was outstanding. On the line the Blue and Gold was slow to get started, but they were too much for the visitors in all departments. White, Cunningham and F. Wagner did the best work for Sayger's men in the opening periods, while the entire Akron line of first stringers worked well in the final minutes.

The most noticeable weakness of the entire squad was their tackling. Upon several occasions the Blue and Gold gridders were unable to drop the Kent runner on the first attempt.

Although the Kent team was completely outclassed throughout the game they displayed good work on the defensive. Their speed in breaking up forward passes saved them considerable yardage, and their ability to tackle also held the score down.

Akron received 35 yards penalties, while Kent was set back only five yards. Sayger's men attempted 11 forward passes, two of which were completed. Kent attempted only one, and that failed. First downs were made eighteen times during the game by Akron and only once by the visitors.

A small crowd of less than three thousand persons witnessed the opening game. The student section in the center of the stadium was nearly filled, and a large number of Kent followers were grouped on the opposite side of the field.

The lineup follows:

Akron U		*Kent*
White	left end	Pyle
Bennet	left tackle	Wagner
F. Wagner	left guard	Jennings
Cunningham	center	Wolcott
Spessard	right guard	Carlozzi
Triplett	right tackle	Tishendorf
Shaffer R.E.	right end	Donnelly
Pfeifle	quarter back	Michaels
Firick	left half back	Swartz
J. Smith	right half back	McDermott
V. Jenkins	full back	Feely

Touchdowns-J. Smith 3, V. Jenkins, H. Jenkins. Try for Point-V. Jenkins (drop kick), H. Jenkins (drop kick). Substitutions-Akron: Schoch for Firick, Vanica for Shaffer, J. Wagner for F. Wagner, Brown for Spessard, Hutchinson for Triplett, Van Berg for Bennet, Denning for Schoch, Long for Hutchinson, Willyard for White, Kregenow for Vanica, Limbach for Hutchinson, Stevens for Van Berg, Minnich for J. Wagner, Barnes for Brown, Thomas for Pfeifle, Stump for Denning, H. Jenkins for J. Smith, Kniffin for V. Jenkins. Kent: Frances for Wagner, Smith for Trotter, Trotter for Pyle, Herrick for Donnelly, Lackey for Wolcott. Referee-Tyler, Reserve. Umpire-Conners, Bates. Head Linesman-Maurer, Wooster. Timer-Ayer, Cincinnati.

November 7, 1923

Sefton's Gridders Defeat Northern Impressive Score

Stump Sparkles in 20–0 Victory with Line Smashes and Punting

Playing within threatening distance of Ohio Northern's goal posts throughout the game, the Buchtel gridders won an impressive 20–0 victory at Ada last Saturday.

A crowd estimated at 5,000, including many loyal Akron supporters, was in the stands to help Northern celebrate Homecoming Day.

Playing the best game of his career, Carl Stump led the Akron attack with a fine choice of holes and consistent punting. He gained at least five yards on every exchange of kicks with Lynch of Northern.

During the first period a punting duel was waged between Stump and Lynch. Akron got within striking distance several times, but was unable to get in a scoring position.

Stump Scores First

This battle lasted until the middle of the second quarter, when Akron suddenly opened up with a few passes which brought the ball to the ten-yard line. Three line smashes, and Stump then went through center for a touchdown. Jenkins missed the extra point when his drop-kick fell short by about a yard.

That ended the scoring of the first half, but Akron kept up its passing game in the third period. For a while Northern was able to cope with the system, but Akron intercepted as many passes as the Polar Bears did, and little was gained by either side in this style of play.

Finally the Seftonites worked the ball down to Northern's 25. On two plays Jenkins and Stump carried the ball to the seven as the quarter came to an end.

It took this same pair just three more downs to put the pigskin over, Stump carrying the ball through center again. He kicked from placement for the extra point.

Northern Threatens

After the next kick-off Northern made their strongest bid for a score when "Cliff" Kerchner appeared in their backfield to heave some passes. Several long tosses were completed successfully and the Norsemen penetrated Akron's 22-yard line before they were checked by an incomplete pass over the goal line.

Stump immediately punted out of danger, and Northern's second test was not so hard to meet. Taking the ball on downs on their own 40-yard line, Akron punted again to gain more territory by the easiest method.

Thomas intercepted a long pass in midfield, and from here Akron started on a march for the last scoring of the day. Stump made a 20-yard gain through left tackle.

Jenkins took his turn and made a first down on two plays, and followed this with a 16-yard sprint around the end that placed the ball on Northern's four-yard line.

From here it was a cinch for "Squirt" to drive through for a touchdown. He drop-kicked for the extra point.

The Akron line played the best game it has put up as a unit this season. With as much improvement this week as it showed after the Mt. Union fracas, Akron's forwards will not suffer anything by comparison with Wooster's vaunted wall that will appear here Saturday.

The summary:

Akron		*Northern*
Willyard	left end	Wander
Stevens	left tackle	Boop
Barnes	left guard	C. Graybill
Mason	center	Terry
Brown	right guard	Herge
Limbach	right tackle	Kattman
Kregenow	right end	Lynch
Thomas	quarter back	Shanks
H. Jenkins	left half back	Greer
Stump	right half back	Smith
J. Smith	full back	Haley

Substitutions-Akron: Wagner for Barnes, Minnich for Wagner, V. Jenkins for C. Graybill, Madorshy for Herkins for Smith; Ohio Northern: Garge, Kerchner for Smith, Evans for Haley.
Referee-Prugh, Antioch. Umpire-Reese, Denison. Head Linesman-McEllory, North Dakota.
Touchdowns-Stump 2, H. Jenkins. Try for Points-Stump (placement), H. Jenkins (drop-kick).

November 15, 1924 (Tel-Buch)

Akron 20 Ashland 14

In one of the most nerve wracking struggles ever witnessed on Buchtel Field, Akron was able to score a narrow victory over Ashland College. The game was a freakish one too, for Akron was able to gain consistently through the Ashland line but because of bad breaks could not score and when Ashland had the ball, they in turn were able to gain at will by the use of the forward pass. So the game resolved itself into chasing each other up and down the field.

Akron scored early in the game on several cleverly executed forward passes. Then the visitors diagnosed the Akron passing game and after intercepting several passes and completing a few of their own for good measure, the score read 14–7 Ashland.

Beginning the second half, Quarterback Schoch switched the attack to line plunging and then it was that Akron began to show superiority but still was unable to score. In the last few minutes of play and by sheer force Jenkins and Smith were

Schoch prepares to pass during the 1924 Ashland game. Courtesy of The University of Akron Department of Intercollegiate Athletics.

able to score and give Akron a safe margin. Wharton's passing to McClintock from reverse end run formations was the best combination seen on Buchtel Field this year.

November 27, 1924 (Tel-Buch)

Akron 17 Kenyon 7

Despite the fact that there was an icy wind blowing across the field and despite the fact that black clouds were hanging low, the largest crowd of the year packed into Buchtel Field Thanksgiving Day morning to see the Blue and Gold defeat Kenyon 17–7.

Coach Coleman's boys played the most brilliant and consistent game of the season against the Purple and although pre-game predictions were in favor of Kenyon, Akron had things all their own way throughout the game.

Akron opened the struggle with a passing attack that took the ball to Kenyon's 35 yard line. A long pass made by Smith was partially blocked by a Kenyon player but Pfeifle snatched up the ball and ran the remaining 20 yards for a touchdown. Jenkins kicked goal.

In the second quarter with the ball in their own territory, Kenyon tried desperately to score by long passes. One of these passes was intercepted and after a few plays Jenkins went over for the second Akron touchdown. The try for point was made good.

It was a different Kenyon team that came on the field after the half. Three successful Kenyon passes brought the ball to Akron's 15 yard line where the Blue and Gold held for downs. Schoch's punt was caught in a strong wind and went straight up in the air and it was Kenyon's ball on Akron's 25 yard line. They made a pass good and Kenyon had 5 yards to go for a touchdown. After three attempts Peters smashed through for the touchdown and the kick was good.

The 1924 team. Photo from Tel-Buch, *courtesy of Archival Services, University Libraries, The University of Akron.*

In the last quarter, with the wind at their back, Akron found easier going. In this quarter Jenkins tried three dropkicks, the last one from the 46 yard line was the most spectacular incident of the game. The ball sailed up and was carried along by the wind, struck the cross-bar and bounced over for 3 points. Score, Akron 17–Kenyon 7.

October 20, 1925

Akron U Whips Case by 14 to 7 Count Saturday, Local Team Improved

Gilleland, Schoch and Haaf are injured; Johnson, Kirn and Smith Score Points

Akron U's more than made up for their two defeats when they whipped Case 14–7 Saturday in the annual Homecoming game at Buchtel Field. The backfield drove through Case's line from the first, while most of Case's gains were around the end. Akron's line showed great improvement, Saturday was the first time in three years that Akron has played Case.

Although outweighed by Case, Akron made most of their gains through the line, making from three to five yards each play. Kirn and Smith scored the touchdowns for Akron. Kirn took the ball over on straight football after Johnson had recovered a fumble on Case's 20 yard line, while Smith broke loose after receiving a long pass.

In the last quarter Case uncorked a desperate pass attack, but was unable to put the ball over. Although Case made some long gains on passes and a few through the line, Akron stopped them whenever they really threatened. The Akron line outplayed Case's, holding the Cleveland team for three downs on the one yard line before Case could pound the ball across for their one score.

Walt Kern made most of Akron's gains through the line. Nubs Johnson also made gains, especially around the end. Schoch, Gilleland and Haaf were the other stars in the backfield.

The 1925 team. Photo from Tel-Buch, *courtesy of Archival Services, University Libraries, The University of Akron.*

Gilleland was taken out in the first period when his nose was again injured. Schoch was hurt in the first half and was replaced. Jenkins was substituted for Haaf when the latter injured his leg.

Johnson guided the team after Schoch left, and directed them in good order. His punting was good and his two place kicks made good the extra points after touchdown.

The line showed much better form than it did at Delaware. Plant, Wargo, and Smith held up their positions exceptionally well, while Cunningham, Taylor, and Kregenow did good work.

Akron got away to a poor start but soon hit their stride. A poor kick by Schoch and a fumble by Gilleland gave Case the ball in Akron's territory. Case was forced to kick and Byrnes, Case tackle, fell on the ball when it hit Akron's scrimmage line. Freshcorn made five and put the ball on Akron's one yard line. Akron held for two downs but Case shoved the ball over on the next play.

In the second quarter Gabala fumbled and Johnson fell on the ball on Case's 20 yard line. Kirn made first down in four plays and then took the ball over in two more. Johnson kicked goal. The ball was in the center of the field most of the time until Johnson threw a long pass to Smith who raced with it for another touchdown. Johnson kicked goal.

The ball was in Case's territory most of the third quarter. In the fourth Case opened up a desperate aerial attack. Schoch averted a touchdown when he forced Focke out of bounds after Focke had received a pass. Parr completed another pass but fumbled it when he downed on Akron's eight yard line. The ball remained in Akron's possession for the rest of the game.

Editor's Note: This game against Case Tech was the only win of the 1925 season (1–7).

Cartoon from The Buchtelite, *1925, courtesy of Archival Services, University Libraries, The University of Akron.*

October 1, 1929

Gold and Blue Zip Out 26–0 Win Over Toledo

Harold Frye, Red Cochrane Flash Long Runs to Take the First Half Lead

Going through their paces in weather better adapted to sun baths, Akron U's 1929 version of a Zipper eleven rolled Toledo University's highly-touted machine underfoot 26–0 to annex their initial victory of the campaign Saturday at Toledo.

It required but little effort on the part of the Gold and Blue gridders to become warmed to their task for the thermometer stood at 95 as the fracas got underway. Soon after the initial kickoff the Zippers had tested the strength of the Toledoans to discover that the torrid sun was to be their chief opponent.

Taking the defensive during the first quarter the Zips kept the pigskin ensconced well into foreign territory. Harold Frye's punting backed the upstaters under the shadow of their goalposts and there they remained while the Blairsmen displayed their offensive tactics.

Early in the second session the elusive "Red" Cochrane ran a punt to the Toledo 45. Quarterback Frye squirmed his way around right end to garner some 14 yards. Then thinking the moment an opportune one in which to open up with his big guns, the brainy "Hare" dropped back and shot a pass to Cochrane who evaded the secondary defense for the first score. Florin rammed his way through right tackle for the extra point.

Frye Dashes 53 yards

Some two or three minutes later H. Frye intercepted a Toledo pass on his own 47 yard stripe and streaked down the sidelines for the second marker. He added the extra point via the drop kick route.

The second touchdown took away from the Toledoans what little pep the sun had not sapped from them and they showed little more than a dogged defense during the remainder of the game. To be frank, with the exception of a good backfield the Petcoffians boasted of little. Their forward wall showed occasional flashes of hard-charging form but they were hardly a match for the Zips scrappy line.

Is Good Kicker

In Dunn, fullback, they possess a dependable kicker and capable tackler. It was mainly due to his long punts that several Akron advances were momentarily checked.

Penalties at inopportune moments kept the Zippers out of scoring distance during the third quarter. Their backs squelched an aerial attack launched by the Toledoans during that period climaxed by Paul Frye's 30 yard jaunt after snaring a Dunn pass. "Peg's" run carried the pigskin to the six yard stripe but a 15 yard penalty forestalled the Gold and Blue.

"Peg" Snares Pass

No sooner had the fourth session gotten under way than the alert "Peg" again pulled down a toss far into Toledo territory to park the leather on their 20 yard line. Another 15 yard penalty carried the Zippers back to Toledo's 30 but this time they were not to be stopped.

"Red" Cochrane tucked the ball under one arm and proceeded to circle left end for the needed yardage and another score. His run was the prettiest of the day. The sorrel-top shook off some five or six would-be tacklers in planting the pill over the final stripe.

Pass is successful

Another Akron advance was climaxed by the fourth and last touchdown, H. Frye tossing a perfect pass to the waiting Oldham over the line. Both of the last tries for the point went awry, the first on the kick by H. Frye and the second on a pass by Cochrane.

A last minute flurry of passes on the part of the Toledoans was brought to a close by the gun.

Play Brainy Ball

Although not working as smoothly as would be expected of an eleven backed up with four or five weeks of practice, the Blair-coached outfit displayed brainy, scrappy ball. Igs Florin at fullback and Paul Frye at the blocking halfback were running interference to the ball-carriers in very effective fashion. The long runs found the two backs blocking out the secondary enough to get Cochrane, H. Frye, and Wilson well under way.

In Harold Frye the Blairsmen appear to have a cool field general well qualified to lead his men. He averaged well over 50 yards on his kicks Saturday and placed them out of the reach of the Toledo safety with uncanny precision. His passing was of the calculated suave variety, the little back picking out his receivers quickly and accurately. His plays were called at the right time and smacked of keen study of the game.

Florin Tears Up Wall

Florin tore through the Toledo wall for consistent gains on the few occasions upon which he carried the ball. His hard-driving, dogged tactics are reminiscent of Ray Huffman, offensive and defensive ace of two seasons back. Aerial thrusts into his zone are doomed to disappointment. He intercepted three tosses, directed his way and backed up the line in excellent fashion.

Of the incomparable "Red" Cochrane little needs to be said. His performance of Saturday proclaims him the "Red" of last campaign—perhaps even more so.

Line Looks Strong

Blair need have little fear for the showing of his forward wall. Although not heavy, they charged hard, blocked cleanly, and above all, flashed a fighty spirit. "Dope" Witwer was a tower of strength while the ends, Oldham and Spessard, look to be consistent performers. Smittkin, the new pivot, relieved the skeptics of considerable worry by handling his position in good style.

Shollenberger and Ensign at guards and the tackle horde; Baker, Falls, Yoder, and Auten seem to be well able to carry their portion of the work. The substitute ends, Hinckle and Winch, look to be comers.

November 15, 1929

Zippers Stand in Fear of Case Machine

Gold and Blue Must Down Clevelanders to Retain Conference Standing;
Will Lead Northern Ohio Loop Should Wooster Drop Muskingum Eleven

By Jimmy Foutts

Shortly after noon Saturday all loyal supporters of the pennant-chasing Zippers will take to their vehicles and start towards the Fifth City of the Land as Akron University observes the first of three Migration Days with Case School of Applied Science at Van Horn field. The Zippers are boasting of the most successful team in years and have a string of six victories and but a single defeat to their credit. Case has a team of great potential strength but has been able to do very little to date in the way of turning in winning scores.

While Akron was downing Ohio Northern last week, the Scientists took a trip to Wooster and rather surprised the Bolesmen by holding them to a 13 to 6 margin in the first half of the encounter. Wooster, however, recovered their poise in the last half of the game and administered a sound drubbing to the Fletcherites. The final count was 46–6.

Case has put up a lot of stiff opposition this year and consistency is bound to be rewarded sometime. Baldwin-Wallace, yet to be defeated, was barely able to eke out a victory over the Brown and White team in the opening encounter of the season.

Lose on Blocked Punts

Oberlin garnered twelve points to Case's six, but these were results of blocked punts and not any superiority of offense. It's up to the Zippers to see that Case does not pull a big upset Saturday and drop the Akronites from the chase for the conference title.

While speaking of conference titles, it might be well to add that a great deal depends on Wooster's ability to stop Muskingum tomorrow if the Zippers are to have a chance. Should the Bolesmen eliminate Muskingum, who are undefeated as yet; and should Akron win the rest of their games, including a victory over Mount in the Turkey Day clash at Alliance, the rest will be easy.

Boast Good Record

Akron by virtue of seven conference wins, one defeat, and no ties will have the best percentage record of the conference and hence a clear title to the championship. The other possibility is that the Muskies will stop Wooster and go through their conference schedule undefeated, which would be bad to say the least.

Case has a wonderful combination for an effective defense and on this they pin their hopes of spoiling a perfect Migration Day for some thousand or two Akronites. The Scientists have a good, heavy line and an excellent punter. What more could be asked to keep down scoring.

Line Is Heavy

The Brown and White line will be somewhat heavier than Akron's. The Cleveland boys average 180 pounds to the man on the forward wall. Tip Tyler, a veteran Case back, is conceded to be one of the best punters in the league. It will bid all Akron supporters to be wary and not become too enthusiastic when placing bets with Louie of Buchtel-Eat fame.

Coach Howard Blair gave his charges a brief respite from their regular drill Monday evening. The Polar Bears were a bit rough and the Zippers were exceedingly fortunate not to lose the services of one or more of their players after last Saturday's fray.

Frye Is O.K.

Harold Frye is apparently O.K. and is practicing with the rest of the squad, but he will not be worked hard until Blair is satisfied that his injury is not serious. His loss would be a serious handicap to the progress of the Blairsmen.

The coaching staff were rather pleased with the work of the linesmen last week and should they show as much improvement this week, Coach Blair can grit his teeth, set his jaw in determination and tell the boys that they are going to beat Mount Union.

Accurate tackling is being stressed this week along with a continued drive for real good consistent blocking. When these things have been accomplished the Zippers will present a team of polished players that need fear no one.

The game starts at two-thirty promptly.

Editor's Note: due to the missing subsequent issue of The Buchtelite, *the article with the game results and overview cannot be presented. The Zips went on to beat Case Tech 14 to 0, giving Akron its 100th victory.*

EXTRA POINT

Football Season

Probably never before in the history of Akron University was a football season so disastrous as the 1925 season.

The season was an extremely muddy one, the team playing practically every game on a heavy field. With this rainy weather, Akron's team, which bragged of a dangerous pass attack, was greatly impeded. The 1925 team was a light, fast crew, and in the mud were practically powerless.

The end of the football season was marked by the resignation of Coach James W. Coleman.

University authorities, after a lengthy and careful consideration of a score of applicants for the position of coach, finally voted to accept George Babcock, assistant coach at the University of Michigan and stellar performer on last year's Wolverine team.

Coach Babcock possesses a very pleasing personality along with an uncanny football brain. Owing to his youth and up-to-date knowledge of modern football, Akron should place one of the strongest teams in the history of the school on the grid next fall. Coach Babcock is also a leader of men and it is this quality which will no doubt serve to break up fraternity politics in athletics.

1926 Tel-Buch

TIME-OUT

The Band & Cheerleading

History of the Band

The University of Akron Marching Band originated between 1900–1910 as an ROTC Band that performed for parades and May Day. Sometime during the early 1920s, the ROTC association was removed from the band and a number of part-time band directors were hired—most notably Francesco DeLeone, James T. Weber, and James Campbell.

In 1938, C. Neil Starr, the director of the music department and a graduate of Northwestern University, thought that the band should perform at football games, and brought the band under the auspices of the music department. Starr directed the band and the twirlers became known as the "Starlettes," a play upon the name of the first marching band director.

In 1941, Darrel "Red" Witters became the first full-time Director of Bands with a band of about 40 to 45 members. According to Don Walcott, Drum Major of the 1940 band, the Marching Band met at Spicer School (a grade school which became Spicer Hall) for one hour before each game to rehearse two or three marches that they would perform at the game. A typical halftime performance consisted of the band marching downfield (in straight lines) while playing these marches. At the end of the field, they would turn around, march back to mid-field, and form a stick-figure "A." They would then march directly off the field.

Between 1943 and 1945, there was no Marching Band or football team due to World War II. The band was reorganized in 1946 and by the early 1950's membership had increased to around 60. In 1951, the band received a bass drum that was inside a rolling Goodyear tractor tire. Although extremely popular at games and very mobile, the drum proved difficult to play. The drum was abandoned after its first (and only) year. The Band, under the leadership of Witters, continued to perform for all home football games, in addition to Cleveland Browns games, parades, and the Soap Box Derby Parade. Witters retired in 1967.

In 1967, Richard Jackoboice became the Director of Bands at a time when the University was changing from a municipal college of 3,000 to a state university of more than 20,000 students. During this period of growth, the band membership jumped from 45 to 100 members almost overnight. Jackoboice, a graduate of the University of Michigan, developed the size and style for which The University of Akron Marching Band is noted.

Left: The 1934 University band. Photo from Tel-Buch, *courtesy of Archival Services, University Libraries, The University of Akron.*

Right: The 1932 University band in A formation. Photo from Tel-Buch, *courtesy of Archival Services, University Libraries, The University of Akron.*

A member of the 1984 marching band. Photo by Bob Wilkey, courtesy of The University of Akron Department of Intercollegiate Athletics.

ued the UA tradition of personally writing and arranging much of the music that the band performed while developing the symphonic sound that has become the trademark of the marching band.

In 1987, Robert D. Jorgensen became Director of Bands at The University of Akron. A graduate of the University of Illinois and Michigan State University, he has helped establish The University of Akron Band program as one of the most highly respected in the Midwest.

In 1992 and 1993, while Mike Golemo was on a two-year leave, Barry D. Martin, a graduate of the University of Illinois and an alumnus of The University of Akron, became the first UA graduate to direct the Marching Band.

In 1994, Michael Golemo returned to The University of Akron after completing his DMA at Michigan State University. He continued the excellence in performance which had been developed during the last decade and helped to change the style from the traditional high step to a more contemporary style.

In 1999, Galen S. Karriker became Assistant Director of Bands at The University of Akron. A graduate of Louisiana State University and Michigan State University, he joined The University of Akron Band Program after serving as the Assistant to the Director of Bands at The University of Wisconsin-Madison. Mr. Karriker continues the excellence of performance of "Ohio's Pride" and its reputation as one of the most respected athletic band programs in the MAC.

During the 2007 and 2008 academic years, while Galen Karriker was on a two-year sabbatical, Michael Beard, a graduate of the University of Memphis and Jody Besse, a graduate of the University of Southern Mississippi, served the University Bands as Interim Assistant Director of Bands and Interim Director of the Marching Band.

In 2009, Galen Karriker returns to The University of Akron after completion of his DMA at Michigan State University. He will again lead (Ohio's Pride) as we enter a new era—the first marching band performance in The University of Akron's new football stadium—Info-Cision Stadium-Summa Field.

Courtesy of Robert D. Jorgensen, Director of University Bands, and Galen S. Karrike, Assistant Director of Bands, The University of Akron

The 1961 Zipettes: Elaine Conrad, Kay Morgan, Mary Jubin, Diane Ceglar, Marilyn Sanderson, Jackie Mallo, Fran Price. Photo from Tel-Buch, *courtesy of Archival Services, University Libraries, The University of Akron.*

Clockwise from top: The 2005 marching band trumpet section. Courtesy of Robert D. Jorgensen, University Bands, The University of Akron.

Akron! Photo from Tobias Studio, courtesy of Archival Services, University Libraries, The University of Akron.

The 1934 cheerleaders: Sid Miller, Bob Greenberger (head cheerleader), Bruce Wert. Photo from Tel-Buch, *courtesy of Archival Services, University Libraries, The University of Akron.*

Cheerleader with megaphone. Photo from Tobias Studio, courtesy of Archival Services, University Libraries, The University of Akron.

The 2008 cheerleading squad. Courtesy of The University of Akron Department of Intercollegiate Athletics.

October 15, 1938

First Girl Cheerleader Brings 'Umph' to Yells

'School Spirit Dead' Rah Rah Girl Declares

By Betty Ann Waugh

"Dates at games cramp style!" Hitler? No. Mussolini? No. No one, in fact but Louise Dill, first and only feminine cheerleader at the University of Akron. "Girls," she says, "are embarrassed to yell at a game when they have a date, and boys feel the same way. I advocate fewer dates at games and more school spirit."

"Maybe I'm too enthusiastic, but it seems to me that all those people should make more noise. Why, even the knot-hole gang yells louder than they do."

Louise Vigorous

Louise is the vigorous little freshmen who led the cheering at the Wabash and Xavier games and who'll be out there cheering again today.

If anyone should know the "Rah-rah" profession, Louise should, because for three years she was cheerleader at Uniontown high school. She likes to yell with the boys, always yelled at the games, and made more noise than the cheerleaders.

Top left: Cheerleaders circa 1970. Photo by Bob Wilkey, courtesy of The University of Akron Department of Intercollegiate Athletics.

Top right: The 1938 cheerleaders: John Byrider, Edward Nicely, Park Myers, Bill Barkley, and the first female cheerleader, Louise Dill. Photo from Tel-Buch, *courtesy of Archival Services, University Libraries, The University of Akron.*

Bottom: Leading the charge. Photo by Bob Wilkey, courtesy of Archival Services, University Libraries, The University of Akron.

Migrate With The Crowd To Baldwin-Wallace

THE AKRON BUCHTELITE

All Campus ... For Dinn...

Akron, Ohio, Friday, October 21, 1938. Vol. 50, No. 8

New Council Deadlocks In Second Meeting

irst row, Robert Secrest, Robert Greenwald, ...llis Friess, James Berry, Marvin McCormick, ...ond row, Mr. Philip Sherman, faculty adviser, ...n Hutchinson, William Schweikert, Conrad Rein-... Richard Greenwald, Frank Kiespies. Third row, Frank Enright, Robert Bertsch, Paul Buzzi, and Edward Nicely.

Not present: Donald Cornell, Frank Simonetti, and Alvis Isner.

...ouncil Is Tied On Party Head

...tudent Council met its first ...dlock of the semester at its ...ting Tuesday when it found it... tied on the election of a ...irman for the University Party ...ch will be held January 18. ...a Noel and Ben Rogers are the candidates who received the ...e number of votes after three ...ots.

...andidates eliminated in the first ...ot were Ruth Heyburn, Alvis ...r, Robert Wiltrout, and Wil... McConnell. Arnold Hanson, ...l, and Rogers were voted upon the second ballot when Noel Rogers first tied. A tie break... ballot was then held but with same results.

...heated discussion took place ...it was finally decided that the ...ision of the appointment would ...postponed for a week. All mem... of the council including James ...ry, council president, voted ...aday except Frank Simonetti ...was not present.

...lvis Isner was appointed dance ...mittee member from Student ...ncil by Berry. A committee to ...e plans concerning Dad's Day also appointed by Berry. Don... Cornell is chairman, to be as...ed by Conrad Reining, and ...k Enright.

...erry named a committee com...ed of Richard Greenwald, chair..., Phyllis Friess, and Robert ...tsch, which is to discuss the ...stion of whether or not it is ...thwhile for the University of ...on to continue its membership the National Student Federa... of America.

...mmerce Students ...o Tour Quaker Oats

...he department of commerce and ...iness administration is sponsor... a tour of the local plant of Quaker Oats Company Tues..., according to David Thomas, ...mber of the Board of Control. ...commerce students, including ...hmen, who are interested in ...trip are to meet at the En...eering building at 1 p.m.

...the tour is a success, several ...of-town trips similar to those last year are being planned. ...tative plans have been made ...a November tour of the ...ngstown Sheet and Tube Com...y.

...nnual election of the Com...ce Board of Control is to be ...Wednesday in E-265. Hold...rs from last year's Board

'Louder And Funnier,' Yells Committee; Win A Cup

By Dick Collier

COLUMBUS discovered America in 1492, and what happened to him? You guessed it. He died broke.

But you don't have to discover America to die broke.

All you have to do is invent the best yell and submit it to the Rally Committee before November 2.

You can pull a Tarzan, if you want to, or a blood-curdling yodel, or anything you care to so long as it's loud, original, and catching. And when you're finished, deposit a transcription in the special contest box in the lobby of Buchtel Hall, and get it in before November 2.

The owner of the most original yell will receive a genuine silver-plated loving cup from the University rally committee, as his permanent possession. Not only that, but it will be engraved with his name and his fraternity affiliation, if he so desires. Presentation of the cup will be made between the halves at the Illinois Wesleyan game. The basis upon which entries will be judged, according to James Brown, committee chairman, are, originality, spirit, and adaptability.

Play Cast Tryouts Call Frosh Actors

Freshman tryouts for a one act play will be held Tuesday, October 25, at 3 p.m. in E-155. All first year students interested in theatre work are invited to attend the tryouts.

All sudents who are interested in scenery painting, construction, or makeup, should report for the meeting, according to Mr. Donald S. Varian, instructor in speech.

The cast for the play will consist of about ten characters, and it will be presented at a meeting of the University Theatre December 7.

Freshmen who participate in this and other freshmen productions will be awarded points that will count toward the necessary 30 required for admittance to the University Theatre. All freshmen who show interest and complete the work assigned to them will receive a bonus of five points at the close of the school year, Mr. Varian said.

Candidates interested in acting should bring along something they would like to read for the tryouts, William McConnell, in charge of the meeting, said.

Panhellenic Banquet Date Set For Nov. 5

The annual Panhellenic banquet will be held at the Mayflower Hotel ballroom November 5. Miss Florence A. Partridge, Dean of Women at Heidelberg, will be the guest speaker for the evening, Jane Bricken, president of the Panhellenic Council, will also speak. Subjects of the speeches have not yet been chosen.

Virginia Thompson is chairman of the committee. Others are: Patricia Nelan, Barbara Shank, Jeanne Benson, Joanna Hoffmaster, and Marjorie Glass.

All money for tickets must be paid to Virginia Thompson, chairman of the committee not later than Friday.

Librarian Attends Convention

Miss Josephine A. Cushman, librarian, is attending a convention of the Ohio Library Association in Cincinnati this week end. Meetings opened Thursday and continue through Saturday.

Student Teachers May Attend NEOTA Sessions

Students may attend the sessions of The North-East Ohio Teacher's Association which is being held in Cleveland next Friday and Saturday.

Student membership tickets are on sale at the office of the Dean of the College of Education at 25 cents.

Rabbi Stephen S. Wise of New York City and Mr. Francis B. Sayre, Assistant Secretary of State of Washington, D. C. will be speakers at the General Sessions.

Tizzy Is Humbug; Tizzy Took A Dare At 6 p.m. Today, Tizzy Will Be There

"Tizzy Lish" is going to crash the Women's League banquet to-

than ever to be one of the guests.

All arrangements have been

Cagers To Play On New Year's? 'Hope Not'--Team

Coach Paul O. Bixler is a very enthusiastic gentleman.

In fact, so very enthusiastic that he scheduled basketball games for New Year's Eve, Founders Day, Washington's Birthday, and on one Sunday.

Taking the floor on Sunday is all right. Taking it on Friday is all right. Taking it on Founders Day and birthday of the Founding Father is all right, but taking it against Ohio Wesleyan on New Year's Eve, when the brave clothes laddies like to cut capers even as you and I—

Coach Bixler announced today that attempts will be made to change the dates of the following games: Ohio Wesleyan, December 31; Baldwin-Wallace, Sunday, January 15; Fenn College, Founders Day, and Ball State Teachers, February 22.

Buchtelite, Dance Committee Get Increase In Fees

The dance committee and The Buchtelite received increases of 5 cents each per student in allocations from the student activity fee, according to an announcement from the treasurer's office.

The Buchtelite will receive 90 cents the first semester and 85 cents the second semester, while the dance committee will get 15 cents and 10 cents.

Other allocations are: Athletic Association: $4.75 first semester, 75 cents second semester. Assembly: 15 cents first semester, 5 cents second semester. Intramural sports: 25 cents first semester, 50 cents second semester. General expenses: 10 cents first semester, 5 cents second semester.

Groups which receive the same amount both semesters are: debate, 10 cents; Student Council, 10 cents; University Theatre, 30 cents; Women's League, 20 cents.

Dean Ayer Cuts No Smoking Rules

Smoking will be permitted in the corridors but not in the classrooms of the new Engineering building beginning Monday.

Four new ash receptacles will be placed on each floor of the building and the "No Smoking" signs will be removed, Dean Fred E. Ayer of the College of Engineering said. Smoking will be permitted on the concrete floor of the old portion of the building as usual.

Dean Ayer said he expected the cooperation of all students in this action. "I don't want to hear of any violations of this regulation," he declared.

Students are especially asked to refrain from using the receptacles as waste baskets.

Blisters Break On Active Feet; Keep Nurse Busy

By Pat Machan

"BUSINESS has picked up considerably since the fraternities have started initiations," thoughtfully reflected Mrs. Emma Henry, nurse in the University health service.

It seems that the health department has been having quite a business in the care and treatment of blisters acquired during fraternity initiations. Either the initiates can't take it, or else 22 miles is too far for anyone to hike in one night. The army is another prolific

Migration Horde Will Invade Be... Parade Forms At 11:30 a. m. Tom...

ROOTERS Blaze Migration Trail To B-W Skirmish

Accompanied by a motorcycle escort of d... the longest Migration Day parade in the histo... versity will follow the Zippers to Berea tomorr... the annual Baldwin-Wallace-Akron game.

Tickets for the game will be 75 cents for st... for others who w... team. The tickets ... the parade lineup...

They will contin... vance sale in the ... fication cards mu... to obtain the tick... duced price.

Lineup On ...

The parade wil... up on North H... diagonally across ... at 11:30 a.m. It ... promptly at 12 a...

Blue and Gold ... other decorations ... free for all the c... in the parade. Th... tributed at the ...

Kickoff At ...

The kickoff will... The rivalry betw... colleges will be k... ago Baldwin-Wallac... defeated Migration ... last year Akron ... 6-0.

Tickets for the ... game at Berea w... at reduced rates ... office at Buchtel ... a.m. Saturday.

Tickets will al... for sale at th... Hawkins Avenue ... ket Street the day... General admission... is 75 cents. Sales ... will close at 12:3...

The parade will ... ing 35 mile route ... 18 to 92. Take 92 i... following it throu... Bath to the junctio... left on 176 to 82... through North ... Strongsville. Turn r... follow north to Be... left on Berea road... to the Baldwin-Wa...

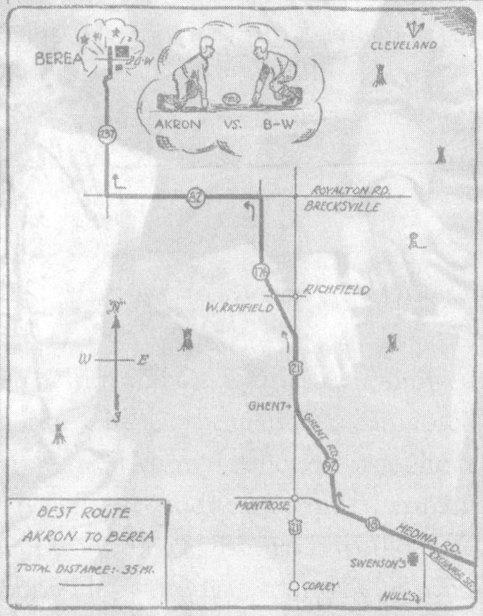

Four Win Leads In University Play 'French Without Tears'

Lucille Paridon, Dana Noel, Gale Richards, and William McIntosh won leading roles in the University Theatre's first production, "French Without Tears" to be given November 17-18 at the YWCA.

Miss Paridon will enact the role of Diana Lake; Noel will play Kit Nellan; Richards will take the role of Hon. Alan Howard; and William McIntosh will be Lt. Commander Rodgers.

The rest of the cast includes; Robert Hunt as Kenneth Lake, Marvin Marquardt as Brian Curtis, Betty Cohen as Marianne, Harold Lionetti as Monsieur Maingot, and Elaine Morgan as Jacqueline Maingot. The part of Lord Heybrook has not been cast as yet.

Members of the cast have held daily rehearsals for two weeks and Mr. Donald S. Varian, instructor in speech, and director of the University Theatre declared that "French Without Tears" will be presented on schedule.

Richard Lockhart has charge of the scenery construction.

Prospective Teachers Must Register Now

All students planning to register for practice teaching next semester should secure their application blanks immediately.

Those interested in secondary school teaching should see Dr. Harold O. Ried, instructor in education. Students wishing to teach in grades 4 to 8 inclusive should see Dr. Hjalmar W. Distad, associate professor of elementary education.

Miss Clara M. Kemler, associate professor of primary and elementary education, will supervise students wishing to teach on the primary-kindergarten level.

AE Will Meet

AE, Evening Session honorary, will have a business meeting of active and active alumni members Wednesday, October 26 at 8 p.m. in B-22.

Dean's Wife In Hospital

Mrs. Donfred H. Gardner, wife of the Dean of Students, was reported as progressing satisfactorily Thursday after an appendectomy Monday at City Hospital.

Carnegie Rally To Feature Music Of Jan Garber

Take a dash of swing or jazz throw in a little of Joe Penner, the cheers of the student body, Mr. C. Neil Starr, director of the glee clubs, leading the singing, gobs of toy horns and 42 cents. Mix them well and set to cool until October 28 at 8:30 p.m. When you remove the mixture you will have the Carnegie Tech Pep Rally at the Palace Theatre.

Swing will be provided by Jan Garber, "idol of the air waves", and his entire stage show.

Joe Penner will cut capracious cajoles with a football in "Mr. Doodle Kicks Off". Toy horns to be sold at the door will add a spice of gaiety. Tickets to be sold at the doors will cost 55 cents.

Football on the stage in the persons of the team will be introduced by Coach Jimmy Aiken. Tickets will be on sale on the campus under the supervision of John Good.

Sophie Recalls The Good Old Days-- But The Freshmen Are Still The Same

TWENTY-FIVE years ago, September 13, 1913, Sophie came to the University to clean the books in the library which was then a single room in Buchtel Hall. When the new building, now the

Council Ca... 'A' Key...

Applications for ... are being accepted ... member of the S... "A" key committee ... of Robert Bertsch, ... Hutchinson, and ... Blank forms may be ... the committee mem...

No definite date ... the keys has as yet ... it will be at a ... sembly in the near ... ing to Bertsch.

To Recognize Cam...

Participation in ... ties and high scho... of students are rec... awarding of "A" ke...

Rules governing ... of the keys specify ... dents must acquire ... women students 25 ... being allowed for ... activities, and sch... applicant must have ... least 77 credit hour... quired quality poin... less than 2.3.

List Ru...

Other rules conce... awards can be fou... in the Faculty ... Regulations Book.

"A" keys are aw... dent Council and a... ing applications for ... by the council. ... awarded twice a y... semester.

Nicely To Atten... Scabbard, ...

Edward Nicely, c... chapter, will atten... first convention o... society of Scabba...

CHAPTER 5
1930–1939

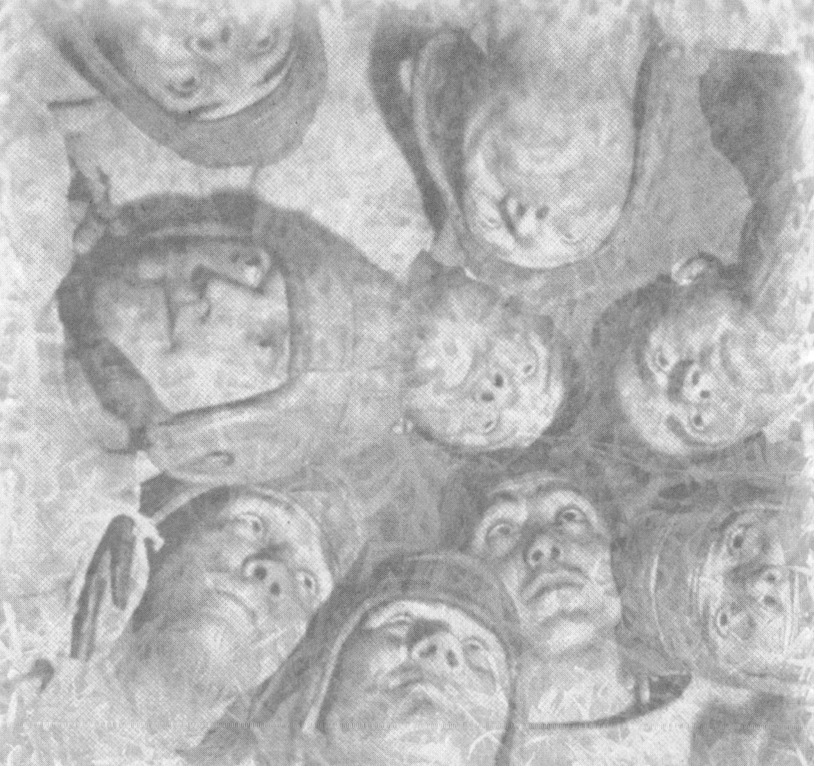

Frank Zazula, 1939-1940. Photo from Tel-Buch, *courtesy of Archival Services, University Libraries, The University of Akron.*

November 25, 1933

Zips Defeat Berea Team in Quagmire

Lindsay Ambles 47 Yards to Make Only Score of Game

One of the biggest football upsets in the Ohio conference this season was staged at Buchtel field last Saturday when the Akron Zippers toppled a highly touted Baldwin-Wallace eleven by a 6–0 score.

In the first quarter Lindsay, with the aid of perfect blocking broke loose for a 47-yard touchdown jaunt which gave the Blue and Gold warriors the lead they never relinquished. The Yellow jackets, however, fought back with a vengeance, and although the field was a quagmire of mud, the light Zipper team stopped the Berean line plunges and B-W was forced to turn to an aerial attack.

Three times in the second half the Yellow Jackets threatened to score by passes but each time the Zipper line tightened and repulsed the threat.

In last Saturday's game the Blue and Gold warriors blasted all B-W hopes for a top notch in the Ohio conference standings.

October 5, 1935

Zippers Smother Otterbein Eleven by 26–0 Score

First, Second, and Third Teams See Action in Second Conference Tilt

By Robert Firestone

The entire Akron Zipper varsity squad toyed with an impotent Otterbein team last night at Buchtel Field and when all the playing about was over, the Zips had tucked away their second Conference victory in as many starts by a 26–0 score.

Coach Howard (Red) Blair took advantage of the Otter's lack of strength to send all of his men into action, and even the so-called "third-stringers" mauled the enemy at will.

Not Particular

Akron was not at all particular how it tallied its touchdowns. After a slow start, the Zips scored late in the first quarter on a 70 yard gallop by Jack Jaques; in the second they sent Carl (Moose) Tsaloff over from the three yard marker after a series of passes and bucks had put the ball in position for the score; and they resorted to Paul Lehockey's perfect passes—passes which floated into the hands of Pat Pontius and Tsaloff, respectively—to ring up their final points in the second and third quarters.

Averages 15 Yards

Jaques, Lehockey, and Tsaloff proceeded to turn the game into a field meet for themselves. Jaques, besides his touchdown run, turned in another effort of 43 yards—and then fumbled. But he averaged 15 yards for every try at the line, and his long spiraling punts kept Otterbein backed against her own goal. Lehockey tossed two touchdown passes, looped several others that missed connections by the narrowest of margins, turned in 27 yards in five tries at the line, and played a bang-up defensive game. Tsaloff scored two of the Zip touchdowns and smashed the line just about as he pleased. Bill Sturgeon, sophomore back, was another who gave a good account of himself while he was in the fray.

Strong Defense

Defensively, the Akron line was just too strong—so strong in fact that in the first half the Otters turned in a net loss of one yard in their line attempts. They did but little better in the second half, gaining 18 yards in nine tries. Earl Hensal, Bob Bauer, Bob Graf, and company, were too capable at turning back all Otterbein thrusts. Hensal further distinguished himself by place-kicking two of the points-after-touchdown.

Bill Anderson, former South High School star, stood out like a shining light for the Otters.

Akron		*Otterbein*
Bostick	left end	Lane
Keller	left tackle	Schiering
Kauffman	left guard	Eastman
Sweitzer	center	Warner
Hensal	right guard	Griffith
Graf	right tackle	McGee
Zemla	right end	Flanigan
Sipes	quarter back	Anderson
Tsaloff	left half back	Booth
Mallo	right half back	Perry
Jaques	full back	Zeigler

October 27, 1937

Clicking Akronites Stop B-W Jackets Homecoming Day

Aiken's Rubber City Iron Men Down B-W without Making Substitutions

The Blue and Gold, lately named the Rubber City iron men, upset the highly favored Baldwin-Wallace Yellow Jackets last Saturday, 7–0, at Buchtel Field.

Top: Cartoon from The Buchtelite, *1935, courtesy of Archival Services, University Libraries, The University of Akron.*

Bottom: The 1936 team's captains: Ernie Kaufman, Mike Krino, Bob Bauer. Photo from Tel-Buch, *courtesy of Archival Services, University Libraries, The University of Akron.*

The 1934 team. Photo from Tel-Buch, *courtesy of Archival Services, University Libraries, The University of Akron.*

The team scintillated with cooperation and extra-bright spots were Zazula's running, Dick Miller's one-man pass defense, and Zemla's blocking, especially on the touchdown play.

The Aikenmen completely bottled up the Jackets' aerial circus, keeping them from completing all but four of their 16 passes and intercepting seven.

B-W's best chance came in the fourth quarter when Davidson broke through and smothered a Zipper punt, recovering it on the 20 yard line.

Akron's touchdown was made after Miller had intercepted one of B-W's many passes and advanced the ball into their territory.

Zazula took the ball on a reverse and went through a hole provided by the combined efforts of Miller, Fisher, and Zemla, the latter then converted the extra point.

The mystery of the game is provided in that Baldwin-Wallace defeated Akron last year 46–7 and led the nation in scoring. They reputedly possess as good a team this year as last.

'Dick' Miller

A strong Baldwin-Wallace team went down to defeat at the hands of the Zippers and Dick Miller in the battle royal at Buchtel Field Saturday. Miller intercepted six of the Streaks passes and opened the hole for "Frankie" Zazula's touchdown that beat B-W.

New Stadium!!

The Zippers may soon be playing "before unlimited thousands in a gigantic stadium at the airport," Jim Schlemmer, sports editor of the *Akron Beacon Journal* commented in his column last Saturday.

"This town of ours is ripe for big time college football," he declared. "If the fact were not generally known or accepted before today, it is now.

"At a luncheon of the 'A' Association at noon initial steps were taken which may lead to completion of a new and gigantic stadium at the airport where our Zippers, two seasons hence, would play before unlimited thousands."

September 27, 1938

Zippers Open 1938 Season with 38–0 Win Over Wabash

By Bill Fogarty

They're singing the "Wabash Blues" in Crawfordsville Indiana, seat of the Wabash College, as the 'Little Giants' coached by Pete Vaughn returned from the Rubber City after taking a terrific beating at the hands of 'Jimmy' Aiken's University of Akron Zippers by a 38–0 score Saturday at Buchtel Field.

Zazula Leads

Led by Frankie Zazula, All-Ohio back who scored three of the touchdowns against the visitors, the Zippers administered a sound pasting to the Wabash outfit. While the score indicates the onesidedness of the contest, the real evidence of the trouncing was in the Wabash players themselves, who took a terrific physical and mental beating from the 'Iron Men.'

Zips Show Power

Outshining the 'Little Giants' in every department of the game, the Zippers rolled up eleven first downs against six for Wabash while gaining 254 yards by rushing to 72 for the losers. In the air they completely outclassed their opponents completing five forward passes for a total of 196 yards, while Wabash tried 15 aerials and completed five for 38 yards.

The Zippers lost no time in proving their superiority over the Wabash squad, marching to four touchdowns in the first half, two in each period. Taking a punt on their own 37 the Akron outfit started their first march with Al Abdulla introducing himself to the visitors by making nine yards in two tries through right tackle.

Frank Zazula went through for five more and Abdulla rammed for 15 to the Wabash 33. "Zaz" tried again at right tackle without success and Ray Sabin tossed 33 yards to Frankie who took it on the five yard strip and went over for the initial Zipper score of the season. Zazula's placement for the extra point was wide. All this happened in the first three minutes of play.

Second Quarter Features Long Run

The second goalward surge came in the latter part of the first quarter when the Hilltoppers capitalized on a nine yard punt and took the ball on their own 46. Ray Sabin carried the ball 27 yards around left end. Zazula made five at the right tackle, and came back with a 27 yard sprint for the second score after a pass failed. Zazula kicked the placement for the extra point to make the score 13–0.

At the outset of the second period, Aiken sent in nine second stringers, and they quickly took up where the others left off. Taking the ball on the Wabash 39 after two fumbles and a bad punt on the part of the visitors, Marshall Meachum, sub quarterback tossed a pass to Keith Culbertson, who grabbed the ball from three secondary men on the 15 yard strip. A buck by Morrison failed but Meachum went through tackle for the score. The kick failed.

Miller Runs Pass to Goal

Only 27 seconds remained in the first half when Dick Miller took a 32 yard pass from Zazula and ran the remaining 20 yards for the score. The kick was wide and Akron led 25–0. Bob Morrison, Wellsville speed merchant, proved his worth to the Zippers while scoring on the longest run of the afternoon for the fifth score. A 'Razzle Dazzle' Zazula to Whitten to Morrison gave Morrison the ball on the 50 and he outdistanced the Wabash pursuers to the strip. Zazula placed-kicked successfully to make the score 32–0.

Dick Miller messed up another Wabash pass for his second interception of the game to put the ball on the Zipper 33 yard line in the last quarter. Zazula faded out to the five yard line and took Sabin's heave for the final score. The kick for point failed but the Zips led 38–0. The game ended with Akron's second and third stringers holding the Wabash club on even terms. The entire squad saw action at some time during the game.

November 2, 1938

Tired Zippers Scare Skibos, Lose 27–13

By Jack Carroll

Over 7000 madly cheering spectators watched the Zipper grid warriors go down to defeat 27–13 to the Carnegie Tech Skibos in the closing minutes of the most hectic football battle ever to be played on Buchtel Field sod Saturday after the Zippers had held the invaders on even terms for 55 minutes of play.

Pre-game predictions rated Tech as high as 30 points better than the Hilltoppers, but the issue of victory was never clearly settled until the game reached its last five minutes of life.

Coach James W. Aiken sent his charges into the fray to "shoot the works", which the Blue and Gold clad footballers took so literally that they were leading the Skibos from Tech, 7–0 with the game only three minutes old.

Abdulla Scores

Tech received the opening kickoff and on the first line play through tackle. Merle Condit, renowned Carnegie back, fumbled and the Zips recovered on Tech's 29 yard stripe.

Frank Zazula and Al Abdulla took turns smashing through the Skibo line with Abdulla taking the pigskin over for the first score. Bob Humphrey converted the after touchdown tally, and an amazed gathering of Zipper rooters went wild in the stands.

Carnegie came back strong and soon knotted the score at 7–7. In the third quarter Coach Bill Kern's pigskin peddlers pushed the ball over the Hilltopper goal line to forge ahead 13– 7. The game went into the fourth quarter and according to pre-game dope, the Zippers should have been completely tired out and at the mercy of Tech.

Whitten Blocks Kick

Instead Humphrey and Jim Whitten tore through the tech forward wall and blocked Frank Jordano's punt and Akron became possessor of the ball on Tech's 34. Zazula passed 17 yards to Ray Sabin for a first down. Coach Kern sent his regulars back into the fray but to no avail as Zazula tied the score on a beautiful run through tackle. Humphrey's try for the conversion failed and the game was deadlocked 13–13.

Skibo's Realize Battle

The Skibos, completely convinced that the University of Akron contest was not a breather, turned on full-steam and rolled through the Zipper defense for two touchdowns in the final minutes to chalk up a 27–13 victory.

Akron rooters contend that Coach Aiken and his lads earned a moral victory, by virtue of their excellent showing in the skirmish and all eyes are focused on this Saturday's contest with Illinois Wesleyan.

Wesleyan Invades

Carl "Tip" Tipton will lead the Titan team when they mix forces against the Zips. Tipton, a miniature whirlwind, who tips the scales at 140 lbs., specializes in broken field running.

Akron		*Carnegie Tech*
Whitten	left end	Betz
Humphrey	left tackle	Dobrus
McCarthy	left guard	Dominy
Fagan	center	Schmidt
Patella	right guard	Reith
Fernella	right tackle	Campbell
Miller	right end	Fisher
Kominic	quarter back	Cannelly
Sabin	left half back	Condit
Zazula	right half back	Muna
Abdulla	full back	Ingalls

Touchdowns: Akron: Abdulla, Zazula.
Tech: Condit, Muha, Moroz, Zawacki.
Try for point: Humphrey (placement); Carnelly 3 (placements).

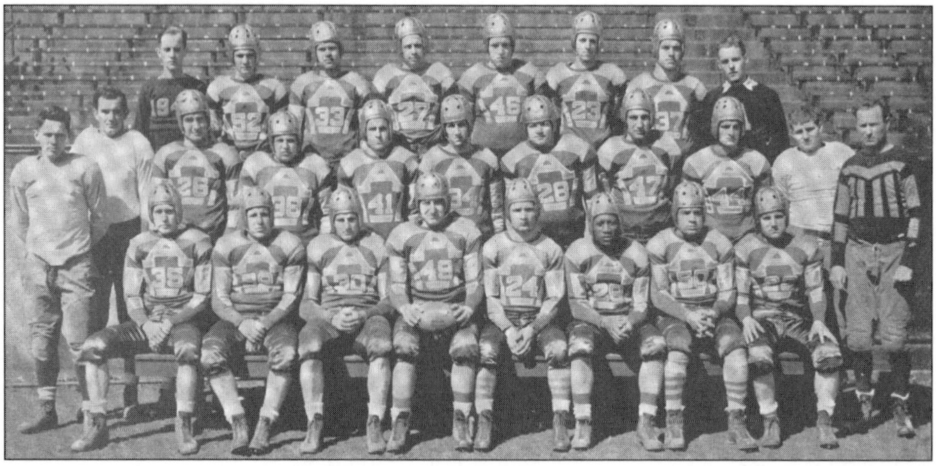

The 1937 team. Photo from Tel-Buch, *courtesy of Archival Services, University Libraries, The University of Akron.*

October 10, 1939

Zippers Beat Wesleyan 13–6 with Last Minute Score; Morrow Tallies Twice

By Bill Good

Although stymied time and again by their victory-hungry opponents, Coach Thomas Dowler's University of Akron Zippers defeated Illinois Wesleyan, 13–6, Saturday at Buchtel Field.

After having been repulsed deep within the Titans' territory no less than four times, the Zippers marched 80 yards to score late in the fourth period. Wade Morrow, slippery Akron halfback, drove over left tackle for the winning touchdown in the final 25 seconds of play.

Two accurate tosses by Zazula enabled Akron to penetrate deep into Wesleyan territory late in the first period. But, when a forward-lateral with Zazula on the carrying end lost ground, the Titans took the ball on downs on their own six.

Titans Score Quickly

Shortly after the opening of the second half, Wesleyan scored suddenly when Wetterlund returned a punt to the Zipper 30. Bob Morrow smashed center for 13 and Wetterlund dashed through right tackle and raced to the goal line behind perfect interference. Bob Morrow's placekick try for point was low.

Twice in the third quarter the 5,500 fans roared forth their approval as the Zippers apparently scored, only to have the touchdowns nullified by decisions of the officials.

Knee Hits Ground

Collie McCombs, 200-pound fullback, climaxed a 55-yard drive when he reeled over left guard into the end zone from the one-yard line. After two of the officials had ruled that McCombs' knee had struck ground in front of the goal line.

Wetterlund then kicked out of bounds on his own 43. Zazula then passed to Morrow, who spun down the sidelines for an apparent touchdown. However, the referee ruled that the Akron sophomore had stepped out of bounds on the 23.

Zazula Fumbles

Late in the final period, Zazula fumbled on an attempted kick on last down. Wesleyan took the ball and drove to the 11 before Akron held. Zazula kicked out but the Titans stormed back to the 20 before Akron tightened its defense again.

At that point, with less than five minutes to play, the Zipper team began its grueling drive which culminated in the deciding touchdown.

October 31, 1939

Wayne Gives Zips 18–12 Walloping

The Zippers were given a lesson in heads-up football Saturday at Buchtel Field. But the experience was costly, for an alert but inferior Wayne eleven defeated Akron, 18–12.

The Tartars, striking suddenly, caught the Zippers "with their pants down" three times in the first half.

Midway in the first quarter, speedy Ed McMullin pranced loose on a sweep around right end and raced 71 yards down the sidelines while his teammates blocked out the surprised Akron secondary.

Intercept Pass

Early in the second quarter, Akron started marching. But huge Jerry Schnelker intercepted Frank Zazula's short pass and, while the Tartars paved his path with vicious blocking, lumbered 85 yards for the second score.

In the final minutes of the same period, the Zippers were caught napping again. On a cleverly executed play, Adams, a substitute Wayne back, started to sweep wide around his own left end, but suddenly wheeled around and passed to Sevick in the end zone.

Akron woke up in the second half and showed some of its real power. Passes, Zazula to Wade Morrow, and Morrow to Al Monzo, were good for touchdowns. Another drive fell inches short of a first down on the Wayne 14.

Three Straight

The loss was the third straight one which Wayne has handed Akron.

Coach Thomas Dowler is hoping that his gridders will play the brand of football of which "they are capable for the whole 60 minutes" next Saturday. For Washington and Jefferson, unbeaten in five games, is said to have a real machine this year.

Mr. George Roark, new W-and-J coach, has molded his offensive around a fast-charging line and three veteran backs, Johnny Macel, Mel Meals, and George Roark.

...ps Tangle With Red Cats Tonight In Rubber Bow...

...e Opens Grid Season ... Western Reserve Team

...iversity of Akron Zippers, with most of the zip ...f them in their first two games, meet the Red ...stern Reserve tonight at the Rubber Bowl, the ...ne for Western Reserve and the first football ...played in the new Akron Rubber Bowl.

...nces to turn back ...s are great, if we ...ds-up ball for 60- ...id Coach Tommy ... Zippers have had ...t work-out, em- ...efense against ... deception plays ...rder to put a phy- ...eam on the field ... Red Cats.

...gaboo Injuries

...ies are still hanging ...ssible that the start- ... the Zippers will con- ...n and Schwartz in ... Wilkins and Bill ... Andy Andreoli will ...by Bob Fellmuth.

...a Lucas received an ... back last Tuesday ... is still suffering a ...ruthwell has a bruised ...n Greenhorn has a ...received in the Col-

...ermen Coming

... Edwards of Reserve ...squad of 27 men. 15 ...

...ued on Page 3)

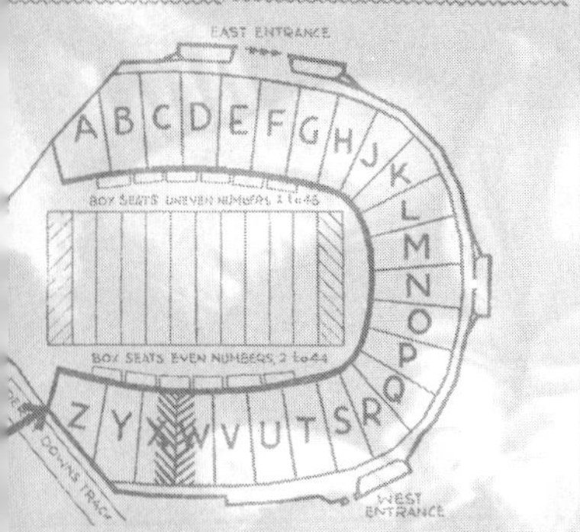

...s will enter the stadium at the west side of the main ...cated by the arrow on the diagram, and sit in half of ... and W.

Tea Hop Rally From 4-6 Today

A "surprise" feature is planned for the intermission of the free tea dance-rally today from 4 to 6 p. m. in the Student Building lounge and cafeteria.

New cheers will be taught students by cheerleaders Richard Caldwell and Louise Dill. "The Akron Blue and Gold" and the "Alma Mater," will be sung, led by William Schwelkert.

Gordon Hagerman will be master of ceremonies and Eric Chedester will sing.

The Rally Committee, composed of Richard Caldwell, Betty Knepper, Pat Machan, Donald McGaughey, and Rex Wingard, is planning the program.

Music will be furnished by the phonograph.

Complete soda bar service will be available until 7:30 p. m. today to accommodate those who attend the pre-game dance and rally before tonights' Western Reserve-Akron game.

...C To Air ... Class Skit

...Words' To Be Pre-...onday At 4:15

...a series of 15-minute ...ns on "The Magic of ... be presented Monday ... over WADC.

...r. Mardelle Witwer, ...Keister, members of ...s under the direction ...le A. Hitchcock, head ...ch department, will ...rogram.

...r 8, in a broadcast ... Robert Keene will ...of Donato Internoscia, ...fessor in Spanish, on ... I Study Spanish?" ...new radio station, ...start a "Let Freedom ... on Tuesday, October ...m. The programs will ...hour long. They are ... the Board of Educa-...

Professor Kraatz Brings 'Em Back Dead, Plenty Dead

NOBODY knows how many rhinoceroses Prof. Walter C. Kraatz brought back from the Carnegie Museum in his Ford this summer, not even Professor Kraatz.

That's because the rhinocerosea have been dead since the Miocenic Epoch of the Tertiary Period of the Anezoic Era, and they're pretty well busted up.

All that may be viewed—they are now on display in the biology museum in Olin Hall—is part of a skull, a vertebrae, and some assorted bones and legs. Originally the parts came from Agate Springs, Forest Quarry, in the bad lands of Nebraska.

Professor Kraatz could have had a dinosaur too, but it was too bulky.

...Enroled In Non-Credit ...mmunity College Courses

...st a week yet to go, ...had enroled in Com-...e courses Wednesday ...Georgia F. Chamber-...y to the director of ...on, said. She expected ...egistered to be great-... by the first meeting ...s.

...tion, directed by Mr. ...rts of the Akron Fire ...and Mr. W. R. LaDue, ...n city water works, ...st enrolment, with 43 ...

...Psychology of Person-... by Dr. C. C. Wood, ...

...ard M. Bertsch; Portrait Painting, Mr. E. L. Novotny, of Kent State University; Advanced Micromotion Study, Professor John Adendorff, head of the industrial engineering department; Blueprint Reading, Prof. Fred S. Griffin, head of the mechanical engineering department, and Shop Mathematics, Mr. Maurice E. Long, of the Guggenheim Airship Institute.

Community College subjects are not offered in regular college, but are offered to all persons who do not desire college credit but who wish additional knowledge of spe-...

THE AKRON BUCHTELITE

UNIVERSITY of AKRON

Akron, Ohio, Friday, October 4, 1940. Vol. 52. No. 5

Buktals Sweep Election, Put 8 In Counc...

Mr. Firestone Will Direct Homecoming

Football, Alumni Luncheon, Open Houses, Dance On Program

Mr. Arden Firestone '29 will be general chairman of the 1940 Homecoming, it was decided at a dinner meeting of the Homecoming Committee Tuesday.

Homecoming, on Saturday, October 12, will include a luncheon, a ceremony at the half of the Akron-Illinois Wesleyan football game at the Rubber Bowl, fraternity and sorority open houses, and a dance in the Student Building.

Eat At Airport

The Homecoming luncheon, sponsored by the "A" Association, will be at 1 p. m. in the Airport restaurant in the Administration Building. Reservations may be made from Mr. Ralph Hartz, "A" Association president.

Mr. Jerome Taylor '28, alumni president, will speak during the half of the University of Akron-Illinois Wesleyan game at 2:30 p. m. in the Rubber Bowl.

Present Flowers

Mrs. Delbert Auten '30 will present a bouquet of chrysanthemums to Mrs. Hezzleton E. Simmons during the half-time ceremony.

All fraternities and sororities will observe open house after the game.

(Continued on Page 3)

Council Dance To Be Tuesday

"Social Improvement" Dance Planned By Lambda Chis

Student Council will hold its second "Social Improvement" dance of the year, Tuesday from 8 to 10 p. m. in the Student Building lounge and cafeteria.

"Due to the large crowd attending the first dance of this type the cafeteria will also be used for dancing," Gordon Hagerman, Council president, has announced.

Lambda Chi Alpha fraternity will sponsor the dance. Don Kreurick, social chairman of the organization, is planning the program.

Admission is free upon presentation of student activity cards.

Mr. Arnold C. Hanson, assistant to the director of adult education, and Mr. Philip Sherman, adviser of men, will be chaperons.

Dance-Rally Today Postpones Concert

The record concert planned for this afternoon in the Student Building lounge has been postponed to next week, because of the tea dance rally.

Arrangements are being made to change the time of the concerts to Fridays at 3 p. m.

The next concert will be a program of classical and semi-classical waltzes under the direction of Fred Brandenstein.

He replaces James McMullin who sponsored the first concert last Friday.

Monday Will Be Deadline For Speakers' Applicants

Monday is the deadline for applications from students interested in becoming members of the Speakers' Bureau, according to Gilbert Thomas, bureau president.

"The pamphlet listing members of the Speakers Bureau and con-...

Red-Headed Frosh Leads 6th Column

THERE'S a sixth column on the campus, but it's no relation to Smilin' Jack, has no Downwind, and definitely, it says, contains no de-icers. The only similarity is that the "Eye" of the outfit is red-headed Helene Mosely, practically a namesake of Zack Mosley, creator of Smilin' Jack.

The column is made up of 11 freshman coeds. The subversive elements they're combating are the kinks in their own personalities, if any. Also they tear apart the men they date.

Helene Mosely, right, who is leading the sixth column movement on the campus, is shown with three of her compatriots, left to right, Betty Carrier, Eileen Schroeder, and Rita Baughman.

Guide 'Til Pledging

The purpose of the organization is to guide them until they pledge sororities. They meet once a week at homes of their members, where they discuss each other's looks, grooming, grammar, clothes, manners and so on.

They also discuss the men they've dated since their last meeting and put them on the approved or otherwise list.

They're all in the freshman social customs class, but they figured they needed a little more personal attention. That's why they're keeping the group small, so they can all get personal attention.

They're In Already

Either the girls over-estimate the amount of coaching they need, or else the column has already done some good work, because members of the group are already establishing themselves in campus activities.

Three of them, Emily Garrigues, Rosalie Borchert and Betty Carrier are trying out for cheerleader. Dorothy Becher is winning a reporter's job on The Buchtelite and Eileen Schroeder was a candidate for Women's League. Miss Mosely, captain of the column, was a model in New York City before entering the University. She now models at a downtown department store.

Other coeds in the organization are Marjorie Meyer, Rita Baughman, Betty Torrey, Dorothy Barnaby, and Melissa Bentley.

Arts Students Are Book Worms; At Least They Carry More Books

By Dick Collier

IF there's a bookworm on the campus, chances are he's an Arts College student, because arts students withdraw more books than any other group on the campus.

Strangely enough, though the arts student who bothers to read a book generally reads 20 a year, only 62% bother to read a book at all, a survey shows. The best-read student by all odds is the typical Evening Session student, for of the 1,245 enroled last year, 1,179, or 98%, withdrew an average of nine books per reader.

But They Bring Their Own

This contrasts nicely with the four engineers who last year withdrew ten books for an average of 2.5 books per reader, or two paragraphs, a sentence, and a semicolon per engineer per year.

While 62% of the Arts students withdrew books, only 56% of the faculty thought it a good idea, withdrawing, on the average, 18 books per reader.

This doesn't necessarily mean that 53 of the 123 faculty members preferred playing bingo to curling up of an evening with the Decline and Fall of the Roman Empire, because the survey only covers books withdrawn from the general circulation desk, and hence excepts the uncounted hordes of faculty members who stormed the departmental libraries, the Upper College reserve room, the city library, and General College reading room.

They are not covered because individual reading records for these divisions are not kept, according to chief librarian Miss Josephine Cushman.

Withdraw 160 Books

Still, 60% of the education majors managed to walk away with an average of 15 books per reader; 24% of the General College students, with 8; and an infinitesimal proportion of engineers.

Probably the queen of readers was Miss Clara Stastny '40, who withdrew 277 books. Other students also took out a few books, of course—one removed 160 but until the survey is completed, Miss Stastny is queen.

Here's The Dope On Game Tonight

Time and place: Tonight at 8:15 p. m. at the Akron Rubber Bowl.

Price of seats: Boxes, $1.70; reserved, $1.15; general admission, 35, 55, and 80 cents; children's general admission, 20 cents. Evening Session students with activity cards, 55 cents.

Tooting A Flute Very Uncertain-- So She Comes To U

SCHOOL teachers are more apt to eat than flute players.

That's why blonde Anita Haines is enroled in the College of Education. She's going to the University as a form of unemployment insurance.

Miss Haines, an accomplished flutist, has had three years at the Julliard School of Music in New York City and has played with the Montreal Symphony, the Brooklyn Orchestra, the Julliard Orchestra and the Orchestra Classique.

Her ambition is to be a concert artist, and she hopes to return to Julliard in a year or two to pursue that ambition, but just in case the fluting field flops, in the meantime Miss Haines is going to learn to be a school teacher.

She had a chance to play with Phil Spitalny's all-girl orchestra, but she refused it because she preferred to play only classical music, and also because it would interfere with learning to be a school teacher.

Wiener Roast Is Planned By Student Y For Tuesday

The Student Y will roast wieners at its outing in Metropolitan Park Tuesday. The group will leave the campus from the Student Building at 5 p. m., and return for the "Social Improvement" dance in the evening.

Mr. John L. Prosser, general secretary of the Akron YMCA, will be a guest at the picnic.

YWCA Plans Cabaret Party

Room Will Represent Cafe Tuesday At 7:30 p. m.

A Cabaret Party, open to all University women, will be held by the University YWCA Tuesday at 7:30 p. m. in the YWCA auditorium.

The room will be arranged to represent a cabaret with dimmed lights, checked tablecloths, and dance floor.

The entertainment will begin with community singing headed by Katherine McCormick and Martha Foster.

A floor show featuring a comic style show, a vocal trio, a piano duet, and a tap dance will climax the party.

Planning the affair are Betty Cooper, Mardelle Witwer, Miss McCormick, Doris Miklashek, and Hazel Hobbs.

Scabbard And Blade Smoker Is October 18

Scabbard and Blade, national advanced military honorary, will hold a smoker Friday, October 18, at 8 p. m. in the Student Building lounge in honor of Col. David H. Cowles, Lieut.-Col. Blaisdell C. Kennon, Major Marvin B. Durette, and Lieut. Ben Logan.

Colonel Cowles was recently promoted from the rank of lieutenant-colonel; Lieutenant Colonel Kennon was promoted from the rank of major.

Major Durette and Lieutenant Logan came to the University military department this fall.

All officers in the junior class have been invited to attend the smoker.

Calling Coed Crooners

Women who wish to enter the ...

Non-Frats Take Onl... One Offi...

Constitutional Amendm... Pass Easily; 800 ... Vote

The Buktal party swa... the Independents in y... day's election as they ... eight of the nine St... Council positions and e... a representative to the ... Committee.

Approximately 800 ... dents voted from an ... ment of 1760.

Two amendments to the S... Body Constitution passed ... huge majority.

Robert Bishop, chosen to ... sent the College of Engin... was the only non-fraternit... didate to weather the landsl... defeated John Burkley, 21-1...

Representatives-at-Larg...

Hollis Allen and Betty ... will be Upper College repe... tives-at-large. Allen beat ... Davis, 133-127, while Miss ... defeated Letitia Dobrin, 17...

General College represen... at-large are: Marthabell ... and Sam Koledin. Miss Rie... feated Juanita Chauncey, ... Koledin outpolled Thomas ... and Robert Tillett. Koled... 159 votes; Denton (I), 12... lett, 32.

Divisional Posts

Arthur Larson, Paul Cobu... William Heepe will repres... spectively, the social scien... manities, and natural scie... visions of the Buchtel Col... Liberal Arts.

Larson won over James ... 95-37; Coburn beat Carmel... etti, 22-14; and Heepe d... Miriam Zimarik, 24-10.

(Continued on Page 3)

Nelson Curbs ... Lounge Chan...

Asks That Students Do... Move Furniture

There will be no more ... of furniture in the Student ... ing lounge, Manager Max ... decreed today.

"The arrangement of furni... the lounge is set up as it ... the maximum of convenien... best appearance," Nelson s...

He suggested that studen... wish to study use the S... Council meeting room, wh... now available for study pu...

"Students may work to... there and the room has a ... table where work may be ... out," Nelson said.

The room may be reserv... student groups by applying ... office of the dean of stude...

Assistant Manager Carl ... announces that applications ... dents who desire waiter jobs ... cafeteria are being received...

Lockhart, Henrich Win ... In Theatre's 'Ghost ...

Albert Lockhart will pl... part of Richard Winthrop... Walter Henrich that of ... Price in the University Th... production "Ghost Train," ... decided Tuesday. Rehearsa... be held every afternoon at ... in B42.

The mystery melodrama ... given on October 30 and ... November 1 and 2 in the S... Building lounge.

CHAPTER 6
1940–1949

The 1940 team in action. Photo from Tel-Buch, *courtesy of Archival Services, University Libraries, The University of Akron.*

October 8, 1940

Reserve Red Cats Edge Score-Hungry Zips, 6–0

Fighting Akron Eleven, Led by John Lucas, Holds Powerful Cleveland Squad to 6–0

By Charles Teter

The "touchdown famine" still haunts Akron's Zippers after their third game of the season Friday night at the elaborate new Rubber Bowl, where the Red Cats of Western Reserve edged out a 6–0 triumph.

After holding the Cats scoreless for three periods, disaster overtook the Zippers early in the fourth period when Bob Fellmuth's pass was intercepted by Paul Anderson of Reserve.

Three plays later Dominic Sanzotta, halfback, broke through Akron's forward wall, dodged three would-be-tacklers, and scampered 45 yards to pay dirt.

Flossie Kicks Beauty

Akron's chief threat occurred in the second stanza as a result of Bennie Flossie's coffin-corner boot, which went out of bounds on Reserve's 1½-yard line.

Flossie returned the Red Cat punt to the 36, picked up 16 on two tries and on a long lateral raced to the 9-yard line. However, Reserve's line braced to halt the Zippers' attack.

Morrow Sweeps Ends

Wade Morrow, Akron's elusive back, gave the Reserve ends a bad night of it as his flank sweeps went for long gains.

The Zipper's fine defensive game was sparked by Center John Lucas, who continually broke up the Red Cats' line thrusts.

About 18,000 thrill-hungry fans turned out for the Zipper's debut in the new bowl, and if cheering was any indication of appreciation, they left the stadium well-pleased with Coach Tommy Dowler's charges.

November 13, 1940

'Weak Spinner, Pass, Punt' Whip Kent 23–7

Coach Starn's Estimation Backfires; Zips Knock Golden Flashes Out of Nation's Undefeated List Saturday in Thriller; Flossie, Latona Lead Drive

What Kent State's Coach "Rosy" Starn called Akron's "two weak spinners, an incomplete pass, and a fairly good punt" came back to haunt him at the Rubber Bowl

The 1940 team. Front row: Harker, Campanale, Latena, Coach Russ Beichly, DiNapoli, Wilkins, Walter, student managers Brickels and Koledin. Second row: student manager Pappano, Hibbard, Christner, Maluke, Capt. Fernella, Mikolashek, T. Sullivan, Monzo. Third row: senior manager DeCora, Coach Dowler, Broge, Andreoli, Greenhorn, McAllister, Humphrey, Grigas, Heller, Coach Otis Douglas, senior manager McCormick. Fourth row: Florin, Nix, Boston, Selby, Lukas, Warner, Moskoff. Photo from Tel-Buch, *courtesy of Archival Services, University Libraries, The University of Akron.*

Saturday, and proved the downfall of his highly-touted unbeaten and untied ('til then) Golden Flashes, as the Zippers came out on the long end of a 23–7 score over Kent.

The victory was an important one in a number of ways. It knocked Kent State out of the nation's list of undefeated teams; it maintained Akron's historic superiority over the Flashes; it put renewed zest in a Zipper team that had bogged down under two ties and five losses.

Kent Started Fast

During the first few minutes of play, it appeared as though Kent was all it was reputed to be. Then, their initial drive was stopped and the Zippers stepped into the spotlight and scored twice in almost as many minutes in the second quarter.

The first Zipper score came after Akron's "fairly good punt" was good for 60 yards and was downed on the Kent 2. Mittiga kicked out of bounds on the Kent 30. After Flossie and Latona had ripped off short gains, a lateral to Flossie around the right end put the ball on the Kent 2. Two line bucks failed, but on the third, Latona drove through over the goal line.

'Incomplete' Pass Clicks

Shortly after, the Flashes attempted to pass from deep in their own territory, but Flossie intercepted on the Kent 45. Akron's "incomplete" pass to Keith Culbertson was good for 35 yards. Latona on a "weak spinner" went ten yards for another score.

In the third quarter, using the two more "weak spinners," the Zippers went down to the Kent 15. Flossie then stepped through the Kent backfield for 15 yards and another score.

The 1941 team moves down the field. Photo from Tel-Buch, *courtesy of Archival Services, University Libraries, The University of Akron.*

Andy Maluke, Zipper guard, kicked perfect field goals after each touchdown and made the score 21–0.

Flashes Score

Then the Flashes unleashed a barrage of passes. One, a sleeper, was good for 35 yards. Another pass on which officials ruled that there had been Akron interference with the pass receiver, gave Kent the ball on the Akron 4. Three running plays netted the Flashes nothing, and on the fourth down, Kilbourne, Flash end, hauled in a pass in the end zone for six points. The kick was good, and Kent trailed 21–7.

On the last play of the game, a Kent pass was knocked down in their own end zone, and the officials ruled that a safety had been scored for Akron, making the score 23–7.

About 8,500 fans saw the game.

November 29, 1940

Zippers Swamp Carroll 47–0 in Season's Finale

The rejuvenated Akron Zippers ended their 1940 football campaign by swamping a bewildered John Carroll team on Thanksgiving Day, 47–0. At least hitting the pace expected of them, the Zippers dominated the whole game, scoring almost at will against the hapless Blue Streaks.

Akron scored in the first five minutes, the touchdown coming on a pass from Bennie Flossie to Bill Selby after the Streaks had fumbled on their own 31 on the fourth down. Andy Maluke booted the placement.

The Zips scored again in the second period on a pass from Flossie to Tom Broge, after a 29-yard run by Flossie put the ball on Carroll's 4-yard line. Bob Humphrey kicked the extra point.

Bennie Flossie halted the Streaks' only scoring threat by intercepting a pass on his own 18 and streaking 88 yards for a touchdown. Felix Latona added Akron's fourth score by bucking over from the 1-yard stripe. With the score 27–0, going into the final period, a complete new team took the field against the Streaks.

The highlight of the game came early in the final quarter when Keith Culbertson batted a Carroll pass into the arms of Bob Humphrey, who ambled seven yards for a touchdown. Humphrey kicked two extra points to take high scoring honors in the game with eight points.

A 63-yard march, with Bob Fellmuth, Joe Campanale, and Andreoli alternating, was climaxed by Andreoli going over for the score. Akron's final score came on a lateral from Mike Fernella to Keith Culbertson.

October 2, 1942

Zips Lost to OW in Last Period Push

Akron Scores Second Touchdown of the Year

By Jack Laraway

Ohio Wesleyan won as expected, 19–7, but it took them until the latter moments of the third quarter as the Akron Zippers opened with their best offensive play of the season Saturday in Delaware, Ohio.

The Zippers, ever trying in spite of earlier reverses, fought hard and well in falling to a superior team. Even an opening 63-yard touchdown march by the Bishops failed to demoralize the Zippers as it had done in the Ohio U and Western Reserve games.

After OW grabbed a first quarter seven-point lead, Akron stopped them cold for the remainder of the half. The booming punts of the Tom Taber were mainly responsible for this.

Zips Click in Third

Akron started clicking in the third quarter. One of the few breaks they have received this year came the Zippers' way as Brentlinger fumbled on his own 35.

After two incomplete passes, Tom Taber connected with Tiny Bohla on the three-yard line, and the Twelve Apostles couldn't have kept them from scoring. Earl Rowe ripped off-tackle for his second score of the year. George Florin kept his placement record perfect and with the score tied, 7–7, it looked like a ball game.

Bishops Score Twice

MacKinnon, Havre, and Richey struck quickly, however, and put the damper on Akron's hopes. After a beautiful 43-yard kickoff return by MacKinnon and three line bucks, Havre went 16 yards around end to score and put the Bishops ahead. Bretlinger failed to convert.

A few minutes later the scoring ended when Richey went off right guard from the T-formation quarterback spot for 81 yards and a touchdown after Taber kicked to the 19.

The 1940 team on the bench. Photo from Tel-Buch, *courtesy of Archival Services, University Libraries, The University of Akron.*

The score doesn't tell of the Zippers' superiority in the second half, however, as they piled up eleven first downs to Wesleyan's six, and gained almost 150 yards.

On one occasion, they marched 65 yards before losing the ball on downs. Another time Earl Rowe broke loose off tackle for 26 yards and almost a score, until Richey tripped him on the Wesleyan seven.

Bohla is Spark

In addition to Taber's kicking and Rowe's sprints were the smashing defensive play of Tiny Bohla and the line bucking of Chick White. Bohla was the sparkplug of the Akron defense throughout the game.

Time and again he messed up the Bishop plays from his line backing position. White made two smashing 12-yard line bucks in succession in the third quarter march.

Coach Otis W. Douglas upset some of OW's offensive plans when he abandoned the five-man center smashing defense which beat OW last year, and shifted his charges to a six-man shuttling line. The Bishops were expecting the same defense, and it was apparent that they were upset somewhat over the change.

The Wesleyanites outgained Akron 282 to 198 and made thirteen first downs to Akron's eleven.

1940 Zipper linemen at the ready: Selby (end), Mikolashek (guard), Fernella (tackle). Photo from Tel-Buch, *courtesy of Archival Services, University Libraries, The University of Akron.*

December 2, 1942

Zips Win 'Moral Victory' in Thanksgiving Battle

After absorbing seven heartless beatings, the fighting Zippers finally came through with the great ball game that "Doug" knew they had in them and tied a heavily favored John Carroll eleven Thanksgiving Day at the Rubber Bowl.

The spirited Zips, who were being spotted from 14 to 27 points by Carroll supports, played truly magnificent football. Led by the punting of Tom Taber and the outstanding line play by Bill Wilkins, George Florin, and Joe Carney, the Hilltoppers outcharged and out-fought the Streaks who were powerless inside Akron's territory.

The 47.7 yard kicking average of Taber was probably the greatest single factor contributing to the Akron "moral victory." Taber's punts, two of them traveling over 55 yards from scrimmage, time and again put Carroll deep in its own territory.

John Carroll had three scoring chances and failed. In a first quarter drive, Joe Meere and Bob Sulky carried the ball in successive downs to the Akron nine, where the Zippers stiffened.

In the second stanza they again dove to the Akron 12, and again the Zipper line threw them back. Their final scoring chance came on a dropped pass on the Akron goal line in the final quarter.

Akron had one scoring opportunity, and succeeded only to have it nullified by a penalty. Carney and Martin Chapman broke through the left side of the opposing line and blocked Meere's punt on the Carroll 22. The ball rolled to the four, where Wilkins recovered. Two line bucks put the ball on the one, and from there Chapman went off tackle to score. A double penalty backfield in motion and offsides resulted in a replay.

Bill Holsberry, ace Zipper passer, received three broken ribs in the last play of the first half. If he had been available in the last minutes of the game, Akron might have scored, as several potential receivers broke clear only to be frustrated by poor passes.

October 11, 1946

Akron Takes Opener 31–13

After a lapse of four years, the university returned to the gridiron on Saturday, September 28 with a victory over Lawrence Tech of Detroit, 31–13. The game was played under a hot and sweltering sun which tended to keep the game from reaching a feverish peak.

The fans had hardly settled in their seats when the Blue Devils had scored. The Zippers received the kickoff and on first down quarterback Bill Holsberry elected to pass. His lazy pass was intercepted by Walerski of Tech. After two futile attempts at the line, Walerski took to the air and completed a 20 yard pass to Brodie, who succeeded in getting beyond our secondary. A desperation tackle on the two yard line by John McMillan failed and the Detroiters had gone ahead six points on a play that covered 64 yards.

The initial quarter ended with the Zips on Techs one yard line, having run up five first downs. The first play of the second stanza found Tony Palermo lugging the mail for a T.D. "Smokey" McMillan's toe put Akron ahead 7–6. This was the beginning of the end for the visitors.

After bogging down short of the Tech goal line on several occasions the Baldacci coached boys scored shortly before the half ended. McMillan, Keenan, and Palermo carried the ball on this drive with Frank Keenan scoring. The place kick failed. Thus the first half was history.

Eight minutes in the third period saw Jim "Mickey" Finn intercept a pass on Tech's 47 yard stripe and outdistance the complete Tech team to make the score 19–6.

To start the fourth quarter, on the receiving end of the punt, McMillan twisted and turned his way up to the Blue Devil's 40 yard marker. With the aid of a roughness penalty, McMillan, Palermo, and Keenan again carried the ball into pay dirt territory. Palermo went the last four.

With about twelve minutes to go, head coach Baldacci began to substitute freely. Kenny Batman, substitute end, intercepted a pass in Tech territory and raced twelve yards toward the opposing goal. A roughness penalty put the ball on the one, from where high stepper Joe Zaher tallied.

With but minutes to go, Lawrence Tech showed their only real offensive threat of the day. They rang up four quick first downs against our third string.

November 15, 1946

Zippers Outlast Scots, Retain Coveted Bell

Scoring in the final two minutes of play, the University of Akron Zippers outscored the Wooster College Scots 26–20 at the Rubber Bowl last Saturday to keep the cowbell in Akron's possession.

Filling the air with passes the Zips managed to push over a score in the remaining minutes of the ball game. A pass from Frank Wahl to Joe Papp covered 18 yards to place the ball on the Wooster 34. Once again Wahl connected, this time to Bob Schumacher unheralded end who leaped high into the air to snare the toss on the Wooster two. Joe Papp then scored his second T.D. of the day as he took the ball on an end around for the winning marker.

The game was a see-saw battle which saw the Zippers opponents once again forging to the lead in the opening minutes of the game.

Scots Score First

The score came as Minnie Busack caught Jim Finn's fumble in mid-air and raced 56 yards for the score. Billy Shinn missed the extra point and the Scots led 6–0.

Akron roared back when Bill Holsberry, whose play was nothing short of terrific, passed from Akron's 45 to Martin Chapman for 33 yards to place the ball on the Wooster 12. Two line plunges placed the ball on the three but a five yard penalty put the ball on the eight. From here Holsberry snapped an aerial to Harold Anderson who stepped over the goal for the score and George (semi-automatic) Chima booted the ball through the uprights and the Zips led 7–6.

On the ensuing kickoff Bill Holsberry recovered Tom Lykos' fumble on the Wooster 30 and promptly tossed a pass to Martin Chapman who scored standing up. Chima missed the point and the score was 13–6.

McMillan Kicks Badly

A poor kick by John McMillan set the stage for the second Wooster score as he booted out of bounds on the Akron 33. The Zips never got out of this hole and after another exchange of punts the Scots marched to the Akron four and from there Shinn plunged over. He also booted the point after touchdown and the score was knotted at 13–13.

Once again Holsberry recovered a Wooster fumble to set up a score, this time on the Wooster 48. A pass to Papp moved the ball to the 32. Another aerial put the ball on the 15—this one to Jack Meiszwiler. The score came on another pass, Holsberry to Papp, who took the ball on the five and fought his way over for the score as the half ended with the Zips leading 19–13

The final Wooster score came as a 40 yard march by the Scots ended with Shinn passing to Busack for the touchdown. Shinn made the placement and the score stood 20–19 in favor of the Scots.

The rest of the third and most of the fourth quarter saw the Scots stopping numerous Zipper drives with pass interceptions and the booting of Busack, his last boot rolling out on the Akron one yard line. On the next play Holesberry slipped a pass from punt formation to McMillen who took it on the scrimmage line and with some beautiful downfield blocking weaved 98 yards for a touchdown only to have the ball brought to the 40 where a clipping penalty occurred. Undaunted the Zips went on to score the winning tally which proved the spirit which they acquired in the Western Reserve game is here to stay.

EXTRA POINT

October 19, 1935
Historical Cowbell is Sought-for Prize

It's a dingy little dinkus to fight for, but it's uppermost in the minds of those 22 men out on the field as well as the followers of both Wooster and Akron in the stands.

The "Cowbell Feud" began back in 1920 when "Weeds" Mason, a University of Akron freshman, attended his first Akron-Wooster football game accompanied by a cowbell, one of the most effective forms of noisemakers. The game was at Wooster, and he quite earnestly vowed that the cowbell would not make the return trip to Akron unless Akron was victorious. "Weeds" returned—the bell stayed.

For three years Wooster retained the trophy, until in 1924, an Akron team captain by none other than Mason himself, a senior then, took a one-point victory over the Scotsmen and brought the bell back to Akron.

"Weeds," now Mr. Kenneth A. Mason, attorney, is to be in the grandstands this afternoon. He's been telling people that he was to be "out of town" today, because he said a trick was played on him last year. "When I said 'of course I'd be at the game,' they made me speak," he complained.

And here's some real, though doubtful, inside dope on the origin of the cowbell (direct from "Weeds"): "So many people have asked where I got the bell; where it originally came from," he said; "well, I'll tell you . . . don't you remember Mother O'Leary, whose cow started the Chicago fire?" Oh yes, now we "remember" and we also suspect a little deviation from the veracious, as the climax comes over the phone: "Well, this cowbell came from the neck of that very same cow!"

The "Weeds" Mason cowbell in its 15 years of sensational existence has become imprinted on the spirit of the University. Mr. Mason perhaps expressed it most simply saying "That cowbell's going to ring in my ears the rest of my life, I guess!"

Editor's Note: Akron lost the 1935 game, but won the following year. The teams didn't meet again until 1946, when the post-war Zips returned to the field, victorious. Akron and Wooster fought for the cowbell off and on until 1966, after which the two teams never again competed. Akron's overall record against Wooster is 18-17-3.

TIME-OUT

The Zips & Zippy

Where Does "Zips" Come From?

One of the most unique nicknames in all of intercollegiate athletics belongs to The University of Akron. Originally Zippers, athletics director Kenneth "Red" Cochrane officially shortened the nickname to the Zips in 1950. Twenty-five years earlier a campus-wide contest had been conducted to choose a nickname for the University's athletic teams.

Suggestions submitted by students, faculty and alumni included Golden Blue Devils, Tip Toppers, Rubbernecks, Hillbillies, Kangaroos and Cheveliers. After a three-way vote—one by the student body, one by the University lettermen and one by the local sports writers and faculty representatives—the winner was decided on January 15, 1926.

The winner, freshman Margaret Hamlin, suggested "Zippers" the name of a very popular rubber overshoe (over 500,000 sold the first year) invented by Akron's B.F. Goodrich Company. She received a prize of $10 for the winning suggestion, which was inspired by the $6 pair of rubber shoes, the "Zipper Boot." Permission to use the name was granted by the Goodrich Company.

Goodrich introduced its rubber galoshes in 1923 and it made a lasting impression on the world. The footwear featured an ingenious invention, a slide fastener with interlocking metal teeth. With a quick pull of a tab, the overshoes opened wide or sealed shut.

The product's original suggested name was the "Mystik Boot," but the name just did not work for Goodrich President Bertram G. Work. "What we need is an action word," he told a group of sales representatives. "Something that will dramatize the way the thing zips." From that he said, "Why not call it the Zipper?"

The Evolution of Zippy

The evolution of Zippy, The University of Akron's mascot, began 56 years ago when the student council, under president Dave Frye and committee for a mascot chairman Bob Savoy (an All-American diver for UA), decided the University needed a mascot.

"Zippy" the kangaroo was officially declared UA's mascot on May 1, 1953.

The selection of the kangaroo for a mascot brought forth the wrath of *The Buchtelite* and the *Akron Beacon Journal* as the name was chosen without the benefit of a campus-wide vote. There was support for the new mascot with defenders saying, "The kangaroo is fast, agile and powerful with undying determination—all the necessary qualities of an athlete."

It is difficult to imagine there was dissent back then seeing as how Zippy is one of, if not, the most beloved symbols of the University. In fact, during an 11-week long national contest, Zippy defeated all challengers. Zippy, after a first-round bye in the playoffs, cruised to

Zippy with cheerleader. Photo by Tobias Studio, courtesy of Archival Services, University Libraries, The University of Akron.

Zippy meets a fan in 1979. Photo by Bob Wilkey, courtesy of The University of Akron Department of Intercollegiate Athletics.

victories over Syracuse's Otto in the semifinals and Minnesota's Goldy Gopher in the final to become the 2007 Capital One Mascot of the Year.

Dick Hansford, UA student council advisor, liked the kangaroo—one of the finalist names when Akron chose "Zippers" as its nickname. He recalled the suggestion was also inspired by a popular comic strip at the time called "Kicky, the fighting kangaroo."

No one recalls who made the arrangements for the first costume, but a papier-mâché head was produced along with a brown furry uniform that zipped up the back. Pete Demming debuted that first mascot uniform in 1954, at the inaugural Acme-Zip Game—not as "Zippy" but as "Mr. Zip."

The first known printed reference to the mascot as "Zippy" was a 1965 Zip football press brochure. *The Buchtelite*'s first use of the name "Zippy" came Sept. 24, 1965, in an identification of a photo of the cheerleaders listing "Mascot—'Zippy'—Charles Huettner."

Zippy challenges Youngstown State's Pete the Penguin. Courtesy of Archival Services, University Libraries, The University of Akron.

Editor's note: Zippy is one of the only female mascots in the nation without a male counterpart. The popular "Fear the Roo" campaign originated in 2005, the same year the Zips football team went to the Motor City Bowl.
Courtesy of The University of Akron Department of Intercollegiate Athletics

Rally 'Round the Roo

Is winning a mascot contest such a big deal? Yes. Yes, it is.

This was not supposed to happen. The 12 schools represented in the 2007 Capital One Mascot Challenge included such big-name players as Virginia Tech, the University of Georgia, UCLA and Brigham Young University. And the list of also-rans from previous Capital One mascot challenges reads like a roster of the NCAA's pantheon: OSU, the University of Florida, Purdue, Washington State, the University of Maryland, Auburn and UNLV.

Yet somehow, Akron's beloved Zippy became the Capital One National Champion on the first try. More astonishing is the fact that Zippy defeated every other competitor in the 13-week competition. No school had ever gone undefeated in a Capital One Mascot Challenge.

And keep in mind, the Capital One challenge is really a competition among fan bases, not individual mascots. Each week on its web site, Capital One paired up the mascots in six contests. Fans were urged to go to the site, register and sign in, then vote in each of the match-ups. To avoid a repeat of a hacking incident years ago, in which one school received 5 million votes in a single week, Capital One said it has invested in safeguards to "detect and discount fraudulent votes from over-enthusiastic fans."

So, how did a humble, Mid-American Conference university, with only one Division I bowl appearance to its credit, outvote some of the biggest and best-known names in NCAA sports? *Akron Beacon Journal* columnist David Giffels '88, '95, provided the answer in a Jan. 3, 2008, column. "This wasn't so much a victory for The University of Akron mascot as it was for a community."
Akron Magazine, *Spring 2008*

Zippy never ceases to entertain. Courtesy of The University of Akron Department of Intercollegiate Athletics.

ENT COUNCIL
SUGGESTIONS
ditorial, Page 2

THE AKRON
BUCHTELITE

Heidelberg Victory
Will Give Zips Crack
At O.C. Crown
See Page 4

The University of Akron, Akron, Ohio, Friday, November 13, 1953—Vol. 65, No. 15

s For
Key Due
xt Week

applications will
t later than 4 p.m.
ay, according to Gil-
, A-Key Committee

n blanks may be pick-
r. Hansford's office any-
today.
-Keys are awarded by
Council once each se-
campus activities and
stic standing. Those de-
honored award are se-
a special committee."

year's committee are
ase, and Dick Maloyan.
dents must amass 30
women students 25
applicants must have
t least 77 credit hours
equired point ratio of
an 2.0.
ber of points possible
any one field such as
holarship, publications,
is limited to two-thirds
required. Unless other-
ied, points for mem-
service in activities are
awarded on the basis
r's work.
ns must be signed by
artment heads in the
ich the work was done.
who is found trying
an A-Key by dishonest
permanently disqualified
ch future award. (Point
A-Key applicants may
in the University A-

Gold-Star
Honored
emorial Hall

nory of approximately
it county veterans who
rld War II will be per-
granite at the entrance
l Hall, the University
$1,400,000-physical and
ation building now un-
ction.
ding will be the only
World War II me-
Summit county.
s will be sandblasted
that can outlast steel,
brick. Each plaque will
red granite, surround-
ebony border. An esti-
man-hours will be re-
erpetuate the names of
county gold-star vet-

Hall is a part of the
00,000-second cycle
ogram which calls for
an Arts and Sciences
d an addition to the

Military Ball Honors Jean

After being escorted through an arch of sabers during intermission at last week's Military Ball, Honorary Squadron Commander Jean McTaggart received the trophy she holds. Miss McTaggart was one of the Hilltop lovelies presented to the dance crowd. Her escort through the arch was Acting Colonel Jack Sheppard.

Mascot Plans Slow But Efficient Is Repo

Plans for putting the Kangaroo into full use a official University mascot are moving slowly but s according to a report to Student Council by Dick B Kangaroo Committee chairman.

Beyer pointed out that the slow movement of the gram was necessary so all the students might a hand in choosing their cot.

"We plan to have the drawing picked from thre sions which will be printed Buchtelite," Beyer said.

During a discussion foll the Kangaroo Committee r Dick Maloyan, Student C treasurer stated, "Student cil isn't seriously considerin Kangaroo."

Maloyan felt that Council giving Beyer their full suppo stated that Student Counci hampering the Kangaroo mov and that they (Council), no er, were responsible for an effectiveness of the program.

Vote Of Confidence Prop

A motion was made for of confidence by Student C for the Kangaroo Committ Maloyan. Bob Savoy seconde meeting.

Alec Thomson, Student C president, agreed with Beye Kangaroo Committee action be slow and thorough in ore do a good job.

"Beyer is doing the job him. This is the first indic that anyone felt there was a in Council toward the Kang or the Committee," Tho stated.

"We needn't pledge our s to the Kangaroo Committee more than any other com of Council. The fact alone th have a committee proves ou port of the Kangaroo," Ted ex-officio member of Coun Tel-Buch editor, said.

Motion Discussed, Passed

Mr. Richard Hansford, f adviser to Student Council, "Last year the suggestion was that we adopt a tangible s as our mascot. This idea wa proved by alumni groups an administration and passed w mously by council."

"If the students want a cot the matter should be t care of this year," Hans added.

Maloyan referred to Ted statement by saying, "The of the Kangaroo Committee any other committee is ridic This is a specific case with a

(Continued on page 2)

Board Approves Student Funds

The Student Activity Budget for 1953-54, amounting to $38,785, was approved by the University Board of Directors at a meeting on October 29, according to Leslie P. Hardy, vice president in charge of finance.

A tentative budget had been drawn up previously by the members of the Extracurricular Committee, composed of students holding chief campus offices and faculty members. The committee is headed by Gordon A. Hagerman, assistant dean of students.

Approved allocations are: Assembly Committee, $1,800; Athletic fund, $12,000; Buchtelite, $7,500; Dance Committee, $300.

Intramural Committee, $1,300; Music organizations, $775; Student Council, $1,360; University Theatre, $1,150; Women's League, $1,600; and Tel-Buch, $11,000.

Approximately $39,500 was expected this year from the payment of student activity fees. A fee of $15 is payed for the first semester and $5 for the second semester.

Cast Commended By 'First Nighter'

By Larry Hawse

The curtain rose at 8:15 p.m. last night on one of the most delightful and entertaining comedies that the University Theatre group has presented in the last few years.

The selection of "The Male Animal" by Director Donald Varian was very wise. The plot is simple and uninvolved, taking place in one location. The excellent set adds to the feeling of realism which is essential to a good production.

The casting of the play was done very skillfully and the actors portray their characters quite well with the possible exception of Fred Bock, whose acting is a little less than that expected of one in a major supporting role.

Top honors in performance should go to Jack Bennett, who gives a perfect characterization of a professor of literature. His drunk scene with John Milford is very real even though Milford is slightly under par on this scene.

Amy Auburn rates high for her

Dot Poses With Army Brass

Kenton Plays

CHAPTER 7
1950–1959

The 1951 team. Front row: A. Dannessa, A. Lionetti, W. Mitchell, J. Mazzaferro, R. Vogt, L. Ahern (manager), P. Scarpitti, D. Holmes, L. Balaj, J. Petracca. Second row: R. Wixcey, J. Kallenbach, H. Johnson, J. Malone, C. Abramski, P. Bickle, G. Ripple, D. Longacre, D. Nicols, 'Doc' Smith (trainer). Third row: Coach Houghton, T. Hillery, L. Keller, J. Cistone, B. Rizzo, T. Anton, G. Shadie, F. Grayden, F. Stams, J. Harlan, 'Doc' Hoffman (trainer). Fourth row: R. Merideth, J. Lytle, L. Sovacol, E. Haddad, G. Preisse, Assistant Coach Maluke. Fifth row: J. Verdon, R. Eckstedt, J. Mazzagatti, T. Conti, J. Janes, C. Keller, L. Hamlin, C. Topalu, G. Manos, E. Conrad. Photo from Tel-Buch, *courtesy of Archival Services, University Libraries, The University of Akron.*

October 6, 1953

Zips Down Muskies 26–13

Rest of OC Takes Notice as Akron Remains Undefeated

By Chuck Blair

For more than 60 minutes last Saturday the World Series atmosphere shifted from the TV set in the Student Building lounge to the well worn grass of the Rubber Bowl. The Bums and the Yanks gave way to the Zips and Muskies.

Horsehide became pigskin and better than 6,000 (a series crowd as far as Zip football is concerned) saw the underdog Blue and Gold eleven soundly defeat the Conference crown contender from New Concord 26–13.

Coach Cochrane's squad now boast three consecutive 1953 wins, more than any Hilltop team since '46, and more in a row than any Akron club since Jimmy Aiken's 1938 edition.

The most important fact the game proved, however, was that the Zips aren't going to be one of those clubs that beats the second division teams and falls apart in the face of real opposition.

Findlay didn't have it. The statistics proved that. Wittenberg was groomed by the press as a possible upset winner in the Akron-Fighting Lutheran contest. Twenty-one points in the first quarter eliminated the Tigers.

But Muskingum … they were another story. On the 26th of last month the Muskies battled Heidelberg to a 12–12 tie. The 1952 Princes won the mythical OC title, which leads Zips to hope that the algebraic axiom of "things" equal to the same thing are "equal to each other," holds true on November 14.

The Muskies had a pass master in quarterback Joe McDaniel, who completed six of 14 for 90 yards, but only one of his aerials netted a score. Akron's pass defense rendered the others harmless.

On the ground Bob Jones reeled off 101 yards in eight carries, better than a first down a try, but the Zip line only permitted one leg score. Four times when the Muskies were knocking on the door inside the twenty the Hilltoppers threw up their own iron curtain and stopped them cold.

There was more drama packed into the final few seconds of the first half than Akron fans have seen in many a season. The Muskies were leading 7–6 and on Akron's seven. They had three cracks at the line before the clock ran out, but the Zips held.

Akron's initial tally came on a Cistone to Conti air mail good for 15 yards and six points. Tom made a great grab while on his knees in the end zone and answered many of Cochrane's prayers as the Zips drew first blood.

John L. Martin, who set up Conti's first period score got one of his own in the third to give Akron a 13–7 lead. Buster Rizzo dashed 20 yards for number three in the fourth and added the clincher in the same frame with Conti's aid.

Rizzo now stands at the seven TD mark for the season. His first TD of the evening was set up by a brilliant 50 yard aerial, Marion Rossi to George Shadie.

Shadie's partner on the other end of the line, Frank Stams, came up with a spectacular grab in the first quarter when he leaped high in the air on the dead run and pulled in a 12 yard Cistone pass with a one hand stab.

With West Virginia Tech on tab for next Saturday, the Zips have an excellent chance of going undefeated into the Homecoming game with Mount Union.

October 27, 1953

Scot Victory Hopes Kilt by Rossi's Conversions

Six in Row by Zips Adds New Page to Grid Records

By Chuck Blair and Ed Kalail

Wooster, Ohio—Throwing everything but their kilts into the game, Wooster's Scots came within two points of snapping Akron's win streak before falling 20–18 at Wooster last Saturday.

It was the Zips sixth win in a row; marking the first time any Akron team has ever won the first six games from opening day.

Coach Kenneth Cochrane, who was on the 1930 Zip eleven that set the six win pace, saw his clip tie the all-time Hilltop win record (also held by 1937 Zippers).

The 20 point output establishes the 1953 Zips as the highest scoring Blue and Gold grid aggregation in modern times (since 1900), with 165 points so far. Previous record holders were the 1927 and '28 teams with 158 points. All-time scoring mark was set by Buchtel College in 1893 when they amassed 276 points.

Akron is finding out the hard way that it's rough to be a winner. Every team you play is up for the game and seems to use the philosophy "if you can't beat 'em bleed 'em."

Things got so rough that Rizzo ran out of bounds on several of his carries to keep the Scot tacklers from piling on his 160 pound frame.

Two Zip scores were called back, one because of a block that they never saw, but called clipping and the other on a fumble that occurred after Jim Horrigan had crossed the goal line.

John Brady suffered the loss on the first called back TD, after a sparkling 52 yard interception run back.

It took championship poise to overcome the bad breaks Akron got from the officials and the keyed up Scots across the scrimmage line, but class plays off in the long run . . . and the Zips have got it.

Besides regaining the cowbell trophy the Zips remained the best club in the state and are still tied with Ohio Wesleyan for the Ohio Conference lead.

Marion Rossi got things underway early in the first quarter when he tossed a 20 yard TD pass to John Vernon in the end zone. It was Rossi's sixth TD heave of the year and Vernon's second scoring snare.

Rossi made the extra point to give the Zips 7–0 first quarter lead.

John Siskowic came back for Wooster in the same quarter with a three yard scoring dash but fullback Ned Martin missed the conversion.

In the second quarter quarterback Jim Ewers scored for the Scots, but Martin again missed the extra point try giving Wooster a momentary 12–7 lead.

The Zips bounced back after an exchange of kicks midway in the second, and Johnny Cistone put Akron on top for the second time with a 26 yard TD aerial to Rizzo who was all alone in the end zone. Cistone made the extra point attempt but it was nullified the officials called a holding infraction against Akron.

Rossi replaced Cistone and booted a 28 yard extra point on the next play for Akron's 14th point.

During most of the third quarter the high-geared Akron offense couldn't get moving, but with less than three minutes remaining in the period Schutzbach crashed over right tackle, headed for the sideline and outraced two Scot defenders to go 74 yards to paydirt. Cistone's kick was no good and Akron led 20–12.

After an exchange of punts Wooster moved to the Zip's 10 yard line early in the fourth stanza but the Akron defense stiffened and held the Scots. On the first play from scrimmage Martin fumbled and Wooster recovered.

After two plays gained only four yards, Hole hit Siskowic in the end zone for the score. The center of the Akron line rushed in to block Martin's kick.

Akron had another scoring opportunity late in the fourth quarter. Rossi flipped a ten yard aerial to Rizzo who made a sensational catch, lying flat on his back at the Wooster four. Schultzbach twice hit a brick wall as he attempted to go up the middle.

The improved play of Bob Schultzbach in the last three or four games was very evident against Wooster. Schultzbach carried 10 times and gained 89 yards, leading all the Zip ball carriers by a wide margin and his 74 yard touchdown jaunt in the third quarter turned out to be the deciding factor in the game.

On the other hand Buster Rizzo has been stopped cold. Against Mt. Union Rizzo gained only 49 yards and against Wooster had a net loss of 17 yards from scrimmage. Of course Buster is a marked man wherever the Zips play and it is becoming very evident that the Akron opponents are determined to get him out of the game.

But although they may bottle Rizzo up on the ground he is definitely the number one pass receiver on the team. He has snared 15 passes good for 304 yards and 4 touchdowns and he scored his lone TD against the Scots via the aerial route.

November 17, 1953

Heidelberg Crushes Akron Title in 26–0 Contest

Akron University's Ohio Conference championship hopes were shattered last Saturday night at Tiffin as Heidelberg rolled to an impressive 26–0 victory.

Led by senior quarterback Jim Lambert whose aerial wizardry and deft ball-handling bewildered the Zip defenders throughout the game the Student Princes scored twice in the second quarter and once each in the final two frames.

The loss, Akron's first in OC play. Coupled with Ohio Wesleyan's victory at Wittenberg makes the fourthcoming game with the Bishop's nothing more than another game with nothing at stake except victory number 7 for the Zips and an undefeated season for Ohio Wesleyan.

The Zips have been on the down grade ever since the West Virginia Tech game and the spark of greatness which they exhibited against Muskingum earlier in the season has been all but extinguished. Kent State started the ball rolling with their crushing defeat and Heidelberg added more fuel to the fire. The Bishops could add the final touch.

Showing no offensive punch whatsoever, the hapless Zips gained only 190 yards. Their vaunted aerial game was slowed to a snail's pace as Marion Rossi and John Cistone completed only three for 12 gaining only 33 yards. The Zips were also blanked in the scoring column for the first time this year. Kent State being the last team to accomplish this feat back in 1949.

The entire first quarter saw both teams scoring opportunities fail due to fumbles and penalties. But with the half almost over Rossi fumbled on the Heidelberg 18 and Bob Warren recovered for the Student Princes. With Walt Livingston carrying the brunt of the attack the Princes moved to the Akron 42 yard line.

At this point Lambert faded back and spotting his receiver in the clear a good ten yards behind any Akron defender he heaved a 42 yard aerial to Bernard Murphy for the touchdown. Lambert's attempted conversion was no good.

Moments later Cistone's pass was intercepted by Lambert on the Heidelberg 38 and behind a host of blockers the fleet back scampered 62 yards down the sideline for the Prince's second score. This time Lambert's kick split the uprights. Both of the Princes scores came with less than four minutes remaining in the first half.

Early in the third quarter the punchless Zips took over on their own 24. After Bob Schutzbach smashed to the 26, Tom Coni on the next play attempting to lateral to Rizzo fumbled and Lee Tyler fell on the lose pigskin at the Akron 30.

Two plays later and the Student Prince's had another touchdown. Warren hit off tackle for three yards. On the next play Lambert faking beautifully faded back and hit his favorite receiver Bernie Murphy in the end zone for the score. Lambert's placement kick was wide.

Akron's sputtering offense just couldn't get rolling and Rossi was forced to kick. Roy King, elusive Negro halfback returned the punt 15 yards to the Heidelberg 45. King and Livingston moved the ball to the Akron 45 for a first down. The Princes

The 1953 team. Front row: John Verdon, Joe Malone, Vince Didato, Jim Horrigan, Tom Hillery, Mario Russo, George Auten, Angelo Rizzo, Tom Conti. Second row: John Martin, Frank Stams, Bill Gaug, Phil Schember, Paul Bickel, Frank Grayden, Dave Longacre, Larry Hamlin, Chet Bekeleski, Joe Mazzagatti, George Shadie, Coach Andy Maluke. Third row: Coach Tom Evans, Dick Cardarelli, Dave McKoski, Jerry Reeves, James Townsend, George Craig, Ronnie Vargo, Howard Spicer, Tony Paris, William Williamson, John Brady, Coach Kenneth Cochrane. Fourth row: Coach Hal Smith, Marion Rossi, Walter Kirn, Bob Schutzbach, Bob Andreyka, Joe Palacek, William Auten, James Foughty, Bill Boalich, John Cistone, Don Grant. Fifth row: Larry Foore, John Costello, Frank Debevec, Clifford Chapman, Tom Daughtery, Dennis Burk, Henry Charno, Dave Harper, Coach Joe Mazzaferro. Photo from Tel-Buch, *courtesy of Archival Services, University Libraries, The University of Akron.*

were momentarily stopped by a 15 yard clipping penalty but King broke loose for 17 yards to the Akron 38 to keep the march moving.

Warren bullied his way to the 30 as the quarter ended. King skirted left end and darted to the 15 yard line for a first down. Livingston, freshman sensation from Ravenna, carried three straight times, the third carry for one yard and the final touchdown of the game. Lambert made it two for four as his kick from placement was good.

For the remainder of the game Coach Cochrane used his second and third string backfielders. Showing fight and courage they moved the ball from their own three yard line to the Heidelberg 43 before the gun sounded ending the game.

The best play of the game for the Zips was a kickoff return by Buster Rizzo in the fourth quarter. The Zip speedster took the pigskin on the six yard line and reversing his field two or three times the flashback momentarily broke into the clear and raced to the Heidelberg 38 before being shoved out of bounds. The beautiful run however was nullified by a 15 yard clipping penalty against the Zips.

The 1954 team. Courtesy of The University of Akron Department of Intercollegiate Athletics.

September 28, 1954

Lutherans Drop Zips before Record Throng

By Ed Kalail

Playing in front of the largest crowd ever to witness an Akron University football game, 23,769, a fighting Wittenberg team edged the Zips 12–7.

The attendance figures eclipsed the old mark of 17,742 set in 1940 when the Hilltoppers entertained Western Reserve in the Rubber Bowl. Last year for the entire season Akron drew a total of 21,213 in four home games.

Paced by the hard running of Don Wood and Gene Urbanski, Wittenberg jumped out to a two touchdown margin at the end of the first half. Wood, senior fullback, led the ground gainers, grinding out 95 yards and scoring one TD.

The Zips new offense couldn't get started in the first half as is evidenced by the statistics. Akron picked up only four first downs to Wittenberg's eight. Only once in the first half did the Zips look like they were really starting to move. After taking the ball on their own 38 the Hilltoppers swiftly racked up three first downs and moved to the Lutheran 21 before giving up the ball on downs.

One of the bright spots in the Akron defeat was the running of freshman backs Wayman Cash and Harold Fuller. After Wittenberg scored their second touchdown, Cash took the ensuing kickoff and rambled 46 yards to the Lutheran 45 before being hauled down, but a clipping penalty nullified the gain. As fate would have it, Cash's fumble in the fourth quarter halted the Zips winning drive on Wittenberg's 27.

Sophomore Jim Townsend, starting in his first game for the Blue and Gold played a superb brand of ball making two spectacular catches from Marion Rossi in the Zips touchdown drive, one on fourth down to keep the march going.

Buster Rizzo, Hilltoppers fleet back and last year's scoring ace was completely bottled up by the Wittenberg defense. Rizzo picked up only 15 yards in 16 carries.

The Lutherans scored the second time they got their hands on the ball. After Jim Ingledue returned John Cistone's punt to the Akron 40, Coach Ralph Ness's charges started rolling goalward.

Quarterback Del Shannon picked up a first down on the Zips 29, but a clipping penalty halted the Tiger drive momentarily. But Wood skirted left end for 24 yards to the Akron 23, where Ingledue and Wood alternated to take the ball to the Zips' six yard line.

Urbanski sliced off right tackle for six yards and the score. A high pass from center stopped John Adler from attempting the extra point.

Near the end of the first period Akron was forced to kick and Ingledue brought it back to the Tigers 42 yard line. Once again the spectacular senior from Crestline, O., Don Wood sparked the Wittenberg offense, as the Lutherans moved the ball to the Zips' nine yard line, as the quarter ended.

A backfield in motion penalty moved Wittenberg back to the 14. Urbanski went to the 11 and Wood to the five. Urbanski carried to the one and on fourth down old reliable Wood hit pay dirt for the Tigers. Adler's kick was wide. No further scoring developed in the second period and the score at halftime read Wittenberg 12, Akron 0.

Coach McMullen's pep talk at half time inspired the Zips as they came roaring back in the third quarter. Rizzo took the kickoff and raced to the Akron 43. From here the Hilltoppers put on a 57 yard sustained scoring march with Bob Schutzbach capping the drive, bulling his way over right guard for three yards and the Zips' lone score. Rossi's conversion was good and Akron trailed by only five points.

During the rest of the game Akron threatened but just couldn't seem to get that one scoring spark needed to push across the game winning TD.

This was the Zips' fourth straight loss over a two year period. The losing streak started with Kent State and then in succession Heidelberg and Ohio Wesleyan. Next week the Hilltoppers face a tough Ohio Wesleyan team which romped to its first win of the season by downing Rochester College 33–7.

The Zips rated in many quarters by four touchdown favorites seemed to lack the finesse and fine polish of a winner and Coach McMullen will have to work hard to sharpen up the dull edges. The same weakness that plagued the Hilltoppers last year is still very evident, a lack of a strong defense. Maybe it was first game jitters or possibly the huge crowd but whatever the cause here's hoping Coach McMullen can smooth it out.

September 24, 1958

First Acme-Zip Victory Sees Gridders Romp Over Mount

The jinx is broken! Akron has won their first Acme-Zip game! These are the cries that rang out throughout the Rubber Bowl last Saturday as the Zip gridders bounced the Purple Raiders of Mount Union 18–0, for their first triumph and their first win in an Acme-Zip game since its origin in 1954.

The 1958 team. Front row: Morris, Wise, Taylor, Burnette, Tausch, Ullrich, Rossi, Rach. Second row: Coach McMullen, Calcei, Townsend, Petrovich, Murphy, Pearson, Wiener, Lupori, Garnett, Adams, Mackey, Coach Evans. Thrid row: Coach Laterza, Stone, Maravich, Daily, Toth, Adolph (captain), Rainey, Semester, Cogswell, Smesko, Bailey, Coach Maluke. Fourth Row: Emerick, Hamilton, Henry, Frampton, Green, Wiley, M. Smith, Gissinger, D. Green, Hoover, Lushbaugh, T. Smith. Fifth row: Yarger, Ripple, Kendall, Pappas, Nelson, Fitzpatrick, Holt, Breiding, D. Smith, Dragash. Photo from Tel-Buch, *courtesy of Archival Services, University Libraries, The University of Akron.*

The crowd of 32,863 shouted their approval for the fine defensive effort of the Hilltop squad in the first period and their devastating running attack that showed its full potential in the final stanza. Three freshmen, Jim Lupori, Owensby Pearson, and Jim Nash received a baptism of fire in the Acme-Zip game and came through like champs. Lupori was the favorite receiver of quarterback Marco Burnette while Pearson and Nash performed ably in the Zip internal line.

The first half was a defensive battle with both the Zip and Raider lines smothering any offensive attack of the other.

After the intermission, the Hilltop squad charged into the lead. The Zip defense forced the Raiders to punt after their first series of downs and Art Bailey returned to kick 27 yards to the Mount 33. Two plays advanced the ball to the 26. On the next play Burnette rolled out to his right and hit Jim Lupori on the 10 and the big end rambled into the end zone untouched.

A Mount punt rolled dead in the end zone in the next series and the Zips began their march for their second touchdown on the 20. Burnette hit left half Ty Cogswell with a pass good for 20 yards. Cogswell figured again in the next key play as he skirted the end for 21 yards to the Raider 27. A Burnette jump pass to Lupori was good for 10 yards. Cogswell lugged the ball another seven and Bailey added the finishing touches on a pitchout from quarterback John Stone.

Dave Adolph, the Zips three year veteran blocked a Mount Union punt a few minutes into the fourth quarter and the ball was put in play on the Mount 32 yard line. With third and seven a pass from Burnette to Ray Green for 16 yards gave the Hilltoppers a first down on the Raiders' 13. Bailey hit the Mount forward wall for 11 yards to the 2 and another first down. Burnette was forced to "eat the ball" on the first play from scrimmage as the Raiders pushed the Zips back to the fifteen.

A 1957 Zips completion in progress. Photo from Tel-Buch, *courtesy of Archival Services, University Libraries, The University of Akron.*

EXTRA POINT

The final game of the 1958 season can be called nothing but the "Mud Bowl." The Zips and Baldwin-Wallace battled to a scoreless tie under anything but football conditions at the Rubber Bowl. The mud and rain made what could have been an interesting game into a game of fumbles and mistakes. For the record it was the first time since 1948 the Blue and Gold had two shutouts in one season recorded against them.

1959 Tel-buch

The 1958 team plays Baldwin Wallace in mud. Courtesy of Archival Services, University Libraries, The University of Akron.

oodyear Pledges $1.25 Million To Challenge

PRESIDENT Norman P. Auburn and Russell DeYoung, Goodyear board rman, look over a model of the proposed Center for the Performing Arts.

The $1.25 million gift announced last week by The Goodyear Tire and Rubber Co. to the university of Akron's $10 million centennial campaign, Challenge '70, is the largest single gift ever received by the university.

The contribution brings the campaign total to $4,490,785 in pledges. It was given in honor of Mr. E. J. Thomas, chairman of the executive and finance committee of Goodyear.

In response to the donation, President Dr. Norman P. Auburn said, "On behalf of the faculty, students and staff of The University of Akron, I want to express our gratitude to the Goodyear Tire and Rubber Co. for its splendid contribution of $1,250,000 to the Challenge '70 program.

"This generous gift raises our campaign total to nearly half of our $10 million goal. It represents a major step forward in plans of the university to develop a cultural center — a much needed public auditorium for the enjoyment of everyone in and around the city of Akron." Dr. Auburn stated.

Mr. Thomas, in whose name the donation was made, is a member of the University Board of Trustees, and is vice-chairman of the Centennial Advisory Committee. Since 1966 he has been chairman of Akron's Citizen's For Progress committee.

Dr. Auburn said, "As a member of the Board of Directors of the university since 1952, Mr. Thomas has played an important role in the university's growth."

Mr. Thomas joined Goodyear as a part-time clerk in 1916. Following his graduation from Central High School in 1917, he became a full-time stenographer and two years later, secretary in the office of the factory manager.

He began broadened training with the company in 1924. In 1932 he was named general superintendent of the Akron plant, and after working for Goodyear in Great Britain, became executive vice-president and was elected to the Board of Directors in 1937. He became chief executive officer in 1956, and two years later, Chairman of the Board. He retired from these positions in 1964.

The objective of t '70 campaign is to million Center for the Arts to be constructed pus and adjacent t Akron, $3.5 million scholarships, profess library learning res $500,000 for renov U's historic Buchtel campus landmark.

Parade Kicks- Acme-Zip Wee

A torchlight para junction with Acme-Z uled for September p.m.

Meet At Conse

All band members cheerleaders, Acme hearts, fraternities, a will meet at the Fi servatory on Fir Hi torches. Leaving fr the parade will tu Buchtel, right onto Rd., right onto Carr Brown, left on Bucht onto College St. to th across Buchtel to Student Center.

Pep Rall

There will be a sn at the dorms and a the Student Center country, soccer, and will be introduced Cochrane will speak.

serving Campus and Community since 1889

the Akron BUCHTELITE

79 — No. 3 THE AKRON BUCHTELITE Thursday, September 21, 1967

It's Acme-Zip Time Again!

Record Crowd Anticipated for Zip Home Opener

It's that time of the year again! Acme-Zip time! And, another capacity crowd will be on hand at Akron's Rubber Bowl for one of the largest athletic and social events of the season. One year ago, a crowd of 40,166 cheered the Zips on to victory over Northern Michigan. This year, with similar attendance expected, the Zips will host the rugged eleven from Tampa.

The gates will open at 3:30 p.m. The first event, starting at 4:50, pairs Randolph-Macon with Akron U's soccer team. Coach Stu Parry rates this year's soccer team as one of his best. At halftime, Woodridge and Field High School bands will entertain.

At 7:00 p.m., there will be more musical entertainment presented by Revere, Hudson, Cuyahoga Falls, and Coventry High School bands. Then, at 7:25, the crowd will be able to release their emotions for the Zip football team as they take the field for warm-up. During the warmup, the Sweetheart Parade will make its way around the track led by the Coventry High band. At this time, the various University organizations will introduce the girls they have selected to honor as Sweethearts for the Acme-Zip day festivities.

The young ladies to be honored are:

Jane Nicholas for Air Force ROTC

PRE-GAME FESTIVITIES are a highlight of the ann extravaganza.

Debbie Van Meter for Lone Star

Eileen McGuckin for Newman Club

Mary Ann Iacomini for Phi Delta Theta

Linda Judy for Phi Kappa Psi

Cindy Horn for Phi Kappa Tau

Debbie Humberson for Phi Sigma Kappa

Ann Vosper for the two residence halls

Chorus will sing Anthem. Then, as b turn to the field, to positions for the op President Auburn Governor Rhodes t tee with the game b

During halftime, tainment by the mous Alliance High tor Band will take the direction of After they are finis

ew Seal And Coat Of Arms Approved

he tradition and history of University of Akron have n re-stated in a new form — official seal and coat of arms roved yesterday by the AU rd of Trustees in their regu monthly meeting held on the pus.

he recommendation was the nination of extensive research the history and traditions of 98-year-old campus along with horough study of heraldry.

he motto, "Fiat Lux" — "Let ere Be Light" — and the open k, used in several AU comncement program dating from 0 through 1916 have direct orical association with AU.

The open book," explained Dr. burn, "was adopted in recogon of the fact that the Unisity's original college curricu-

the shield containing the identifying symbols of the University and the motto. The principal color scheme is azure (blue) and or (gold) in keeping with the traditiona colors of the University.

The coat of arms is a re-creation of AU's history.

The first element is the phoenix, a mythical eagle-like bird with deep red and gold wings. It is often regarded as an emblem of excellence.

Affixed in the shield, the heart of the coat of arms, are representative components of the University — the open book, three cortises or stripes and the lamp of learning with a city skyline.

The three diagonal cortises bisecting the shield represent the three stages through which the

CHAPTER 8
1960–1969

The 1968 team. Courtesy of The University of Akron Department of Intercollegiate Athletics.

October 28, 1960

Inspired Zips Upset Wooster in First Win

Great Team Effort on Part of All Zips

By Jim Main

"If continuous or consecutive winning would be functional ubiquitous experience in your personal coaching faculty, then you could never achieve the ultimate realization of triumph after chaos or pleasurable readjustment from desperation to exuberance."

This is what Coach Joe McMullen uttered after the University of Akron Zips upset Wooster last Saturday at the Rubber Bowl. Freely translated, the above statement means IT FEELS MIGHTY GOOD TO WIN!!!

There is no doubt about it, Saturday's win over the Scots was a team victory all the way. The real surprise of the whole game was the fact the Zips beat Wooster at their own game, on the ground!

The Zips, headed by Frank Lomax's 78 yards for 13 carries, piled up a total of 193 yards rushing. George Deo had 46 yards on 11 carries followed by Senior Tom Murphy with 45 yards on 18 carries. Steve McClellan was the top runner, as usual, for the Scots.

Akron drew first blood in the see-saw battle, with Murphy scoring from the one, after Wooster's McClellan had fumbled on his 13 yard line in Wooster's first play of the game. It was the first of four fumbles lost by Wooster in the game. Mike Dudock circled left end for the two points.

Wooster came roaring back minutes later as Jim Turner scored six from six yards out. Gary Williams added the two extra points on a pass from Bill Washburn. Never say die Akron again came back with Marco Burnette at the helm drove 65 yards to have Murphy fumble in the end zone, but due to the alertness of center Bob Dyser Akron scored. That ended the scoring in the first period.

Late in the second quarter, Wooster quarterback Washburn threw a 39 yard rollout pass to his left end Al Cooksey for six points. The half ended with the score knotted at 14–14.

After a scoreless third quarter, Wooster finally went ahead for the first time with 7:08 remaining as McClellan ran untouched from 13 yards out. A holding penalty nullified the extra point try, and their kick from the 21 was short.

This set the stage for a great comeback by the Zips. Driving to the Wooster 35 yard line, Frank Lomax took a hand-off from Marco Burnette and burst into the line. For a moment it seemed like he was stopped but then (shades of Jim Brown) he broke

In the 1961 game against Denison, Akron's Joe Richardson eludes the opposing defense as he snares a Mackey pass. Photo from Tel-Buch, *courtesy of Archival Services, University Libraries, The University of Akron.*

free, was nearly stopped again by two Scot defenders, but shook them off and just as he was about to cross the goal line was hit from behind yet still fell into the end zone for the score. A great superhuman effort on his part.

This wasn't all for up steps senior halfback Nelson Eddy to take the spotlight in the heroes role. With the pressure on, Eddy calmly (so it seemed) kicked the extra point that decided the ole ball game. What a tremendous finish!!!

December 2, 1960

Zips Go Down Fighting in Loss at Youngstown

By Ken MacDonald

Akron's relentless Zips were defeated for the eighth and final time this year by the Youngstown Penguins, 34–21, but as usual they went down fighting. If the Zips had played in the first half like they played in the second, they might have ended the long season on a winning note.

After scoring a quick touchdown, with George Deo's seven yard jaunt, Akron was literally run over, especially by halfback Frank Horvath who picked up 134 yards and scored three six-pointers. Before the Zip gridders could get back into the scoring column again, the score was 34–7, with the score at the half being 27–7.

After a scoreless third quarter, Akron came rearing back with sheer determination and within two minutes time had scored two touchdowns. It was truly a great team effort led by the six departing seniors, especially by Nelson Eddy who played his finest game of his career on the Hilltop, scoring both touchdowns.

During the final minutes of the game, the inspired Zips had recovered a fumble, recovered two onside kicks, and intercepted a wayward Penguin pass, proving that never-give-upness that has characterized them throughout the long season.

Coach Joe McMullen, along with Nelson Eddy, journeyed to Erie, Pa. Thanksgiving Day for the Gem Bowl and helped the West All-Stars defeat the East All-Stars. Captain Tom Murphy also was invited to participate but declined the invitation so he could remain eligible for track.

Another Zip received an honor last week, that being the naming of Frank Lomax to the first team defensive safety on the All-Ohio Conference team. Honorable mention was bestowed on Jim Lupori, Marco Burnette, and Bruce Mackey. Thus ended a somewhat disheartening, yet somehow memorable, season.

October 6, 1961

Denison is Akron Zips' Victim before 35,061

By Steve Coleman

The University of Akron Zips smashed Denison, 28–0, in a thrill-packed Acme-Zip extravaganza last Saturday night. Some 35,061 fans saw Akron unleash its new Split-T offense to grind up the Big Red.

Deo Scores First TD

Both teams played a close first half, with the Zips taking a 7–0 lead a few minutes before the intermission. Akron's first score of the season began when linebacker Tom Lowry intercepted a stray Denison pass on the Akron 39 yard line. Fourteen plays later, fullback George Deo crossed the goal line after a ten yard gallop, for the first of his three touchdowns.

Zip Defense Tightens Up

Akron came back in the second half a much stronger defensive unit and had an offensive attack that almost busted the game wide open. Defensively, the Zips gave up only three first downs in the entire second half, allowing none in the third period.

Meanwhile, the offensive unit was scoring almost at will, adding three more scores, including a fine 50 yard TD pass play from Joe Mackey to Tom Adolph.

Richardson Sparkles

Both halfback Joe Richardson and Deo did fine jobs in eating up the yardage. Richardson had 91 yards in nine carries and Deo compiled 87 yards in 22 carries. Yet, Denison's fine hard-running fullback, Nick Musuruca emerged as the game's leading ground gainer with 92 yards in 26 carries.

October 5, 1967

Defense Shines

Freshman Lead Attack; Zips Flatten Marines

By Harry Movsesian

Akron displaying a fine offensive attack and using an exceptional defense never let the Quantico Marines launch their attack as the Zips won their second game in a row Saturday night, 20–0.

Ron Lemon and Jack Beidleman, both freshmen, treated the 6,000 fans who turned out for the All Service Night game to some very fancy running behind fine blocking from the Zips offensive line.

Beidleman rushed for 154 yards in eight carries including a dazzling 53 yard touchdown run in the third period. Lemon, who was subbing for the injured Tony Moro, gained 61 yards in sixteen carries including a five yard run for the Zips' first score.

The Zips defense completely stymied the Marines running attack in allowing the Corps a total of only 37 yards net rushing and a mere 81 yards passing for a total of 108 yards total offense. Twice the Marines invaded the shores of the Zips' goal line only to have their attack fizzle out.

Akron rushed for 265 yards and Don Zwisler passed for an additional 87 yards to give the Zips a total of 352 yards total offense, their best offensive effort of the campaign.

The Zips' first serious threat ended on a "sour" note when Lemon fumbled on the Marines' 30 yard line in the first quarter. Akron forced Quantico to punt and on the next series of downs Zwisler hit end Jerry Malizia for a dazzling 35 yard reception and put the ball on the Marines' 5 yard line. Lemon then scored the Zips' first touchdown of the game pushing over from the five on the last play of the first quarter, Dave Kosoy added the extra point and Akron led at halftime 7–0.

The Zips began to move once again midway through the third quarter when Beidleman taking a handoff from Zwisler on the Zips' 42 yard line circled on his right end and turned on the speed to outrace the Marines on a 58 yard touchdown gallop that enabled Akron to increase its lead to 13–0, once again Kosoy added the P.A.T. and the Zips led 14–0.

Moments later, Quantico aided by a pulling of the face mask penalty that nullified a pass interception by the Zips' Lynn Livelsberger and an additional 15 yards against the Zips' Gordon Larson for disputing the call, gave the Marines a first down deep in Zip territory. Once again the Zips held, with cornerman Ron Skowronek breaking up a fourth down pass play from the Zips' 6 yard line.

Akron took over and in eight plays once again scored on John Vargo's seven yard jaunt. The big play of this march was a 55 yard run by Beidleman. The point after touchdown was no good and the Zips won their second game in a row 20–0.

Next week the University of Youngstown invades the hilltop, which will prove to be one of the biggest games of the year. So get out and support the Zips, they deserve it.

The 1964 team in action. Photo from Tel-Buch, *courtesy of Archival Services, University Libraries, The University of Akron.*

October 18, 1968

Zwisler Shines in Zip Victory

By Joe Natoli

Don Zwisler threw for two touchdowns and ran for another as Akron University came to life in the second half after trailing 7–0 at halftime to beat Bradley University 27–13 Saturday in Peoria, Illinois.

John Vargo started the Zip comeback by dashing 40 yards up the middle minutes after the second half started. John Harrison's conversion tied the score.

QB Don Zwisler then got into the act by engineering a drive to the Braves 5-yard line where he calmly hit John "Home-run" Hoover for the T.D. Harrison's conversion gave the Zips a 14–7 advantage.

Early in the fourth quarter Zwisler scrambled 42-yards for the Zips third T.D. as the Zips took a 21–7 lead. Zwisler completed the Zip's scoring for the day by unloading a 52-yard touchdown bomb to Wayne Fox. Bradley pushed a final score across with a minute left in the game.

QB Don Zwisler turned in another fine job and the offensive line, the men nobody ever hears about until they flub up, turned in a sensational job. Not many people realize the importance of the offensive line except for their parents, their girl friends, or the offensive backs, but without their hard work there wouldn't be an offense. Without the "cracking" of guys like Mike Kura, John Travis, Dave Parker, Ken Delaney, and Barry Schaad, Zwisler, Ruff and Co. might just as well stay home.

E. Kentucky Next Test

This week the Zips have a Saturday afternoon game with Eastern Kentucky in Richmond, Kentucky. Eastern Kentucky, who has 35 lettermen back from their

Ohio Valley Conference champion team, defeated Middle Tennessee 49–21 Saturday. Eastern's defense, which allowed only 70 points last year, second best among all college football teams last year, has returned for another season and might cause trouble for the Zips.

November 14, 1968

Zips Sting Yellow Jackets, 59–19

By Joe Natoli

Damon Runyon, a famous writer of the past, once wrote a little poem about the greatest jockey of his time, Earl Sande, one of the luminous names of the era of Jack Dempsey, Babe Ruth, Bill Tilden, and Bobby Jones. If Runyon would have been at the Bowl Saturday, the poem might have gone something like this:

Maybe they'll be another
Maybe in 90 years
Maybe there's a twin brother
With more brains above the ears
Maybe, I'll lay against it,
A hundred bucks to a fin
Never a team like the Zips
Bring those victories in.

Akron University led by Dan Ruff, Jack Beidleman, Don Zwisler and the fine play of the interior offensive line of Kura, Travis, Parker, Delaney, Schaad, and Flaherty jumped off to a 21–0 first quarter lead and coasted home to a 59–19 football victory Saturday over Baldwin-Wallace in the Rubber Bowl.

Akron, victorious in the last four games, travels to Bowling Green next Saturday to face Western Kentucky, the number five ranked small college team. W. Kentucky's strength lies in their strong defense led by the team captain, all OVC tackle Walter Heath along with linebackers Bill Hope, end Lawrence Brame, defensive halfback Jim Garrett and linebacker Tom Vanest.

W. Kentucky's question mark is whether the offensive line can give the necessary pass protection to get their aerial game going. The offensive line is composed of all first year men except for end Steve Rusnock. They must have a good passing game so that fullback Dickie Moore, the nation's top college-division rusher last season can be truly effective. Handling the passing are two QBs Mike Egan and Johnny Vance.

A strong victory Saturday would bring the Zips a notch closer in getting a bowl bid.

September 23, 1969

Zips Tromp Tampa 40–0

By Greg Varley

Gordon Larson leaves little undone.

But the question that most people are asking is just how does he do it?

With the loss of an All-American quarterback in the graduation of Don Zwisler and with a tougher schedule than in 1968 prospects for 1969 was simply a matter of individual speculation.

Speculation ended last Saturday night.

It ended with the arm of a freshman quarterback and with four touchdowns by a 155 pound halfback.

In two games the Zips have amassed 92 points against none for the opposition. Coordination between offense and defense is as carefully tuned and as smoothly running as an assembly line.

There are few mistakes.

And mistakes that are made happen at times or places that have little or no effect on the score.

Before 43,000 Acme-Zip fans Akron displayed this machine at its finest.

Quarterback Mic Hutton combined his arm with the running talents of junior halfback Jack Beidleman to make the Rubber Bowl seem hotter for the University of Tampa than the 85 degree temperatures the Spartans left behind in Florida.

Beidleman scored four touchdowns tying the Acme-Zip record in that category. Three of those scoring efforts came on short runs, but one, a 72 yard touchdown pass from Hutton to Beidleman, four plays after a Tampa pass was intercepted by Dick Bozicevich, seemed to be the sign for Tampa to call for plane reservations.

This type of play is the secret of winning football—the offense being able to capitalize on mistakes forced on the other team by the defense.

Mistakes by the opposition seem to be the trademark of the Akron defense as they have forced five fumbles on the Spartans, recovered two of them and came up with three interceptions.

But, even if the other team doesn't make a mistake it seems that they're not going to get very far anyway.

In their first two games the Zips have seen fit to give up only 40 net yards rushing. Butler gained only four net yards on the ground.

The reason for eight 0's in eight quarters for the opposition seems a little more understandable in view of these statistics.

All faces point to a team which could erase many of the records set by the Grantland Rice Bowl team of 1968.

Already this year one thing has been accomplished which wasn't last season—Tampa has lost to Akron.

But what of the rest of the season?

1969 teammates take a breather on the bench. Photo by Bob Wilkey, from Tel-Buch, *courtesy of Archival Services, University Libraries, The University of Akron.*

This week the Zips travel to Eastern Michigan.

Last year the Hurons were ranked seventh by the Associated Press and this season the team looks even stronger.

Another thing about the Hurons of "68," they along with Tampa were the only two teams to beat Akron.

And Tampa has already been sent home—beaten.

After Eastern there are seven more games left, five of those games are home games.

Four of those games are to be played at the Rubber Bowl. The fifth game, against Youngstown, is scheduled for Barberton.

It's true that Gordon Larson leaves little undone—but his team leaves even less.

Eastern Michigan will find out Saturday.

Extra Point

First Bowl Game

As it turns out, The University of Akron's first-ever bowl appearance was a star-studded event. Little did the Zips know that the quarterback they faced that day would go on to become one of the most successful players in NFL history.

The Zips and Louisiana Tech met up for the College Division Mideast Region Championship in the 1968 Grantland Rice Bowl in Murfreesboro, Tenn. It was the first bowl appearance for both teams.

Both squads came in with highly-touted quarterbacks. For Akron it was senior Don Zwisler who entered the game ranked fourth in the nation in passing. For the Bulldogs, it was a junior named Terry Bradshaw who ranked first in the country.

Tech jumped out to a quick 21-0 lead behind a 16-yard TD run and 36-yard TD pass from Bradshaw. The Zips managed to get on the board with 1:50 left in the half on a 1-yard run from junior John Vargo. At 28, Vargo was the oldest running back in the country.

The Zips cut the lead to 21-13, but two more Bradshaw scores sealed the Bulldog win. This college quarterback is the same one who went on to lead the Pittsburgh Steelers to four Super Bowl championships and was inducted into the NFL Hall of Fame. Not quite an easy opponent for the Zips' first bowl.

Courtesy of The University of Akron Department of Intercollegiate Athletics

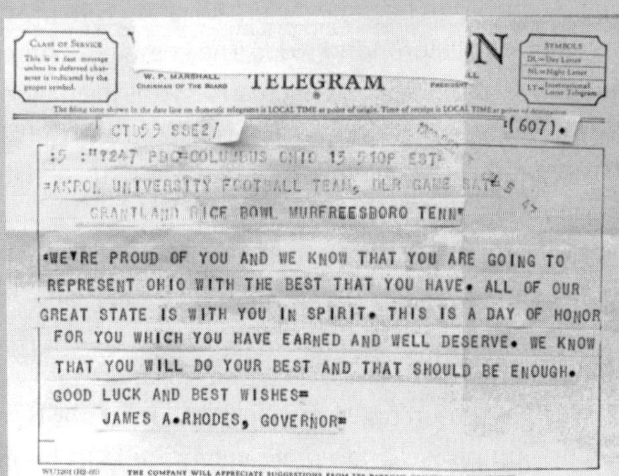

W. P. MARSHALL, CHAIRMAN OF THE BOARD — TELEGRAM

CT059 SSE2/ (607).

:5 :"7247 PDC=COLUMBUS OHIO 15 210P EST=

=AKRON UNIVERSITY FOOTBALL TEAM, DLR GAME SAT=

GRANTLAND RICE BOWL MURFREESBORO TENN=

=WE'RE PROUD OF YOU AND WE KNOW THAT YOU ARE GOING TO REPRESENT OHIO WITH THE BEST THAT YOU HAVE. ALL OF OUR GREAT STATE IS WITH YOU IN SPIRIT. THIS IS A DAY OF HONOR FOR YOU WHICH YOU HAVE EARNED AND WELL DESERVE. WE KNOW THAT YOU WILL DO YOUR BEST AND THAT SHOULD BE ENOUGH. GOOD LUCK AND BEST WISHES=

JAMES A.RHODES, GOVERNOR=

Telegram from Governor James A. Rhodes to 1968 team before Grantland Rice Bowl. Courtesy of Archival Services, University Libraries, The University of Akron.

TIME-OUT

The Acme-Zip Game

Knowing Northeast Ohio would not tire of good football, marching bands, and fireworks, four imaginative and farsighted Akronites gave birth to the Acme-Zip Game in 1954. The phenomenal growth of Acme-Zip into the 1980s was regarded as one of the biggest success stories in intercollegiate sports. It became one of the Akron area's great family entertainment bargains and a much-awaited yearly event.

Acme-Zip was born with a promotional idea the late 'Red' Cochrane brought back with him from Philadelphia in 1953. Ambrose 'Red' Dudley, athletic director at Villanova, had successfully promoted its opening game by selling tickets through a local food chain—97,802 fans turned out.

With this idea in mind, the Zips' athletic director called a meeting of Fred C. Pockrandt, President of Acme Stores, Inc., a local food chain, Ben Maidenberg, executive of the *Akron Beacon Journal*, and University of Akron President Norman P. Auburn to evaluate this plan.

Out of this meeting, Acme Stores became the organization with the drive, foresight and means of making the unique ticket proposal work. The company's supermarkets and later its discount stores throughout the Akron area were to serve as the major distributing points for ticket sales. These men figured that a decent crowd would turn out at the Zips' opening home game is there was good entertainment, the price was right, and the whole idea was promoted with enthusiasm.

Don Plath, a sportswriter for the *Akron Beacon Journal*, in reporting the outcome of the meeting, referred to the game as Acme-Zip. It was called the Acme-Zip game from that point on.

The Acme-Zip game featured a buy-one-ticket-for-a-dollar-get-one-ticket-free gimmick. For the first game of the 1954 season (vs. Wittenberg), Acme stores put up a guarantee of $10,000. Since the Acme-Zip project was community-wide in its boundaries, the *Akron Beacon Journal* and Acme staged an all-out promotional campaign and built up tremendous community awareness of the coming game.

The first Acme-Zip game had 23,796 pass through the Rubber Bowl turnstiles—more than the 21,828 that the Zips drew for the entire 1953 season. Over its early history, crowds steadily climbed to a high of 43,171 in 1971. The Zips' overall record in Acme-Zip games is 32-15-1, including an 11-year unbeaten string from 1961 to 1971.

Courtesy of The University of Akron Department of Intercollegiate Athletics

Top: The Acme-Zip game often draws the largest crowd of the entire season. Photo by Tobias Studio, courtesy of The University of Akron Department of Intercollegiate Athletics.

Left: Zippy is always on hand during Acme-Zip festivities. Photo by Tobias Studio, courtesy of Archival Services, University Libraries, The University of Akron.

niversity of Akron

BUCHTELITE

y,
r 26, 1976

Volume 88 Iss

A commuter student teaches Gung-Fu

by Carl Lewis

intense and exhausted ts are performing side ver a stack of seven scoop trying to develop a form.

ir instructor very vely observes, and then nts, "Throw the kick and make the turn. Your foot is going to burn, but let it burn. You've made the kick and got your man and after that you can let it burn."

And so go the teachings of George Moore, a commuter student from Cleveland, presently instructing a class in Gung-Fu for Black United Students weekdays from 5 to 8 p.m.

Moore, who has been studying the art for 13 years, initiated the class at The University of Akron out of a desire to expand the membership of his original group, the Imperial Gung-Fu Club of Cleveland.

Moore stated that due to the fact that the art is so beneficial to those participating, "The members of the club want to introduce it as widely as possible."

According to Moore, Gung-Fu originated over 2,000 years ago in China. The art was primarily used by religious monks to relax the body and discipline the mind.

"All forms and stances are basic, and though the basic forms may be strenuous, the art breaks into a fluent form," Moore said.

He continued by indicating that the forms of the art are patterned after the tiger, leopard and crane. The various animal forms are combined to create new forms which make each individual's style a little different.

Each member of the class is pushed to perform to the limit of his or her endurance. Warm-up exercises performed by the class are designed to use muscles not normally used.

While sueprvising a sparring match between two of his students, Moore emphasized the reed for accuracy of blows and power in delivery. While being conscious of your opponents blows he stressed that you should not be afraid of them. During the workout the blows were often hard, with few attempts to pull the impact.

Speaking of the prospective fruits resulting from the hard training to be enjoyed in the future, Moore remarked, "It's no magic, it's no dream, it's real."

According to Moore, during his introduction to Gung-Fu he really didn't know what he was getting into. He thought it was a joke, but for him it is no longer a game.

Moore has accomplished getting his entire family "off into the art."

According to Moore, he is seeking students "who want to train and train hard, and want to teach themselves how to fight, and I will show them so the things I know. But the must show themselves."

True commitment by st is not only demonstrat attending the class but a sacrificing time from activities, he said. Michael a consistent member of th declared that, "Since we every day, the hardest p the training) is getting the together; other than everything is fun at 8 p.m.

Vince Dorsey, another to the class, is one of th students who has had pr experience in the martia Dorsey openly claim preference for the presen of Gung-Fu as opposed to Karate forms.

For those individuals wh they are not physically enough to engage in the p of Gung-Fu, Moore easily that notion by stating th present grand master, Cle Jonathan Wom, is 72-yea

Persons interested in up for classes with the Im Gung-Fu Club Cleveland/Akron may c George Moore through th office, room 8, GS

nn says laughter is best medicine

Dear Ann Landers,

d your talk last night at homas Hall. I must say k was truly an enlight- xperience. The picture of at appears in our news- everyday just doesn't do tice.

aps that's because you smoke or drink, as you d I don't think you look d either "for an old who is 58-years of age." really true that you can phony letter a mile away people in real trouble take time to compose a piece. You said, "A would have to be a tic to make up the phony you receive; Well I am a orried.

phony letters always too contrived and too tten? You said that real have a tone of humility xiety that is difficult to d are usually not expres- ccinctly, brilliantly and tly. Well if that's the nn, believe me, this letter

as glad to hear you say ese are difficult times in to live and that you have nerves of steel even to be otic. You know, I agree, th all the changes that aken place in the last 25 with television, affluence permisiveness of society, g person would naturally tle disturbed, maladjusted rotic.

as glad to hear that you hat people are creatures

Your law states that if you think of your three closest friends and they seem OK, then you are the one. Well all my friends seem nuts. Is this say, truly be an awesome respon- sibility. People really do need help, or just someone to lean on or listen to them. This exactly describes what you and your staff of experts do. You said that if you had the wisdom of Solomon you could not pull out of your head the answers to some of the questions you get. But you said that you love trying to help people.

You say that you have always been a proponent of programs like Alchoholics Anonymous and Recovery and other groups that offer continuous long term help to people like the people that write to you for advice. This you said has been your primary job and service to your 60 million readers for the last 21 years; What influence you have!

As you said, some of the letters crack you up. You also stated that you don't write letters to roll 'em in the aisles but if it amuses as well, its all the better.

"A good laugh can take the stink out of misery," you said. And that may be the best advice that you, Ann Landers, have ever offered.

Signed,
N.E.P.R.

College Press Service

Now you, too, can own the best of Richard Nixon. Posterity Tapes in Illinois has released a 60 minute tape that

Ohio enrollment figures

Preliminary headcount to Chancellor James A. (Dolph) Norton of the Ohio Board of Regents show that 350,410 students, 10,718 more than last fall are enrolled on public campuses in Ohio.

What that means to the University of Akron is a 1.1 percent gain in enrollment from 1975.

This is the second straight year that Ohio's public institut- ions of higher education have shown substantial enrollment growth.

All types of state-support colleges and universities show increased numbers of students on their campuses. The overall gain was 3.2 percent; over the two-year period of enrollment growth. The cumulative gain was 17.3 percent.

The technical colleges reported the largest increase in number of students. Technical colleges gained 3,850 (16.5)perce last year.

The technical colleges ed the largest increase in of students. Technical gained 3,850 (16.5)perce last year.

Community and state and technical colleges with a gain of 2,830, (percent from last year.)

University main ca reported a gain of enrollees from 1975.

CHAPTER 9
1970–1979

The 1970 team charges against Indiana State. Photo by Bob Wilkey, from Tel-Buch, *courtesy of Archival Services, University Libraries, The University of Akron.*

October 17, 1972

Gridders Devastating in 49–0 Romp

By Mike Peticca

If Friday the 13th wasn't an unlucky day for the Northern Michigan Wildcats, then Saturday the 14th more than made up for it. For the fates had decreed that on that night the Wildcats would meet an Akron University team—a team ready to explode in frustration after being denied victory in all but one of four previous encounters.

The Zips, who had two weeks to smart over the past disappointments, attacked the unfortunate visitors with a vengeance and determination that had been missing. By pounding out 392 yards on the ground and limiting Northern's total offense to 89, Akron obliterated the opponent 49–0. It wasn't really that close.

While performing this astonishing about-face, every aspect of the Zip game was in top form. The blocking of the offensive line was sometimes awesome, and always crisp. Gleefully following the men up front were Sophomore halfback Barry Eisome, rejuvenated tailback Ernie Calhoun, fullback John Mather, and quarterback Eric Schoch.

Eisome, a replacement for offensive captain Calvin Pierce, punctured the Northern line for 74 yards in 19 thrusts, five of the yards accounting for Akron's initial touchdown.

Calhoun gained 70 of his total 102 yards in the first quarter, effectively establishing the Zip attack. Ernie chipped in with the fourth in Akron's parade of seven scores.

Playing a new role was Mather, who usually has to be content with leading his backfield mates through the holes with strong blocking. John slashed for 93 yards in 12 carries, and much of this came off the double slotback formation of a new Gordon Larson wrinkle featuring Maher as the only back behind the quarterback.

Then there was Schoch. The junior signal caller contributed 46 yards in 11 runs, but included were Akron's second and third touchdowns, more importantly, Eric's ball handling was almost flawless in directing the attack. Because of the success on the ground, Schoch went to the air but ten times, completing five for 73 yards. Tim Flaherty latched on to three of the aerials for 48 yards, while Bon Clayton's only catch—a 21 yarder—resulted in touchdown number five.

Wayne Sovlansky and Pierce added the final scores, while Tom Budziszewski was perfect on seven extra points.

Sharing the spotlight with the offense was a swarming defense. This unit, shaken by five lineup changes and upset with yielding 51 points in the past two games, played with the fire and reckless abandon reminiscent of the 1971 defense. Though Northern lost their fine quarterback Pete Spieier to an injury early in the game, one can't help but think it wouldn't have been any different even if the Wildcats had him all the way. The fact that Northern could manage only two yards per offensive plays speaks for itself.

Also, Akron's defense forced Northern into losing four fumbles and an interception, while Akron committed no turnovers—a pleasant turnabout from the first four games.

After both teams could not move on their first possessions, Akron moved 80-yards in ten plays for a 7–0 lead. Though Eisome got the points, it was Calhoun's 51 yard running that highlighted the drive.

Northern's sole scoring threat followed as they reached the Akron 20. But the Zip defense, helped greatly by a holding penalty on the Wildcats, stiffened and forced a punt. It was on this drive that Spieier sustained his costly injury.

Akron moved 85 yards in 14 plays following the punt. Featuring the march were Schoch passes of 23 and 14 yards to Flaherty. Barely a minute of second quarter had expired when Schoch pushed in from a yard out, Budziszewski's conversion making the score 14–0.

The defense helped set up the third score. Keeping Northern's offense bottled up deep in its territory, the Zips got the ball back at their own 48. The distance was moved almost routinely in eight plays, all on the ground, capped by Schoch's one yard score. The drive was keyed by the running of Maher out of the double slot formation. The score stood at 21–0 at intermission.

Akron's first half totals showed 254 yards, including 219 running. The story of both halves can easily be summed up in Larson's simple post game explanation: "our offensive and defensive lines both had control of the line of scrimmage."

The 10,042 in attendance figured the Zips couldn't be as good again in the second half—but indeed they were.

Denny Hamad started Akron again with a fumble recovery at his own 42. Mixing the plays beautifully, the Zips took eight plays in moving the 58 yards to pay dirt. Calhoun got the score, his first of the season, from five yards out.

Northern again fumbled following an exchange of punts with Denny Blake falling on the loose ball at the Northern 22. The now panic-stricken Wildcats saw Clayton gain a couple steps on his defender and haul in Schoch's pretty throw in the left corner of the end zone. The score board now showed Akron up 35–0.

The onslaught continued as Rich Madden fell on yet another Wildcat fumble at their 26. Schoch, now the only starter remaining in the backfield, handed to Sovlansky who scored from two yards out on the first play of the final quarter.

Northern received the kick and, that's right, fumbled again. Blake recovered the slippery pigskin on the Wildcat 27, and the score stood at 49–0 after Pierce scored on a three yard jaunt.

Though 10:49 still remained, the Zips chose mercifully to close out the scoring. The 49 point margin is the biggest the Zips have rolled up since they annihilated But-

The 1972 team. Photo by Tobias Studio, courtesy of Archival Services, University Libraries, The University of Akron.

ler by 52–0 in the 1969 opener. Akron's record improved to 2–1–2, while Northern fell to 2–4. The Zips hope for an encore as they travel to meet a tough Youngstown State squad Saturday night.

October 2, 1973

Defense Better but Zips Still Lose 16–14

By Mike Peticca

Buoyed by the fine efforts of a quartet of freshman starting their first games for the University of Akron, the much maligned Zip defense responded to all the criticism with a very respectable performance against Ball State at the Rubber Bowl Saturday night.

However, it was all in vain as, surprisingly, the Zip offense chose on this night to be the culprit and don the goat's horns heretofore reserved for the defense, in a 16–14 losing cause.

Akron lost two fumbles which led directly to Ball State's first ten points, and also gave up the pigskin three times on intercepted passes.

Despite its improvement and grittiness, though, the defense could not assert itself at the game's most critical moment, when Akron had scored the game's final touchdown with 7:04 still left to play in the contest.

Ball State was allowed to convert several third down situations at this point, and managed to run out the clock, denying the Zip attack one final chance to win the ballgame. The failure of Akron's defense here was even more glaring in light of the fact that the Cardinal march started way back on its own five yard line. Sixty-six yards later, after yielding the necessary yardage on three crucial third down situations, and even once on fourth down, the Zips were saddled with their third defeat in four games.

To the dismay of the 9,755 fans who came expecting an exciting display of offensive fireworks, the game's first quarter somewhat resembled a middleweight boxing match with the contestants probing for weaknesses in the early rounds.

Ball State was no doubt disappointed in this testing-out period, for the one deficiency that they expected to take advantage of—Akron's surrender to the opposition's running game—had obviously been reckoned with by Zip Coach Jim Dennison.

After the 47–33 debacle in Philadelphia, the rookie tutor was determined to shore up the Akron defense, and he did so successfully. Freshmen Banks Johnson at linebacker, Chuck Cullins at middleguard, and Bob Wolf at end plugged up many of the holes through which the Cardinal runners expected to rampage, and cornerback Ira Perkins did a good job in turning in the wide stuff, preventing long bursts outside.

But the Akron star of the night was Gary Yost, whom Dennison had moved to linebacker because of his quickness and toughness. Though light for the position at 185 pounds, Yost came through with a brilliant effort, showing great pursuit and instinct throughout.

While Akron was making it rough for the Cardinals to mount an effective attack, the Ball State defense did likewise, and in fact proved to be the catalyst for Ball State's jumping to a 10–0 lead in the second quarter.

Akron quarterback Eric Schoch, who undid much of his good work (92 yards running and 112 passing) with four turnovers, fumbled on the final play of the first quarter, with Ball State recovering on the Zip 34.

Moments later Cardinal field general Rick Scott, playing in his first series of the game, called flanker Kyle West's number on the reverse, and the speedster motored 15 yards to the Akron 15, and might have scored had not one of his own blockers knocked him down.

Scott followed with a run to the seven, and a penalty on the Zips gave Ball State a first and goal inside the four.

But the Akron defense rose to the occasion and allowed nothing on three straight plays, the Cardinals being forced to settle for a 21-yard field goal by Paul Mills.

Midway through the quarter, Zip halfback Barry Eisom lost a fumble on his own 29, and this time the Cardinals hit paydirt easily, as it took only four plays to capitalize, with fullback Tony Schmid getting the points from seven yards out, giving Ball State its 10–0 lead with 5:00 left in the half.

Schmid ended up as the Cardinal's leading ground gainer, totaling 63 yards in 17 carries. As a team, Ball State managed just 173 yards in 58 carries. In last year's 21–21 tie with Akron, Schmid had 191 of 346 Cardinal yards gained on the ground.

Akron's offense responded with determination, striking for 64 yards in eight plays. Key gains were Schoch's 16-yard run after being pressured, Eisom's 20-yard jaunt on a well-executed draw, and a third down aerial of 12 yards from Schoch to Bob Clayton to the Cardinal 14.

Schcoh came through again on third down from the six, running the option play into the end zone. Brian Ellis' extra point brought Akron within three at 10–7, and the half ended 2:42 later.

Wolf made a big defensive play moments after Ball State took the second-half kickoff. Scott had just found Cardinal end Kevin Canfield with a 40-yard bomb to the Akron 20, but Wolf crashed through the line on the ensuing third down to sack Scott for a 15-yard loss, forcing a Cardinal punt.

Akron could not move, and Scott, who completed 7 of 12 passes for 146 yards, hit West, all alone, at the Akron 25 on the first play. West continued to the Zip nine before being hauled down after the 47 yard advance.

On fourth down from the two, Jeff Harrison bulled off right tackle for the score. Mills' conversion attempt sailed outside the cross bars, and Ball State led 16–7 with 7:49 remaining in the third period.

Ball State almost locked up the game early in the fourth quarter when defensive back Claude Riley pilfered a Schoch pass and jetted 54 yards to the Akron six, before he made too many moves and lost control of the ball, with Zip guard George Anderson recovering on the six.

Akron was forced to punt, and again Ball State couldn't quite drive the final nail in the Zip coffin, as Card back Jeff Merry fumbled on the Akron ten, with Dave Laubacher falling on the loose pigskin.

The Zip offense, suddenly aroused by the nine-point deficit with time slowly but surely eroding, quickly moved the 90 yards for the score. The blitz was spearheaded by six Schoch completions, mostly to Clayton, with the fine wide receiver teaming with Schoch for the touchdown from 11 yards out. This last pass was especially well-thrown, finding its target which was literally sandwiched between several Cardinal defenders. Unfortunately though, it also marked Akron's last hurrah for the night.

October 21, 1975

Evan Scores with 18 Seconds Left

'Hollywood Writes Zips Script'

By Rich Martorano

To say that the Zips gave the meager but enthusiastic Homecoming crowd their money's worth is quite an understatement. Certainly, Hollywood must have written the script because a more spectacular finish would be hard to come by. Amidst the utter bedlam that rocked the Rubber Bowl last Saturday night, a dramatic last-second, 24–23 victory over favored Temple was just beginning to be savored.

Such a celebration seemed most unlikely as the playing time dwindled down to a precious few ticks of the clock. Pinned by the Zips at their own six yard line, Temple quarterback Pat Carey put the ball up for grabs and his tight end Jeff Stempel gathered in the lob for a first down at the Temple 44. Trailing 17–16 with approximately a minute to play and desperate for a score, Carey caught the Zip defense sleeping and dumped a short pass to pudgy running back Kevin Grady coming out of the backfield. Grady was gone and so was the Zips' lead.

Dead silence cast its shadow over the Rubber Bowl as Temple's superb placekicker Don Bitterlich booted the extra point that gave the Owls a 23–17 edge with only 53 seconds left in the game.

Bitterlich squibbed the ball on the kickoff and the Zips got possession at their own 22. Summoning that last amount of grit and pride that distinguished winner from loser, Akron prepared to mount one last drive.

Field Marshal Tom Kot quickly hit wide receiver Glen Evans on a square-out to the 38, good for a first down. On the next play, Kot hit Evans running down the sideline and he moved to the Temple 24 before being dragged down.

Thirty-two seconds now remained. Two incompletions followed and the Zips faced a third and ten predicament. Fading back to pass, Kot threw for Evans who grabbed the toss near the ten.

The svelte receiver then slithered his way into the end zone with :18 showing on the clock, knotting the score at 23–23. Jim Embick then came through by splitting the uprights and Akron was ahead once again 24–23.

A masterful last ditch effort it was, racing 78 yards in five plays and using only :34. Temple did nothing following the kickoff, and the delirious Zip gridders poured onto the field jumping for joy.

Judging from the game's opening moments, a Temple rout was in the offing. Receiving Embick's opening kickoff and starting at their own 16, the Owls opened the game with an option play to the left side of the Zip defense. Quarterback Carey pitched the ball to Kevin Grady and it seemed as though it would take him forever to turn the corner. Once he did, there wasn't anyone wearing blue and gold in sight. Eighty-four yards later, Akron was down 6–0 with only 19 seconds elapsed in the game. Bitterlich's conversion made it 7–0.

Louie King returned the kickoff to the 22. On third down, a Billy Mills' fumble was recovered by Temple's Joe Geise at Akron's 3. However, the tough Akron defense held. Bitterlich came in and kicked a 39 yard field goal, increasing Temple's lead to 10–0 with 10:07 remaining in the first period. The teams traded punts for the remainder of the quarter.

As the second period began, Akron gathered in a punt at their own 44. They moved to a first down at the Owl 44. From that point, the Zips converted on three consecutive third down situations and found themselves at Temple's 10. They stalled unfortunately, and Jim Embick put the Zips on the board with a 22 yard field goal. The Zips went the distance in 15 plays and trailed 10–3 with 6:40 remaining in the half.

Temple answered that score with one of their own at the end of the quarter. After an Akron punt, the Owls began at their 20. On second down, running back Bob Harris ripped off a big gain to the Zip 41, an effort that put the Owls in possible field goal range of Don Bitterlich's magic legs. Probable was more appropriate because on fourth down, the left-footed Temple star launched a 56-yard rainbow through the goal posts, breaking a Rubber Bowl record.

Bitterlich's three-pointer gave Temple a 13–3 lead with 1:06 playing time left in the half, and that's the way the score stood at intermission.

The Zips took the second half kickoff and marched to a touchdown. Starting on their own 19, Tom Kot directed the drive goalward. Once again, the Zips kept their

A 1974 Zip tackled by the competition. Photo by Bob Wilkey, from Tel-Buch, *courtesy of Archival Services, University Libraries, The University of Akron.*

drive going by converting on key third downs. On second and goal from the four, Kot hit Tom Enright with a short pass for Akron's first touchdown of the evening. Embick's PAT capped the 15-play, 81-yard march which also chewed up 7:15 on the clock. The gap was now closed to 13–10 with 7:45 remaining in the third period.

Temple countered approximately five minutes later. Following a short Akron punt, the Owls took over at the Zip 41. They advanced to the 22, but could manage no further progress. Bitterlich entered and booted what must have seemed like a chip shot. His second 39-yarder widened Temple's lead to 16–10 with 2:34 remaining in the third period.

Yet the Zips came right back. King returned the kickoff to the 28, and Tom Kot went to work again. One must be careful to note that it was largely the play of the Akron offensive line that enabled them to fight back continually. Undaunted by the accolades accorded Temple's big defensive, the Zip interior consistently beat their opponents off the mark and clearly won the battle of the trenches. Temple's possible All-American candidate Joe Klecko spent a good deal of the evening on his back.

Moving methodically downfield, inspired by the running of Billy Mills, the Zips closed in on the goal line.

Mills enjoyed quite an evening. He rushed for 151 yards in 44, yes, 44 attempts, and in the process stamped his name into the Akron U record book. The 44 carries eclipsed the old mark of 42.

On second and seven from the nine, Mills took the ball on a counter and slipped into the end zone. The crowd erupted. Mills' scamper tied the score at 16-all.

Embick's conversion iced the 12-play, 72-yard drive and Akron led for the first time with 11:37 remaining. Neither team moved well until the final fireworks.

Akron's sensational victory should provide the team with sufficient momentum for the remaining games on the schedule. First, however, they must topple Youngstown State this Saturday night at 7:30 P.M. at the Rubber Bowl, a team that whipped the Zips last year 30–0.

October 5, 1976

Akron Blitzes Indiana St. 34–7

For the University of Akron it was not just another ordinary victory, but an impressive showing against probably the second toughest opponent on the 1976 schedule.

The 34–7 score also looked pretty good considering it was in front of 8,318 fans at Memorial Stadium in Terre Haute, Ind.

The key factor in the outcome of the game was the fact that Akron capitalized on six of Indiana State's seven turnovers.

Akron jumped out to a 13–0 lead by scoring on three Sycamore fumbles. ISU running back Tom Johnson fumbled on the second play of the game and Cheo Akili recovered the ball for the Zips on the Sycamore 41 yard line. Akron moved down to the 15 where the ISU defense held and the Zips had to settle for a 32 yard field goal by Jim Embick.

Akron got the ball back late in the first period on a punt by the Sycamores. The Zips drove from their 35 to the ISU one-yard line. The defense which had stopped Akron on their previous drive rose to the occasion once again and with third and goal the Zips were stopped on two successive rushing attempts.

Just like an instant replay on television, ISU's running back Johnson on the second play from scrimmage fumbled for the second time with Akili once again recovering the ball on the one.

On the second play, quarterback Marty Bezbatchenko went in from the one and with Embick's conversion the Zips led 10–0.

Sycamore quarterback Dave Pearre fumbled on the Akron 43 as he was running around right end and linebacker Fred Miller recovered the ball for the Zips.

Akron moved the ball to the 14 but then two straight plays for minus yardage pushed the Zips back to the 24 where Embick came in and connected on a 41 yard field goal to give Akron a 13–0.

Both teams scored in the third quarter. Akron's came first on a 12 yard pass from Bezbatchenko to split end Glen Evans. The drive took the opening kickoff and took it 62 yards in 15 plays before the touchdown pass. Embick's kick made the score 20–0.

In the fourth quarter, Akron threatened by driving to the ISU 23-yard line, but after the drive was halted Embick came in to boot a 41 yard field goal that was wide to the left.

Indiana went to the air on the first play after the missed field goal and middle guard Jim Meyer intercepted the Sotak pass and returned it for a touchdown. Embick's kick was good and with 7:28 left in the game Akron led 27–7.

Both teams traded punts and then on ISU's next possession, Pearre fumbled with the recovery made by Dobrezeniecki for the Zips on the Akron 39.

It took Akron 10 plays to move the 61 yards with running back Dave Axner going in from the seven. Embick's kick was good and Akron closed out the scoring for the game leading 34–7.

October 11, 1977

Defeat Dayton 31–24

Zip Football Team Finds 'Big Play' in Winters

By Mike Elliot

The University of Akron football team has been looking for "the big play" all season, and finally found a number of them Saturday night against Dayton. The game played before 9,100 wet fans at Dayton's Welcome Stadium ended in a 31–24 Akron victory.

The Flyers got on the scoreboard first as senior quarterback B.J. Dailey hit junior tight end Charles White with a 46-yard pass to put the ball on the Akron 15. Four plays later, Dailey scored from the one and with the extra point the Flyers led 7–0 with 5:57 left in the first period.

The Zips couldn't get anything to go right offensively until sophomore halfback Paul Winters supplied the first big play. Winters broke through the line and sprinted 70 yards for a touchdown. This run was the longest run from scrimmage by the Zips this year.

Winters ran for 121 yards and two touchdowns. Winters' burst came at 0:28 left in the first period and at the end of one quarter the Zips and the Flyers were deadlocked 7–7.

Akron's second big play came in the second quarter after the Flyers had driven from their own 38 to the Zip 43. On fourth and inches the Flyers gambled for the first down. Flyer fullback Brian Dorenkott got the call but the Zip defensive line got him at the line of scrimmage for no gain and the Akron offense took over. On the next play, quarterback Rick Beeman took advantage of a brisk wind at his back as he hit senior split end Ron Fuller with a 48-yard bomb. Fuller made a spectacular catch on the Flyer nine to give the Zips a first and goal, for the third big play, Winters carried the ball over from the eight on the next play for his second touchdown. With 12:11 left in the half, the Zips led 14–7.

The lead didn't last for long as the Flyers drove to the Akron 17. An offsides penalty gave Dayton a first and five on the Zips 12. Dayton ran the ball down to the eight for a first and goal but the Zip defense nailed quarterback Scott Terry for two consecutive losses and all of a sudden the Flyers were faced with a third and goal back on the 10. Terry's pass fell incomplete on third down and it looked as though the Zips were out of trouble. Akron was called for pass interference and Dayton was back in with a first and goal on the three. Dorenkott then ran it in and with the extra point the game was tied again at 14–14 with 3:15 left in the first half.

Senior John Dobrzeniecki returned the ensuing kickoff back to the Akron 39 for good field position. Akron then drove to the Flyer 24 where Jim Embick put the Zips ahead with a 41-yard field goal at 0:25 left in the half. The first half ended with Akron holding a 17–14 lead.

The second half was played in a steady rain. The Flyers tied the game with a 32-yard field goal by German-born placekicker Harmut Stecker with 3:44 left in

The 1978 team. Photo from Tel-Buch, *courtesy of Archival Services, University Libraries, The University of Akron.*

the third quarter. The teams exchanged punts and the Zips were faced with a third and four on their own 22. Beeman pitched out but the ball was fumbled and Dayton recovered on the Zip 12. The third period ended with the score tied at 17–17 but the Flyers were threatening.

On the first play of the final period, Dayton quarterback Scott Terry ran 16 yards for a touchdown and the Flyers led again 24–17. A short Flyer punt gave the Zips the ball on Dayton's 37-yard line where the Zips drove down to the 22. From there, Beeman and Fuller teamed up again for yet another big play. Beeman hit the split end with a 22-yard touchdown pass to tie the score for the fourth time, 24–24, with 10:21 left to play in the game.

On the next series of downs, junior linebacker Keith Luck intercepted a Dailey pass and the Zips had the ball on Dayton's 31. The Zips drove to the Flyer 22 and it was time for the final "big play." On fourth and one on the 22, Akron brought out the field goal team to attempt a 39-yarder. Ron Fuller, who holds for Embick on field goal tries, took the snap from center and attempted a pass. The pass was incomplete but Dayton was called for pass interference and the Zips had a first and goal from the three. Halfback John Montgomery ran it in from the one for the winning touchdown giving the Zips a dramatic 31–24 victory. The win was the fourth of the season for the Zips who are now 4–1–1.

October 18, 1977

University Football Team Stumbles, Waddles Against Youngstown's Penguins

By Mike Elliot

The Youngstown State Penguins proved that steel is stronger than rubber Saturday night as they defeated the Zips 28–10. The game was played before 8,874 at the Rubber Bowl.

The Penguins took the "Steel-Tire Trophy" back to Youngstown by winning what was billed as the NCAA Division II championship of Ohio. The Zips were outplayed by a fired-up Youngstown team that dominated every aspect of the game.

After receiving the opening kickoff, the Zips could manage only one first down and were forced to punt from their own 37 yard line. Andy Graham then suffered his first blocked punt of the season. Penguin linebacker John DiDomenico blocked the punt and Maurice Reynolds picked up the loose ball and ran untouched for an 11 yard touchdown.

That was the first time this season the Penguins scored in the first period.

Akron started to come back as they drove the ensuing kickoff to the Akron 49 where halfback Paul Winters ran 42 yards to give the Zips a first and goal on the Youngstown nine yard line. The Youngstown defense then closed the door and the Zips had to settle for a 20 yard field goal by Jim Embick with 8:34 left in the first quarter and the Zips trailed by only four points 7–3. After the teams exchanged punts, Youngstown quarterback Keith Snoddy drove the Penguins to the Zip 33 but a 50 yard field goal attempt fell short and the first period ended.

The Zips opened the second period with no offense and after a short punt, Youngstown had good field position on their own 48. After a four yard run put the ball in Akron territory, Snoddy drilled the ball to wide receiver Jim Ferranti who made the catch between two Zip defenders and raced 48 yards for the Penguins' second touchdown. With the extra point, the Penguins led 14–3 with 13:35 left in the half.

Youngstown's defense shut off the inside run and Akron seemed reluctant to try anything else. The Zips had problems getting yardage on first downs and were frequently faced with third and long situations and couldn't get the big play.

Youngstown defensive back Fred George picked off a Rick Beeman pass and returned it 36 yards to the Akron 23 yard line. After the Penguins drove to the Zip 13, Snoddy threw his second touchdown pass, this time hitting tailback Marschell Brumfield with a strike in the corner of the end zone with 10 seconds left in the half. The extra point was good and Youngstown led 21–3 at the half.

The third period was a defensive struggle with neither team getting on the scoreboard. The Youngstown defense that was good in the first half was better in the second half as the Zips could muster only one first down in the third period. Youngstown threatened as the Penguins drove to the Zip 19 but a 36 yard field goal fell short.

Marty Bezbatchenko, who had taken over as quarterback late in the third quarter, mastered a drive that gave the Zips their first and only touchdown of the night.

Akron got the ball after linebacker Steve Cockerham recovered a fumble with 11:00 left in the game.

The Zips then drove 45 yards in 12 plays with Bezbatchenko scoring from the six on a keeper and the Zips trailed 21–10. Youngstown came right back on their next series as Snoddy ran for 26 yards in three plays and Brumfield added 5 more before the tailback scored his second touchdown of the game from the Zip 20 with 3:31 left in the game to make the final score Youngstown 28, Akron 10.

Snoddy was the game's leading rusher with 93 yards to go along with his six pass completions for 118 yards and two touchdowns. Brumfield was held to 30 yards in 7 carries but also scored two touchdowns. Paul Winters led the Zips with 60 yards in 18 attempts.

The loss put the Zips record at 4–2–1 and has hampered their playoff chances. Youngstown State is now 4–2 and hosts Dayton next week while the Zips travel to Central Michigan.

November 21, 1978

Score Five TD's in 39–28 Win

Cameron Sets Record, Steals 'Senior Night' Show

By Steve King

It was "Senior Night" at the Rubber Bowl Saturday, but freshman tailback Terry Cameron stole the show in Akron's season-ending 39–28 victory over Northern Iowa before 5,522 fans.

Cameron, a 6'1, 173-pounder, set a new school record by scoring five touchdowns in helping the Zips to break a two-game losing streak and avert a losing season. UA finished 6–5 overall and 4–1 in the Mid-Continent Conference, and the latter mark assured them of second place. The win was Akron's 100th at the Rubber Bowl. Northern Iowa ended in the league cellar with 2–9 and 0–5 ledgers respectively.

Ironically, Cameron's tallies, all of them coming on the ground, were earned almost by default. Paul Winters, the Zip's leading rusher this season, did not carry the ball and participated in only about ten plays against the Panthers after severely bruising his right ankle last week against Eastern Kentucky. Redell Windley, the second-leading ground gainer, did not even suit up after suffering two separated shoulders in the same contest.

"Without Paul and Redell in there," Cameron said afterwards, "someone had to step in and do the job. But give credit to my offensive line, because they were opening up some big holes." On the night, Cameron gained 121 yards in 33 tries.

Still smiling in the Akron locker room, head coach Jim Dennison, who got his 40th career victory at UA, wasn't ready to close the book on '78 just yet. "We've got a young team," he related. "I'm not sure I want to stop playing now. There are great things in the future for this club."

Dennison agreed when it was mentioned that there was a lot of difference between records of 6–5 and 5–6.

"I told the whole squad before the game that this was the most important game they would ever play in and that includes the national championship game some of them participated in two years ago."

"They practiced as winners all week," said Dennison. "We were not going to be beaten."

"Even though we were only 6–5 this year, our seniors led us well," he continued in reference to eight players who were playing their last game for Akron (quarterback Marty Bezbatchenko and Windley are not included in the list, because both were hurt). "If our disappointment is going to be a six-win season, we'll take it."

The Panthers made it 7–0 on Kelly Ellis' 97-yard touchdown dash with 10:40 left in the opening period—the longest scoring run ever against the Zips.

However, the lead was set-up quite unusually. Akron's Rick Holman blocked a punt by Mark Witver and recovered it at the Northern six. UA couldn't score in four rushes, though, including a fourth down attempt from only a yard away, and the Panthers gained possession.

The Zips tied it at 7–7 with 1:09 remaining in the quarter when Cameron capped a 14-yard play, 73-yard drive by going in from a yard out.

Akron then took a 14–7 lead the next time they had the ball. Cameron got his second tally on a two-yard run, culminating a 43 yard, 10 play march with 9:38 left in the half.

Northern, which rolled up 486 yards total offense against the Zips, knotted the score when quarterback Terry Allen went untouched for a 45-yard touchdown on an option keeper around right end.

It looked as if the score would remain 14–14 at the half as UA got the ball at their own 36 with just 44 seconds left in the period.

But fullback Dan Simon gained ten yards on a run, and then Akron wide receiver James White made a spectacular catch of a Bob Maxwell pass at the visitors 16. A roughing penalty against Northern took it to the eight, and with 16 seconds remaining, Maxwell hit tight end Doug Blanchard for a touchdown on the next play. Andy Graham missed the extra point attempt, and Akron led 20–14.

The Zips weren't through yet, however, thanks to some shoddy play by Northern on the ensuing kickoff. Ellis and up-man Norm Montgomery looked like two infielders on the 1962 New York Mets trying to field a ground ball, because Dave Pruner's line drive kick rolled untouched through both players' legs. The Zips Mark Fedorisin recovered the ball on the Northern three, and Cameron got his third touchdown three plays later on a one-yard plunge over left guard, with one second left.

Blanchard was called for offensive pass interference on the two-point pass attempt, and the lead remained 26–14.

Akron got another tally early in the third period when cornerback Rick Holman intercepted an Allen pass and returned it 36 yards for the touchdown with 8:52 left.

Akron and Kent State face off in 1979. Photo from Tel-Buch, *courtesy of Archival Services, University Libraries, The University of Akron.*

It was Cameron's most spectacular run of the night as he broke a tackle at the 28 and galloped down the right sidelines past the remaining Panther defenders. Graham's extra point was no good again, so the margin stayed 32–14.

Whitver had another punt blocked after the visitors' next series. Akron's Mike Valencheck smacked the ball straight up into the air, and teammate Mike Williams caught it in full stride and ran it back to the Northern four.

UA scored on their first play as you know who went over the left tackle with 6:34 still left in the third quarter.

Northern made it reasonably close, though, with two touchdowns in the final period. The first came with 12:13 left as Ellis caught an Allen pass in the right flat and raced 70 yards for the score. Dana Deines got two more points on the conversion run, and the Zips lead was narrowed to 39–22.

Rick Ellingson then picked-off a Maxwell pass and brought it back 27 yards to the UA 38. Three runs and a personal foul penalty against the Zips moved it to the eight, where Allen found tight end Jeff Hamilton alone in the end zone. Allen couldn't connect on the extra-point pass, though, and the score of 39–28 was the final.

EXTRA POINT

Chris Angeloff. Courtesy of The University of Akron Department of Intercollegiate Athletics.

THE CHRIS ANGELOFF SCHOLARSHIP

The Chris Angeloff Scholarship was established in memory of Chris Angeloff, a junior starting tight end, who collapsed and died of cardiac arrest during UA's 20-8 victory over Marshall in the Acme-Zip game on Sept. 6, 1975.

His teammates voted to retire his jersey, the first such tribute paid to a UA football player.

Angeloff, 20, was leaving the field on a possession exchange midway in the second period, got to the sidelines and collapsed. As many as seven doctors tried to revive him.

A native of Erie, Pa., Angeloff had become a starter as a sophomore. An accounting major, he carried a 3.20 GPA. He was the son of Carl and Mary Angeloff.

At the request of the family, income from the endowed fund is applied to athletic scholarships. Funds are derived from memorials contributed to Angeloff.

AKRON HAS NCAA FIRST IN '76 BOWL

The first overtime game in the history of the NCAA playoffs occurred at Akron's Rubber Bowl on Dec. 4, 1976 when the Zips met Northern Michigan in the second round of the Division II playoffs—a game called the Knute Rockne Bowl.

Northern Michigan scored first in overtime—a 39-yard field goal, but Akron answered with a touchdown—a one-yarder by quarterback Marty Bezbatchenko—to win 29-26.

While Akron won the first two rounds of the NCAA Division II playoffs at home in the Rubber Bowl, one week after the history-making Knute Rockne Bowl, the Zips traveled to Wichita Falls, Texas to play in the Pioneer Bowl, where they lost to Montana State, 24-13, on Dec. 11.

Courtesy of The University of Akron Department of Intercollegiate Athletics

Take the Bierce Library tour — Whitehouse style

See Page 3

Zips blank Salem in home opener

See Page 5

Daryl Hall's solo debut goes hog wild without Oates

See Page 7

The University of Akron

THE BUCHTELITE

uesday, September 9, 1986 | Established 1889 | Vol. 98, No. 1

uspects ndicted n rape- nurders

KRON, Ohio (AP) — A Summit ounty grand jury yesterday urned criminal indictments ainst three Akron teen-agers in e slayings of Wendy J. Offredo d Dawn McCreery, two female iversity of Akron students, who re slain after they were beaten d raped in the early morning urs of Sept. 2.

A fourth teen appeared in Sum- t County Juvenile Court yester- y on charges filed against him by lice in the slayings.

Summit County Prosecutor m Slaby said the grand jury urned a 12-count indictment ainst Richard W. Cooey II, 19. was charged with four counts aggravated murder with death nalty specifications, two counts kidnapping, four counts of e, two counts of aggravated bery and one count of onious assault.

Under Ohio law a person can be licted for aggravated murder h death penalty specifications two ways. One, the murder must e place during the commission an aggravated felony. The addi- nal charges against Cooey of lnapping and rape are classified aggravated felonies. Second, a rson convicted of murdering two more individuals with "prior lculation and design" can receive e death penalty.

COOEY HAS BEEN charged a grand jury with four counts murder, because according to aby, "the facts would fit either " of the two possible conditions r which one could receive the ath penalty in Ohio. Cooey can indicted on both sets of cir- nstances; he cannot be con- cted of both.

"An election (will be held) as to hich set indictments will be us- d," said Slaby.

Slaby said all four aggravated urder charges carry a possible eath penalty.

The grand jury also charged enny Horonetz, 18, with one unt of felonious assault and one unt of obstruction of justice and erry Grant, 19, was charged with struction of justice.

The felonious assault charges em from an incident during hich the teens allegedly threw a ncrete block from a freeway erpass onto Offredo's car, Slaby id. Three teens then approached d offered assistance. The women ent with them, police said. Two

See 'Suspect,' page 6

Zip-a-dee-do-da!

Zip fans Steve Collins, Mark North and Kirk Olsen showed their Zip pride when The University of Akron Zips met the "not that bad" Salem Tigers in "the closest 35-0 game ever played."

Alarming disparity in health services

by Robin O'Brien
Asst. News Editor

Nearly twenty people provided testimony on the sharp disparities which exist in both health and use of health services between minority and non-minority Ohioans at a public hearing last Saturday in Olin Hall.

The hearing was sponsored by UA's Outreach Office of Human Services, the Akron Black Nurses Association and Universal Nursing Services Inc.

"Health care should be available to all, regardless of their ability to pay. By the year 2000 the needs of the elderly will triple. What are we doing for those needs," R.N. Gladys Hall, said.

Currently, the infant mortality rate for black and minority Ohioans remains nearly twice that of white Ohioans.

THERE IS ALSO a higher incidence rate of alcohol-related illness, heart disease and diabetes for blacks compared to whites.

Black and minority deaths resulting from cancer are increasing four times the rate of white Ohioans.

Also, homicide is the leading cause of death for 15-to 44-yea old black and minority males.

Ann Cormany, of the Goo Samaritan Hunger Center at 42 S. Hawkins Ave., said the pro gram initally assisted women wit children. However, now the pro gram is curving towards sing men in the 25-to 40-year-old ag bracket.

"At least 98 percent are blac men who seek food," Corman said.

"THIS TIME LAST year I wa making $35,000. . . .The factor jobs are gone. There is no plac for us to turn. I can no longer into a high tech societ Everything is not all right. M family is hungry and my shoes a worn," Howard Rooker, a Rosly Avenue resident, said.

He now makes $4 an hour support his family of four.

"If you really want to have seminar you (the Task Force) ha to talk to people in the streets . .I am tired of listening to wh people say they are going to do Rooker said.

Glen Proctor, a business wri for the *Akron Beacon Journ* urged that the media become m sensitive to minority issues.

Also, Akron Deputy May Dorothy Jackson said senior

See 'Disparities,' page

Capital projects taking shape

by Mark Humphrey
Buchtelite Contributor

The cost of attending school rises every year. This is an accepted and expected fact. Where the additional money goes is not always as evident. Capital improvement projects, however, are a visible sign of our tuition at work.

The Department of Physical Facilities is responsible for all capital improvements on the University of Akron campus.

Randy Richardson, the University architect, is a member of this department. Richardson, along with Donald L. Bowles, the Vice-President of Administrative Services, provided a summary of projects the University is currently completing and those which will be started in the near future.

The University is currently working on several projects. The most notable one is the Oliver Ocasek Natatorium. The natatorium, located next to Spicer Hall, is scheduled to be completed in September of 1987. Presently the project is 30 percent complete. The construction of the buildings outer shell is making visible progress daily. However, a considerable amount of the natatorium will be built underground during and after the outer shell is completed.

THE NATATORIUM will house a 50 meter pool, a weight room and nine handball/racquetball courts. The new facilities will be available for general student use.

Another important project is the Memorial Hall renovation. This project is 88 to 90 percent complete. Work was originally scheduled to be completed this October but difficulties with a separate water/heat contract has set this date back to January.

A refurbished research building next to the physical plant is also slated to be ready by January 1987.

In addition to these projects there are several smaller projects which are being completed. An electrical bank has been added to the new art building, thus putting it under University power. A second substation to be built on Carroll Street is also being considered. This additional substation would provide back-up in the event of a power failure.

There are several projects in the works which have not yet begun construction. The first of these is the law school addition. Construction on the addition is planned to begin July 1987.

> *"We have grown quickly. The University is now the 52nd largest in America."*
>
> *Donald L. Bowles*
> *Vice President of Administrative Services*

THE OTHER NEW projects are being funded with money the University has just secured from the state. The largest of these is the construction of the new polymer science buildings. This project consists of building both a nine story tower and a twelve story tower. The buildings will contain 130,000 square feet. It will be built at a total cost of $17.5 million, including $10 million from new funds recently appropriated. Construction will begin in November 1987, at the earliest.

The polymer science buildings will be located on the triangular plot of land bordered by Center Street and Buchtel Avenue. These buildings, along with the law school addition, will eliminate parking areas already in existence.

"We recognize the need for additional parking," said Bowles. The University has already begun searching for additional areas, according to Bowles. A nearby church is allowing the University to use 350 additional parking spaces for the next three years.

Another large project is the estimated $8.825 million college administration building which is slated to be built on the site of the old Greyhound terminal. The building will contain 84,000 square feet and will eventually be connected with the Buckingham Center.

The Greyhound project could also provide a source of additional parking for the University.

"IT MAY ALSO connect to the Polsky parking deck," said Bowles. Plans for connecting the new building to the parking deck are still tentative.

An addition to the Auburn Science Center is also being planned. Most of the informati on the project is tentative and a chitects are still being selected f the addition. The addition w cost approximately $2 million. T addition will be built in an op court between the towers addi about 14,700 square feet of spa to the science center.

The University also receiv $2.5 million in utility renovati funds. This money has been fu neled into several projects. The projects include repairs to wa utility lines. Smaller projects i clude the acquisition of the Bel warehouse at Lincoln and M Streets. It would then be used f storage. The Fir Hill Center w also be renovated for gradua study and research.

Some of the state funds ha been channeled to the Way County branch of the Univers of Akron. These funds are goi toward building the John E. Bo Health and Education additio The $1.5 million in funds will p vide the branch with gymnasium.

"We have grown quickly," s Bowles. "The University is n the 52nd largest in America." U is the third largest university in state of Ohio.

CHAPTER 10
1980–1989

An early 1980s team loses the ball. Courtesy of The University of Akron Department of Intercollegiate Athletics.

November 8, 1983

Youngstown Gets 'Black'ened by Gridders

By Beckie Kern

To say it was a night of surprises would be an understatement. And, while a game between two intense rivals like Akron and Youngstown State is bound to produce some excitement and surprises, for the 9,146 fans it was more than they probably ever thought would happen.

In their last game of the 1983 season at Akron's Rubber Bowl, the Zips razzled and dazzled the visiting penguins from play one and never looked back, winning 49–21.

Well, maybe the Zips did do some looking back at the first quarter since they had 44 minutes in the locker room to reflect on it. That 44 minute delay was caused when a car hit a utility pole and knocked out power in Ellet, Kenmore, and much of South Akron—including the Rubber Bowl.

But the blackout wasn't the only surprise or cause of excitement. A tremendous ground performance by tailback James Black and an exciting passing game from freshmen quarterbacks Steve Stams and Vernon Stewart kept the fans so interested that the cold and delay weren't enough to make them leave.

Black carried the ball 40 times for an Akron single game rushing record of 246 yards. He also recorded his longest run from scrimmage in his college career with a 57-yard scamper.

But now to the passing. After Akron's defense stopped Youngstown on its first series, the Zips offense went to work. With Steve Stams at quarterback, backup quarterback and wide receiver Vernon Stewart lined up at the tailback position. Stams pitched the ball to the right for Stewart who let go with a 65-yard touchdown pass to senior wide receiver Rick Bailey. Dennis Heckman added the point after at the 12:04 mark.

"We had planned that play on the Sunday before, after watching Youngstown's films," said Zip Head Coach Jim Dennison. "A lot of things had to click, though, since it was a 'go-for-broke' play, and they did."

But it didn't take long for the Penguins to startle the Zips with a Ken Kuhn to John Goode pass for 80-yards and a touchdown. Paul McFadden's point after attempt was good at the 11:53 mark.

After linebacker Tim Fowler recovered a fumble by Goode on a punt return, the Zip offense capitalized on the mistake. From Youngstown's 36 yard line, Stams connected with Bailey for Akron's second touchdown of the night. Heckman added the extra point with 6:46 left to play in the first quarter.

After four plays by Youngstown, Penguin tailback Robert Thompson dropped the ball in the backfield, where UA defensive linemen Dan Kreighbaum fell on it at YSU's 34.

The Zips ran off three plays before Stams connected on his third touchdown pass of the evening—a tight end delay to freshman Ron Taylor.

On Akron's next possession, things went black—literally. Black ran two plays before the entire Rubber Bowl went black because of the power failure. It took 44 more minutes before Akron could run its second and 11 play.

Three plays later, Heckman kicked a 47-yard field goal with 53 seconds left in the first quarter.

Youngstown came right back with another touchdown, this time on a sweep with John Murphy carrying the ball eight yards for the points. McFadden added the extra point to make it 24–14 at the 12:20 mark of the second quarter.

"Going into the game we had expected to score at least 24 points," noted Dennison. "What we didn't want to do was to trade touchdowns back and forth. But the defense really shut them down in the second half." Going into this game, Youngstown had been averaging more than 28 points a game.

Heckman boosted the Zips' score to 27–14 on a 20 yard field goal at the 10:33 mark. That field goal also tied Heckman with former UA kicker Andy Graham for most field goals in a season.

On the Zips' next possession, Black gained 50 yards on three carries before Stams kept on the option for UA's first touchdown of the evening on the ground. Heckman added the extra point to make it 34–14.

The Penguins, however, came right back with a touchdown of their own. Kuhn hit Goode on a 41 yard scoring strike to bring the score to 34–21.

But Akron also had more points on its agenda. Driving 80 yards (with Black gaining 57 on a sweep left), Stewart, who replaced the injured Stams, handed off to Black for the four yard score up the middle. Stewart then hit wide receiver Tom Park in the end zone for the two-point conversion to make it 42–21.

The Zip defense tightened its belt in the second half and also did the only scoring in the half.

Defensive back Robert Johnson picked off Kuhn's pass at YSU's 48-yard line and returned it the length of the field for the six points. Heckman's point after attempt was good, making the final score 49–21.

Zip notes: Bailey, in his last game at the Rubber Bowl, finished the night with three receptions for 111 yards and two touchdowns. Jim Reynolds, also in his last home game, had one reception for 65 yards. Linebackers Tim Fowler and Jeff Lake led all Zip tacklers with 19 and 17 total tackles, respectively. Lake had one pass break-up, while Fowler recovered a fumble. Senior tri-captain Dave Arango had 10 total tackles and four tackles-for-loss for minus 19 yards.

November 22, 1983

A Record Breaking Day for Zip Gridders

By Beckie Kern

Clarkesville, Tenn.—When the Zips walked on to the field at Municipal Stadium here Saturday, what they had their minds focused on was to finish the regular season with eight wins. What they got was their eighth win (to become only the fifth Zip team in 83 years to win that many in a season) and a re-writing of several Akron and Ohio Valley Conference records.

Akron, which finished 8–3 on the season with its 26–3 victory over Austin Peay, was led by James Black in the record setting with kicking specialist Dennis Heckman also adding his name in several categories.

From the first play, Black was ready, taking a pitch from quarterback Steve Stams and scampering for 13 yards. When the game was over, Black had carried the ball 52 times for 295 yards and one touchdown. The effort topped the 256 yards he gained against Youngstown State two weeks prior for the most yards rushing in a single game.

"You never actually feel a guy can gain that many against any team," said Head Coach Jim Dennison. "When he got close (to the record), we wanted him to get it so we kept running him. Actually, we ran him about eight more times than we had planned to."

For Heckman, the records were tallied in the field goal category and in place kicking points. Heckman hit four of four field goals on the day and added two extra points to give him 35 career field goals and 160 career place kicking points. Heckman also finished the year with the most field goals in a season for the OVC with 17 and the most points place-kicking in a season for Akron with 72.

"Our goal for the whole team was to get eight points out of the kicking game." said Dennison. "Even though the team didn't know it, those were all the points Dennis needed to break the record."

After the Governors won the toss, they elected to start on defense and kick with the wind at their backs. But the move didn't affect the Zips, and especially Heckman, who was the first to score points for the Zips when he connected on a 37-yard field goal into the wind in the first quarter.

Then, after six plays at the end of the first quarter, Akron was ready to score again. On the first play of the second quarter, Stams connected on a pass to senior wide receiver Rick Bailey. Bailey made the catch for the 54-yard score after the ball hit off his hands twice between two APSU defenders.

On the Governors' next possession, Akron's defense went to work. Linebacker Tim Fowler recovered a Willie Johnson fumble at APSU's 49-yard line. The Zips turned the mistake into another Heckman field goal, this time from 27-yards out, to make the score 13–0.

Two series later Heckman connected on his third field goal of the day. The 49-yarder at 3:31 gave Akron a 16–0 lead.

The 1983 team. First row: D. O'Conner, M. Supplee, G. Housos, D. Morgan, D. Arango, J. Black, T. Park, J. Reynolds, R. Bailey. Second row: S. Peterson, D. Heckman, T. Fowler, T. Spikes, J. Anderson, G. Spencer, D. Sutter, B. Clark. Third row: L. Small, R. Vargo, B. Pasquale, F. Simon, R. Pasquale, E. Sovacool, T. Hodges, D. Dillon, R. Brant. Fourth row: K. Swartz, B. Sparks, J. Huth, N. Rock, G. Dennison, N. Lademarco, T. Romantic, M. Stephens, S. Lemons, D. Gilbert. Fifth row: T. Fowler, B. Wurts, M. Petrus, G. Reed, R. Holmes, E. Schooler, T. Lauro, B. Hagenmaier, T. Swing, S. Stams. Sixth row: V. Stewart, A. Green, G. Thomas, J. Long, K. Kline, D. Lombardo, V. Homan, T. Wallace, T. Seislove, G. Gilbert. Seventh row: A. Johnson, M. Blaser, R. Allen, B. Manning, D. Boggs, J. Lundy, T. Brown, B. Moran, M. Stricklen, G. Kalis. Eighth row: C. Kelley, W. Dotson, M. Clark, E. Andrade, S. Rafac, D. Kreighbaum, M. Paramore, M. Teifke, K. Grisdale, J. Fordyce. Ninth row: R. Taylor, H. Hopkins, W. Grant, R. Johnson, G. Stephens, C. Kelly, K. Baker, W. Davis, E. Dellemonache. Tenth row: Assistant coaches D. Fletcher, P. Winters, D. Axner, T. Flaherty, W. Rollinson, J. Durbin, D. Newell, T. Forbes, J. Ling, and Head Coach Jim Dennision. Photo from Tel-Buch, *courtesy of Archival Services, University Libraries, The University of Akron.*

"Our defense is just so team oriented, it's hard to come up with one play that stands out in my mind," said Dennison. "But the fumble recovery after we had 10 points gave us a chance to score again so that stands out."

That team play by the defense enabled the Zips to hold Governors to two first downs in the first half and 63 total offensive yards. They also held APSU's offense to only nine minutes with the ball during that time.

The only scoring of the third quarter came off the leg of Heckman, this time from 28 yards out.

Then, on its first series of the final quarter, Austin Peay scored its lone three points. The Governors had to settle for a 34 yard field goal after UA's defense held them to one yard in five plays.

But Akron still wasn't finished with its scoring. The Zips drove 63 yards for Black's three yard touchdown run, making the final score 26–3.

"Every one of our seniors had an outstanding performance, and I'm not just saying that," said Dennison. "Watching the films right now (Monday) they all had a very good game.

"Eight and three sets you apart. I've been associated with four of those five teams with eight wins or more and this team has to take a back seat to none of them."

However, the season seems to have come to an end with the 8–3 record, even though Dennison considers this team to be a very good one right now in Division I–AA.

"Our team is on a roll right now," said Dennison, "The problem is not how good we are, but rather, there are too many good teams in our district," Eastern Illinois (9–2–0), Indiana State (8–3–0), Eastern Kentucky (the OVC champion at 7–2–1) and from Akron's district." "If we were in any other district, I'd say we'd be going to the playoffs."

Records Set at APSU

Dennis Heckman, OVC—Most FG, season-17 (previous record, 14, by Murray Cunningham, TTU, 1975) ... Akron U—Most FG, career 35 (previous record, 31 by Andy Graham, 1978–80) ... Most points place kicking, season-72 (previous record, 66 by Graham, 1979) ... Most points place kicking, career-160 (previous record, 153 by Jim Embick, 1974–77).

December 3, 1985

Zips 'Aired Out' by QB—Ehrhardt in I–AA Playoff

By L.C. Johnson

Kingston, RI—The University of Akron football team was literally aired-out of the NCAA Division I–AA playoffs by the University of Rhode Island before a rambunctious crowd of 7,317 at Meade Stadium. URI quarterback Tom Ehrhardt passed for 472 yards and five touchdowns to lead the Rams to a 35–27 first-round victory.

Perhaps more than Ehrhardt's 'airing it out' was the Zips' simply 'erring it' in the early goings, as two interceptions by free safety Mike Cassidy thwarted Akron drives. After taking the opening kickoff, UA's offensive contingent proceeded to move the ball at will—driving 77 yards to the URI 4-yard line until Cassidy picked off a Vernon Stewart pass in the end zone after Stewart's intended receiver, Willie Davis, had slipped on the wet natural turf.

Just as they had started off the game, the Zips took over at the outset of the second quarter and moved the ball with an equal amount of success. However, they were unable to cash in on the scoring opportunity as Cassidy intercepted his second pass of the game in the end zone.

As it turned out, these drives would only give the Zips an advantage in time of possession—not the scoreboard, as the Rams led 14–7 at the half, despite having control of the football for 11 fewer minutes.

This proved to be more than enough time for Ehrhardt who passed 70 times, completing 43 with only two interceptions. In the first half alone, the All-American signal caller lofted 35 aerials and did not attempt a single rushing play. This still did not make him easier to defend.

"We just couldn't get to him," said Akron Head Coach Jim Dennison. "He used a three-step drop and that's tough to defend. He's a good quarterback, I have to give him credit. He didn't throw into our coverage. Quite frankly, we thought we'd get a few more interceptions against him."

Dennison had no illusions of stopping the Rams' high-powered passing attack (which ranks number one in the nation averaging 384.3 yards per game); instead, he attempted to contain it.

"We wanted to take (Brian) Forster and (Dameon) Reilly (URI's two top receivers) out of the game," said Dennison. "If they were gonna beat us, they were gonna beat us left-handed. We made him throw to the other side and he hurt us."

The *he* that Dennison was referring to was tight end Tony Dimaggio who caught 11 passes for 88 yards and four touchdowns—three of which came after intermission. Reilly and Forster didn't have too shabby a day themselves as they combined for 16 catches for 208 yards. And another receiver, Bob Donfield, caught seven passes for 99 yards and go-ahead touchdown just prior to the close of the half.

"I've never seen anything like it," said Akron linebacker Jeff Lake. "He had four or five receivers to go to every time and they were just finding the seams. And (Ehrhardt) had such a quick release we couldn't get to him."

Still, the Akron defense had no need to feel apologetic as they were actually doubling as the Akron offense. Leading 7–0, the Rams were attempting to pad the lead, but Mike Griffin's 32-yard field goal attempt was blocked by outside linebacker Greg Thomas and recovered by linebacker Bill Hadden who raced down the sidelines then lateralled the ball (just as he was being tackled) to defensive halfback Gary Tyler, who carried the ball to the end zone for the touchdown.

Dimaggio scored his second TD of the game early in the third quarter and the Rams led 21–7. The Zip defense answered back when defensive tackle Steve Rafac intercepted Ehrhardt's pass deep in URI territory and returned it 16 yards for the touchdown.

This game marked the return of tailback Mike Clark to All-OVC form as he rushed for 172 yards on 33 carries and a third quarter touchdown that tied the score at 21–21. Unfortunately, Clark was carried off the field mid-way through the third quarter as he was re-injured, and appeared to have carried the Zips' chances for victory to the sideline with him.

The Zips' comeback at this juncture made the early turnovers seem nonessential—at least as far as Dennison was concerned, as he was unwilling to concede that the miscues were the Zips' primary downfall.

"No, we came back and tied it up and had time to win it," said Dennison. "It didn't help us, but it didn't cost us the win either."

What did cost the Zips were Dimaggio's final two scores. His 8 yard TD reception in the third quarter enabled the Rams to regain the lead 28–21. But the Zips' chance for a tie came up short as Russ Klaus' extra-point attempt was blocked following Anthony Green's fourth quarter 1-yard touchdown making it 28–27.

For Klaus it marked the first time during his UA career that he had failed to convert a point-after. He had been successful on a record-setting 49 in-a-row.

A Mike Knapp shanked punt later in the quarter set the stage for Ehrhardt's game-winning scoring drive as he drove the Rams 46 yards in six plays—culminated by a 7-yard pass to Dimaggio.

"We've got nothing to hang our heads down about," said Dennison. "We've had a good season. And I'm proud of the fact that we came back against the number one scoring team in the country from a 21–7 deficit. We could have folded the tent, but we hung in there, and it says a lot for our team."

September 9, 1986

Fiery Zips Whip Salem Tigers 35–0

By Mike Popovich

The score might not have reflected it, but Saturday's 33rd Annual Acme-Zip game had its share of thrills and chills for both The University of Akron and Salem College.

Unfortunately for Salem, the thrill of victory probably went down with All-American quarterback Jimbo Fisher who left the game with a strained knee in the first quarter. The fiery Zips then used that as an incentive and promptly whipped the pesky Tigers from West Virginia 35–0 before 35,202 in the Rubber Bowl.

This game was also seen in the eyes of the of the nation as a large number of media personnel gathered in the press box and on the sidelines to watch Gerry Faust's debut as head coach of the Blue and Gold. And, after a shaky start in the first quarter, they saw a pretty good show.

"Anytime you win, it's a thrill," Faust said. "I want to thank the student body. They were there in full force and they were really great. In 29 years of coaching, I've never seen more electrifying enthusiasm than I saw Saturday night. It reminded me of 'Death Valley' down in Clemson."

Indeed, Salem, which virtually had nothing to lose in this game, gave the sellout crowd and the Zips fits early in the first quarter as Fisher, on the strength of a 23-yard pass completion to Robert Smith and a 19-yard run after scrambling out of the pocket, engineered a drive to the Akron 28-yard line.

On fourth and eight, the Tigers looked to take the early lead but Barry Chilers' field goal attempt never came about as holder Eric Alkire fumbled the snap to thwart the drive. That, however, was still an indication that it would take more than the luxury of a national spotlight and tradition to put away this team.

"They presented some problems for us early in the game by jumping around in different formations," Faust said. "We felt that by watching some of their passing game, they would jump their backs around which they did. We did a good job covering their formations but we felt that we didn't contain the quarterback as much as we should."

Fisher, in only six minutes of action, racked up some impressive numbers, connecting on three of five passes for 41 yards and rushing for 25 yards on only three carries.

"He's the key to our season," said Salem Head Coach Corky Griffith. "The poor little 17 year-old freshman who then came in there was outstanding. That kid came in there and did an excellent job. I'm certainly proud of him."

That was Bernard Rembert, who may never be a Fisher but who definitely kept the Tigers in the game throughout the duration of the first half.

The Zips unveiled their new offense on their second possession when senior quarterback Vernon Stewart threw a perfect touchdown strike to senior tight end Chris Kelley. Freshman Bob Dombroski added the extra point to give Akron a 7–0 lead with 5:56 left in the first quarter.

"We got out passes when we needed them," said Stewart who completed seven of 16 passes on the evening for 141 yards. "We needed them especially since our running game wasn't going as well as it should have in the first half.

"On the touchdown, we faked to the tailback on play action and that brought their linebackers up a step or two," he added. "It was just a choice for me. Kelley was my primary option but after they (the Salem defense) began to key on him, it opened up other people."

"Their defensive backs were playing three deep and were 10 yards off the wide receivers," Kelley commented. "Most of my patterns were underpatterns and that was leaving me open all night. I felt that if I could get the ball and catch it, I could run some of them over."

The Zips' first drive of the second quarter stalled at their own 25 but the Blue and Gold received a break as the Tigers were penalized for having too many men on the field on Mike Knapp's punt. Four plays later, Knapp and Akron got another break when Salem was once again penalized for illegal participation after Knapp mishandled Mike Teifke's snap.

The Zips took advantage of those two miscues by moving the ball to the Tiger four on the strength of six and 13-yard completions from Stewart to Dan Hampton and Kelley respectively. Four plays later, and following yet another Salem illegal participation penalty, Hampton scored straight ahead from one yard out. Dombroski's kick made it 14–0 with 6:44 left in the first half.

"I never saw so many flags," lamented Griffith. "I thought we should have been better prepared. We got the ball in good field position after Knapp fumbled the punt but our nose guard forgot to come out. That's uncalled for and it's my fault. Good coaching makes the difference in situations like that."

The Tigers then found themselves in a position that probably any coach could not handle on their next possession. After Brian Moran coughed up a Childers punt at the 30, Salem engineered their best scoring drive. On fourth and goal from the six, Rembert apparently hit wide receiver Mark Dills with a TD strike but the play was wiped out after officials concurred that a whistle accidentally blew before the snap.

"I didn't hear any whistle," Griffith said. "They said that someone allegedly threw ice on the field and hit our center. After that, the game got out of hand.

Top: The 1985 team's Mike Clark blasts through with help from offensive guard Nick Lademarco. Photo by Allen Boley, from Tel-Buch, *courtesy of Archival Services, University Libraries, The University of Akron.*

Left: The 1983 team's James Black led the offensive attack with nine touchdowns. Photo from Tel-Buch, *courtesy of Archival Services, University Libraries, The University of Akron.*

"I don't feel that we got ripped off," he added. "The officiating didn't beat us. But I saw some calls that I didn't agree with."

Akron erupted in the third quarter and took a 28–0 lead on one and two-yard touchdown runs by Hampton and fullback Tony Lauro respectively. The Zips then iced the game on the first play of the fourth quarter when freshman Pierce Joiner picked off Rembert's only interception of the evening and returned it 24 yards for a touchdown.

Individually, Hampton paced Akron offensively with 44 yards rushing on 12 carries. Tailback Mike Clark, who didn't start because of bruised ribs, added 36 yards on seven carries. Kelley was the Zips' leading receiver with four receptions for 101 yards.

Rembert capped a fine evening by leading the Tigers in rushing with 51 yards on 13 carries while completing three of 11 passes for 41 yards.

Total yardage favored Akron 346–170 while first downs also favored the locals 16–8. Faust knows that those numbers will have to improve especially going into Saturday's game against a Kent State team that rattled Toledo 18–16 in Head Coach Glen Mason's debut.

"We have to get better in all phases of the game," Faust said. "We have to improve immensely this week. The time between the first and second game is the key time for improvement."

September 30, 1986

History Times Two in UA Victory

By L.C. Johnson

The Zips' style of play versus the University of Central Florida started out very much like the weather that preceded the 7:30 P.M. kickoff.

Even kickoff time was altered back one-half hour from the original 7 P.M. starting time—largely due to the weather and partially due to the fact that the majority of the 12,186 fans who turned out for the ballgame had yet to come through the turnstiles.

However, even more threatening than the weather forecast were the visiting Knights of Central Florida, who were clinging to a 14–13 halftime lead.

The Knights were leading by virtue of two touchdown runs by senior tailback Elgin Davis. And they clearly stole the show in the first half of play. In fact, they managed to put a damper on what turned out to be two milestone performances by Akron's Mike Clark and Vernon Stewart.

Clark, a 5-foot-9, 175-pound senior tailback from Cleveland and Stewart, a 6-foot-3, 175-pound senior quarterback from Ferrel, PA, both became the all-time UA statistical leaders for most yards rushing and passing, respectively.

Clark, who entered Saturday's game needing 66 yards to surpass Jack Beidleman's mark of 3,080 yards rushing, had already done a yeoman's days work by halftime, with 147 yards rushing and a touchdown on 19 carries.

Meanwhile, Stewart needed just 42 yards to eclipse the standard of 3,335 yards passing that was set by Don Zwisler. Stewart also would have his name etched in the UA record books prior to the end of the half, on the strength of 3 passes for 63 yards and a touchdown.

At the time, though, those records had to be the farthest thing from the Zips' minds, as they were in jeopardy of having their season record drop to 2–2.

For the record, the Zips (3–1), on the strength of a couple of old reliables, came back to win 20–17—thanks largely due to Clark's and Stewart's unwillingness to rest on their first half laurels.

It took a late fourth-quarter touchdown by Clark, who rushed for a career high 255 yards and two touchdowns on 31 carries. And Stewart who completed 9 of 15 passes for 104 yards and a first quarter touchdown, helped engineer the game-winning nine-play 80-yard drive.

The Zips' first score resulted from the game's opening drive, which saw the Zips march 57 yards in just eight plays.

Clark, and senior fullback Tony Lauro, combined to pick up 32 of those yards on seven consecutive rushes. Stewart then hit senior flanker Larry Small with a perfect throw in the right corner of the end zone. Bob Dombroski's point-after gave the Zips an early 7–0 lead.

UCF answered back and ultimately took the lead with Davis' two scores midway through the second quarter to go up 14–7, as their successful two-point conversion

The 1986 team brings down Austin Peay. Courtesy of The University of Akron Department of Intercollegiate Athletics.

following the second score made up for Ed O'Brien's first extra-point attempt that was blocked by UA strong safety Robert Lyons.

Clark scored his first TD of the game and the season, late in the second quarter to cut the deficit to one point, but Dombroski's point-after attempt sailed wide of the crossbar and was no good.

Still with time remaining in the first half, the Zips got another chance to score following a UCF punt after an apparent 38-yard touchdown pass from Darrin Slack to wide receiver Ted Wilson was ruled out.

Akron eventually drove all the way to the Central 11-yard line, but with time running out, Dombroski missed on a 28-yard field goal attempt. Both the missed extra point and the field goal were Dombroski's first of the season.

Central came right back at the outset of the third quarter and extended their lead to 17–13 as O'Brien booted a 25-yard field goal. The score would remain that way through the remainder of the third quarter and set the stage for Stewart and Clark's late fourth quarter heroics.

Akron took possession with about six minutes left in the game at their own 20-yard line. From there, Stewart passed four times for 35 yards. However for the most part the game-winning drive—and the entire game plan, marked the return of the tailback-oriented offense that had become the trademark for the UA offensive attack.

And attack it did, sandwiched in between Stewart's aerial assault. It featured Clark, who ran inside, outside, and on sides of the Rubber Bowl that many of the Zips' fans didn't even know existed.

In the end though, Clark managed to burst through a hole vacated by the right side of his offensive line and dash 37 yards to pay dirt to end up in an all too familiar place—the end zone with the game-winning score.

Zip Notes: The Zip gridders are idle this week but next week they will take to the road where they'll face the defending Ohio Valley Conference Champion Middle Tennessee State University Blue Raiders in Murfreesboro, TN.

September 22, 1987

Blocked Field Goal Enables Zip Win

By Mike Popovich

My, doesn't winning taste sweet! After its last four games, bitterness was the only flavor to which The University of Akron football team was accustomed. In that span, the Zips were an unimpressive 0–4 and on the road to becoming 0–5 when they took on the 28th-ranked Eastern Michigan Hurons Saturday night at the Rubber Bowl.

But someone forgot to tell this young Akron team that they were playing an Eastern squad which was highly-touted after it scored a decisive 33–17 victory over defending Mid-American Conference champion Miami of Ohio.

The Zips used that as an incentive to upset the Hurons, 17–16, before 10,032 fans who braved the rain and cloudy skies.

This was a game that literally looked as if it would come down to the final second. And guess what? It did.

With one second left, following a 28-yard pass completion from Eastern's senior quarterback Ron Adams to senior tight end Bill Kupp at the Zips' 35-yard line, the Hurons called upon placekicker John Laupp to attempt a potential game-winning 52-yard field goal.

Laupp, a slender 5-foot-9, 159-pound sophomore, has been handling the back-up kicking chores behind starter Tim Henneghan. In his first collegiate field goal attempt against Miami, Laupp netted a 51-yarder which proved that the attempt was within his reach.

However, Laupp's boot was a low line drive shot that was "pierced" and batted down by sophomore lineman Pierce Joiner as time expired.

"As soon as I heard the thud, I said 'I can't believe we blocked the darn thing,'" said Akron Coach Gerry Faust.

Eastern boss Jim Harkema said it best when summing up the close contest.

"One point, one inch, this and that and that's the game," he said. "We had a chance to win the game in the last minute. That shows you what kind of football team you have."

Harkema will get an even better look at what the Hurons are made of when they return to Northeastern Ohio next Saturday and face Kent State in the Golden Flashes' home opener.

And all Kent did Saturday, after defeating Akron 27–23 last week without starting quarterback Patrick Young, was thump Kansas of the Big Eight Conference, 31–17, on the road.

"We're still 1–0 in the MAC and that's where we want to be," said Harkema.

Meanwhile, the Zips must contend with a short practice week before they travel to Philadelphia Thursday to meet the Temple Owls in Veterans Stadium (ESPN, 8 P.M.). The Owls stunned 16th-ranked Pittsburgh, 24–21, in the Steel City Saturday.

"We'll just enjoy tonight and go to work and look toward Temple tomorrow," said Faust after hearing the Temple score. "But the one thing that we can count on for that game is everyone being healthy. We came out of this game without any serious injuries."

"We still need to go to work on everything. We still need to go in and scrap. The kids played a hard, good game on both sides of the ball. But we also made some dumb mistakes."

"Despite that, we think that we have improved over 300 percent since we played Western Michigan at the beginning of the season. The people who have come out to the games have seen two exciting football games and we could very well be 3–0."

The scenario for this game, though, was written as if Akron may have had to look at a 0–3 start after three weeks.

Put on your seatbelts and get ready for the final 6:42.

With the Zips leading 17–10, and Akron driving into Huron territory, sophomore tailback Derek Alston sprinted up the middle for 11 yards but fumbled the ball into the hands of EMU sophomore defensive back Dan Bennett at the Eastern 35.

With the help of two pass interference penalties against the Zips, a 12-yard pass completion from Adams to wide receiver Mark Ziegler and a key 9-yard run on fourth down by the Hurons' speedy 5–8, 182-pound senior tailback Gary Patton, the Hurons suddenly found themselves in scoring position at the Akron 5.

On the ensuing play, senior tailback Jimmie Johnson, a 6–0, 201-pounder, plowed through the final five yards for the touchdown with 1:58 left in the game to complete a 12-play, 65-yard drive.

Harkema elected to gamble and go for the two-point conversion and the win. On the conversion attempt, Adams rolled right and was stopped short on the 1-yard line by Zip senior defensive lineman Doug Knepp.

"The decision to go for the win was entirely mine," Harkema said. "I would not be happy with a tie. I thought we had a good play and that we played it good. If it would have been a league game, and depending on who we would have played, we probably would have kicked the extra point."

With the Hurons down to their last timeout, Akron needed just one first down to run out the clock. However, the Zips wasted a play when sophomore quarterback

Akron and Kent State battle for the ball in 1989. Courtesy of The University of Akron Department of Intercollegiate Athletics.

Andy Kubik threw incomplete on the first play of the drive that was meant to be the option.

Faced with fourth-and-six on the Zip 46, sophomore punter Bill Rudison shanked a 17-yard punt out of bounds that set up the drive culminated with Laupp's missed field goal.

With the exception of the first and last Huron drives, the Akron defense played exceptionally well, holding Eastern's two giant killers, Patton and Adams, to a combined 239 yards total offense. Patton netted 101 rushing yards on 23 carries while scoring one touchdown. Adams completed only 9 of 24 aerials for 138 yards. Both were instrumental in last year's 24–21 victory over the Zips in Ypsilanti.

"I'm especially happy with our defense because Patton killed us in the game last year," said Faust. "We limited a good football team who was averaging 34 points a game to 16 points. Our defense is getting better. We knew that last week."

Eastern took a 7–0 lead with 7:56 left in the first quarter when Patton stepped right and struck pay dirt from seven yards out to complete a 14-play, 91-yard drive.

The Zips tied it at 7–7 when Kubik connected with sophomore tight end Kurt Latell for a 13-yard TD with 8:49 left in the second quarter to complete a 4-play, 62-yard drive.

The Hurons answered with a 9-play, 47-yard drive that culminated with a 25-yard field goal by Henneghan with 51 seconds left in the first half. The score remained 10–7 at halftime.

Sophomore placekicker Bob Dombroski tied the game at 10–10 with a 41-yard field goal with 6:21 in the third quarter to complete a 6-play, 12-yard drive.

Akron then took the lead for good on the first play of the fourth quarter when Kubik scored on the option from six yards out.

Kubik finished the evening with 15 of 28 pass completions for 195 yards. Sophomore fullback John Motton netted 77 yards on 13 carries to lead the Zips' ground game. Latell caught nine passes for 97 yards. Defensively, Knepp led Akron with 12 tackles.

The Zips led in total yardage 358–280 and in first downs 18–15.

November 14, 1989

Akron Mangled by Tennessee, 52–9

Vols' Depth Too Much

By Mike Perkins

Knoxville, Tenn.—The real numbers indicating the story Saturday were Tennessee 95, Akron 75.

Those are the number of scholarships which are given to the respective schools. What it adds up to is that the Volunteers had more depth than the Zips.

The only numbers that really mean anything are the ones on the scoreboard: Tennessee 52, Akron 9. But like the Auburn game a year ago, the Zips made a good showing before 91,883 at Neyland Stadium.

It looked as though it would be anybody's game in the first quarter as the Zips gave the Vols all they could handle. The Vols took a 7–0 lead following a 32-yard touchdown run by Chuck Webb, and were threatening for more when Webb fumbled on the Akron 14.

The Zips capitalized by driving 86 yards in 14 plays, culminating with a three yard pass from Mike Johnson. The usually reliable Bob Dembrowski, though missed the extra point, and the score was 7–6.

The Zips had a chance to take the lead when Tony Thompson fumbled on the Akron 45, but Daron Alcorn's 53-yard field goal attempt was wide to the right.

By the time the second quarter rolled around, Tennessee's depth was having an effect on the Zips. Quarterback Andy Kelly took advantage of a weakened Zip secondary for some long strikes, and Webb was virtually unstoppable as he rushed for 168 yards. All told, the Vols had 588 total yards.

The Zips moved the football against the 11th-ranked Vols to the tune of 368 total yards. Alston was the leading rusher with 114 yards and Johnson passed for 201 yards to become Akron's all time passing leader.

Both of these seniors would gladly trade impressive stats for a victory, and both of them said the Vols did not intimidate them.

"We made a giant step from last year," Alston said in reference to the Auburn game. "We had no confidence last year. This year, we felt we couldn't be beat. We just made mistakes."

In a 1989 clash of rivals, Akron halts the Kent State line. Photo by Michael Parks, from Tel-Buch, *courtesy of Archival Services, University Libraries, The University of Akron.*

Alston had no trouble running the ball between the tackles, and he took advantage of holes left by his linemen.

"We felt we could run off tackle," he said. "I was able to cut up the middle at times, too. We were prepared for everything they showed us."

For Alston, the game had a bittersweet taste.

"There was specialness for me just playing Tennessee," he said. "It was our last game, and we wanted to go out in style."

Though some satisfaction could be derived from the fact the Zips scored, they also squandered a number of scoring opportunities.

"They had good defensive match ups to our plays," Johnson said. "The thing that really hurt us was that they had three big plays in the first half. If not for those, we might have only been down by five."

When Johnson was informed he was now Akron's all-time passing leader, he responded, "What passing record? Oh well, records are nice to have, but I'd rather have a victory."

Head Coach Gerry Faust said he knew the numbers game was going to have a tremendous impact on the contest.

"We felt we had to have a supreme effort," he said. "We had to have intensity, but we also had errors and we got banged up," he continued. "Losing Pierce Joiner was a big loss, and we don't have that depth yet."

Faust said the final score is not a measuring stick of the play of the Zips.

"The score doesn't indicate how well we played," he said. "I'm very proud of our young men. We moved the ball against an excellent football team. They have great team speed and they are just a great team."

Faust made somewhat of a pitch for more scholarships, something the program needs if it wants to compete with schools like Auburn and Tennessee.

"As you know, we only have 75 scholarships," he said. "Today was an example of that. We just couldn't keep fresh guys in there. I thought we played pretty well but we were worn out."

Faust has to look at the positive fact the Zips finished the season at 6–4–1, their first in Division I–A, and for at least one period, they not only competed, but also gave a tough time to one of the top teams in the country.

Extra Point

The Moving A

Among other changes he has made in the UA football program, Gerry Faust has designed a new logo for the golden helmets and the pants his players will be wearing this fall. The logo features a modernistic blue A with lines streaking from it indicating forward movement.

Faust got the idea after reading this statement by Oliver Wendell Holmes, "The greatest thing in this world is not so much where we are going, but in what direction we are moving."

"That's our theme, moving ahead," said Faust.

Courtesy of The University of Akron Department of Intercollegiate Athletics and Archival Services, University Libraries, The University of Akron

TIME-OUT

THE COACHES

JOHN HEISMAN

The story goes that Buchtel College's quarterback, 6-foot-4 inch Harry Clark, had trouble bending low enough to pick up the football when the center snapped it to him.

Squirted it to him was more like it.

At that point in football history, 1893, the center transferred the ball to the quarterback by putting one hand over the front of the ball and pressing down on the back with his other hand. When he released the front hand, the ball would flip up and back in the general direction of the backfield.

It was an awkward maneuver, to say the least, and resulted in many fumbles.

Buchtel's coach had a better idea. Why not have the center simply pitch the ball back through his legs? Shotgun-style, we'd call it today.

It worked.

Clark saved his back, and Buchtel cut down on its fumbles. No one objected, and by the end of the season all colleges were using the new center snap.

So how did Heisman end up in Akron?

After the 1892 season, the students again besieged the Reverend Orello Cone, Buchtel's president since 1880, pleading with him to convince the Board of Trustees to hire someone to coach the college's club teams. Cone pushed the measure through.

The students' first choice was Heisman, and they moved quickly to get him. The young coach was invited to campus in January, and after inspecting the facilities he spelled out the terms under which he would render his services. The weekly student newspaper, *The Buchtelite*, ran the headline "HEISMAN! HEISMAN! Rah! Rah! Rah!"

Alas, John W. Heisman's association with Buchtel wasn't a long or especially satisfying one for him—the faculty and trustees got together and legislated his job out of existence. But it did have its moments. In 1894, when he technically wasn't even working for the college, Heisman engineered a 12-6 win over Ohio State. He played quarterback in the game to boot.

After retiring from coaching, Heisman served as the New York City Downtown Athletic Club's first athletic director, starting in 1930. The club awarded its first trophy to the nation's top college football player in 1935 and "renamed" the trophy in memory of Heisman when he died a year later at age 66.

Story reprinted with permission from Akron Magazine

Fred Sefton and Howard Blair. Courtesy of Archival Services, University Libraries, The University of Akron.

Kenneth "Red" Cochrane. Photo from Tel-Buch, *courtesy of Archival Services, University Libraries, The University of Akron.*

Joe McMullen. Photo by Tobias Studio, courtesy of The University of Akron Department of Intercollegiate Athletics.

Gordon Larson. Photo by Tobias Studio, courtesy of The University of Akron Department of Intercollegiate Athletics.

Dwight B. Bradley

Dr. Dwight B. Bradley was born in Bangkok, Siam, June 10th, 1882, and came to the U.S. at the age of six. He started to school in the Oberlin Public Schools at the age of seven.

In the Oberlin High School, he played football, baseball and was on the track team. Upon entering Oberlin College he played left end on the football team for four years, making the all Ohio team three years. He was also on baseball and track teams here. He later took up a medical and dental course in the U. of P., where he played left end on the football team. While here he was catcher on the baseball nine, a member of the swimming team for two years, and made the basketball team two years. Graduating in '07, he has practiced in Philadelphia until coming to Buchtel to take charge of athletics.

He came to us, well recommended as a good athlete and trainer and has certainly made good. A man who can take a green bunch of men and after seven days' training have them holding down a strong team like Wooster, is certainly a coach!
October 1908 Buchtelite

Coach Haggerty

Two years ago Haggerty came to Buchtel to put the institution on the athletic map. Whether he has succeeded or not the records will show. Last year's work resulted in a football championship, a near basketball one, and a number one baseball team. This year, although there are some defeats registered, the football status of Buchtel has been strengthened by the kind of game she has played against the big Ohio elevens, notably Reserve and Case. Haggerty looks for a championship basketball team and a stronger baseball nine than that of last year. Track work seems also about to be revived. Hats off to our coach.
December 1911 Buchtelite

Coach Sefton

Coach Fred Sefton has now been with us for two years and during that time he has made his way into the hearts of all loyal Akronites. He has already made a name for himself in the State as an able coach in every line of athletics.

Compared with other colleges, the number of men from whom the teams are to be picked is small. Yet "coach" has succeeded in putting out teams that have been the envy of other schools.

In basketball he was the main factor in giving Akron a near champion team. His football teams have been unexcelled in conditioning and in coaching.
1917 Tel-Buch

Kenneth "Red" Cochrane—He Saved Akron Football

With just nine wins over five seasons from 1947-51, The University of Akron football program was in danger of being discontinued. It was in the fall of 1952 that the University looked to Kenneth "Red" Cochrane to revitalize the dying program. He had been the athletic director at Akron since 1948.

"No question about it, Akron football exists today because of 'Red' Cochrane," former Zip SID Ken MacDonald told the *Akron Beacon Journal*.

"We had only 19 guys in spring practice and hardly anyone went to the games," said Frank Stams who played for UA from 1951 to '53. "And on top of that, there was no head coach. It certainly didn't look good."

With campus pressure mounting to drop the program, Cochrane stepped in as head coach and admitted in a September, 1952 newsletter he was not excited about his return to coaching: "However, after two weeks' work with our fine squad and the excellent help given me by the staff, I find myself becoming really enthused and liking it . . . I want to take this opportunity to thank everyone for being so helpful to us in this fall's endeavor. The administration, faculty, students, and community have all gone out of their way to help us which is most encouraging in our present task."

That first year was rough as the team finished 2-6-1. It looked like even Cochrane would struggle to turn the program around. Then, in 1953, the Zips began to click. Akron's six wins were the most since 1938 and they compiled a 4-2 mark in the Ohio Athletic Conference.

With the Zips back on track, Cochrane turned over the coaching reigns to Joe McMullem in 1954 and turned his attention to the attendance problem. Akron had averaged just 5,457 fans per game in 1953 as attendance at college football games around the country was in decline. That fall, he began brainstorming ideas to boost attendance and soon the Acme-Zip Game was invented.

Courtesy of The University of Akron Department of Intercollegiate Athletics

Gordon Larson—A Winning Tradition

For Akron U the first victory of the season was achieved by scoring the most one-sided victory since the 1955 Hilltop squad took apart Otterbein 58-0.

For Gordon Larson, the 58-0 signified the second most points scored in a single game by any of his eight previous Akron seasons—hopefully the start of his ninth winning season.

From 1961 on the Zips have yet to find themselves on the short end of the record stick as they have through the second game of the 1969 season turned in a 49-23-7 record under Larson's leadership.

But winning is not something that Gordon Larson developed just during his tenure at Akron.

In a coaching career that spans 20 years Larson has recorded 90 wins against 50 losses and 11 ties.

Included in those 90 victories are those of the 1958 Marion Harding High School team which won the title of the top high school team in the state and won for Gordon Larson the title of "Ohio High School Coach of the Year."

As with many football mentors who win the title, he found himself in the college coaching ranks the next season.

A move to Columbus found him as defensive backfield coach for Ohio State—a position held for two years before his coming to Akron.

His 1968 UA team was the first team in UA football history to play in a post-season bowl game and its 327 points were more than any other team amassed in a single season.

September 23, 1969 Buchtelite

Zips Get Gerry Faust

Speculation of where Gerry Faust would be coaching in 1986 ended Dec. 18, 1985 when he was named the 23rd head football coach at The University of Akron.

"In my book, Gerry Faust is a winner," said Dr. President William V. Muse. "He has proved it on the football field at Cincinnati Moeller and at Notre Dame. More importantly he's a winner as a human being and exemplifies what college athletics is all about. We believe he's the kind of individual around which the University can build a strong NCAA IA football program."

Faust replaced Jim Dennison, who resigned after 13 seasons as UA's head coach. Dennison has accepted the position of associate director of athletics.

Faust brought with him 23 years of head coaching experience. During 18 seasons at Cincinnati Moeller he produced a glittering record of 174 wins, 17 losses and two ties. His last five seasons were at The University of Notre Dame. He left the Fighting Irish after posting a 30-26-1 mark, including 7-5 seasons in 1983 and 1984 and a 6-4-1 record in 1982.

"We have left our mark on Akron football and it has been a positive one," continued Dennison. "We're proud of that!"

Indeed, Dennison, his staff and players have accomplished many milestones since taking over the Zip football program in 1973. He guided his 1976 squad to a 10-3 season, his 1983 team to an 8-3 mark and the 1985 squad to an 8-4 record—three of the six best records in UA's 85-year football history.

In 1985, the Zip gridders were picked sixth in the Ohio Valley Conference, but surprised many by finishing second on the way to an 8-4 mark. UA's effort was rewarded with a ranking of 10th in the final national poll and a berth in the NCAA IAA playoffs. Unfortunately, UA lost to Rhode Island, 35-27, in the first round.

The 47-year-old Dennison became the winningest football coach in the school's history with a 34-32 victory over Western Kentucky on October 5, 1985. Dennison's 13-year record was 80 victories, 62 losses and two ties.

He was UA's first coach to win 10 games in a season, the first to win a post-season game and the first to play for a national championship—all in 1976. That same season, Dennison became the first UA grid coach to be named Ohio Coach of the Year and the first to be named Kodak National Coach of the Year. In 1985, he was selected a Co-Coach of the Year in the Ohio Valley Conference.
1986 Tel-Buch

End of an Era

By Casey Moore

The firing of head football coach Lee Owens proves two clichés true: Nice guys *do* finish last, and *winning is* everything.

What exactly has Owens done to constitute staying, you ask?

Some refer to the shape of the program when Owens took over in 1995. The Zips had just come off a 1-10 season, and Owens helped put them on the map. He led them to seven wins in 1999, the most by a Zips team in almost a decade. The following year, he would lead Akron to a share of the Mid-American Conference crown, a three-point loss to Mar-

Jim Dennison. Photo from Tel-Buch, *courtesy of Archival Services, University Libraries, The University of Akron.*

Gerry Faust. Photo by Russell D. Sibert, from Tel-Buch, *courtesy of Archival Services, University Libraries, The University of Akron.*

Lee Owens. Courtesy of The University of Akron Department of Intercollegiate Athletics.

J.D. Brookhart. Courtesy of The University of Akron Department of Intercollegiate Athletics.

shall in the closing seconds being the only thing stopping the Zips from a trip to the MAC Championship game.

He posted a 22-16 record within their underrated conference during the past five seasons and has helped recruit some pivotal local players, none more noteworthy than star quarterback Charlie Frye who may have been hit the hardest by the transaction.

Others will tell you that he encouraged excellence in the classroom, which is why the team's graduation rate hit 70 percent and never dipped below 50 percent during the past four years. I realize football is played out of the classroom, but we're all in college to walk across a stage, not across a goal line, and that was something Owens knew.

Owens had also always been one of the nice guys in the athletic office. Accommodating to any interview and quick to acknowledge a student-newspaper to be as important as a major newspaper.

But the truth of the matter is it's not at all surprising that Owens is no longer a Zip.

Athletic director Michael Thomas' job is to bring about winning sports programs by any means necessary, and he has justification for letting Owens go. Thomas' worry about the status of the program struck last season when the Zips started 0-6, including disappointing losses to Central and Eastern Michigan. After an extended evaluation at the end of the season, Thomas surprisingly spared Owens his job.

It took just one game into this season for the buzz to come back. After the Zips failed to beat Kent State for the first time in seven tries, you could almost hear Thomas preparing the guillotine.

It would seem the thing that put Owens on the chopping block was his inability to lead the Zips to that all-important win.

Now Thomas gets to find his own man. Whether or not the new head coach will come from inside the program will all be up to him. But one thing is for sure: Unlike when Owens got here, a good foundation is already laid out.

November 18, 2003 Buchtelite

J.D. Brookhart

J.D. Brookhart was born in Pueblo, Colorado in 1964 and earned his B.S. degree in 1988 at Colorado State, where he played on the field as a three-year starting wide receiver. His coaching experience includes working with the Denver Broncos as a coaching assistant (1995-96) as well as at The University of Pittsburgh as an assistant coach (1997-2003). He became the head coach at The University of Akron in 2004.

2009 marks J.D. Brookhart's sixth season as Akron's head football coach. His philosophy towards college football is much like the approach taken by a CEO to a Fortune 500 company, viewing success on the field in the same context as the bottom line in the board room.

It is that philosophy which led Brookhart to be a 2007 Distinguished Sales and Marketing Honoree, as given by the Akron chapter of Sales & Marketing Executives International. He has additionally used his salesmanship to land the top-rated recruiting classes in the Mid-American Conference in 2005, '06 and '07 by various publications—all of which produced Freshman All-Americans at season's end.

Sideline advice is given during a 1981 game. Photo by Bob Wilkey, courtesy of The University of Akron Department of Intercollegiate Athletics.

The mood around the Akron football program is similar to what is found in corporate America, where constant productivity and forward progress is a must and employees are held to the highest level of accountability.

The 43-year-old Brookhart, who has a career record of 27-33, views himself not only as a coach and teacher, but also as a manager of people.

The role of a manager and the parallels between business and the gridiron come easy to Brookhart, because prior to his move to the coaching ranks he was a highly successful member of the corporate community from which the UA program is modeled.
Courtesy of The University of Akron Department of Intercollegiate Athletics

WHAT'S HAPPENING . . .

ı CAMPUS

ɔrm numbers down

AKRON, Ohio (AP) — The economy a declining pool of 18-year-olds go-to college have reduced the number tudents living in campus dormito-

ɩ the University of Akron, trustees ned that the school ran a deficit of rly $1 million on its dormitory and eteria programs.

Residence halls fell $466,195 below enue projections for the last fiscal r. Dining services were down 7,016.

he numbers led Charles E. Taylor, rd finance chairman, to look into the n vacancy rate in campus housing.

Two reasons were cited, the *Akron con Journal* reported Sunday: the nomy and demographics. Many stu-ts who might have lived on campus v can afford only to commute, and re are fewer 18-year-olds.

We're just in one of those cycles," said ry Schwarzmueller, executive direc- of the 800-member Association of lege and University Housing Offic- International in Columbus.

He said reduced college enrollment l on-campus housing use is not just a ional trend. "I've talked to more who they are down than at any time ce the big dip in the mid-1970s."

He said the economy is the "big driv- factor."

et some students are choosing other sing over dormitories because they afford it.

Michael Mills, assistant director for rations at the University of Toledo, l students in urban areas are mov- to off-campus housing.

He said more students are working l they can pay for an off-campus rtment by the month and live there r-round.

For Jay Hershey, the University of ron's director of residence halls, "it nes down to a numbers game."

The number of 18-year-olds will in-ase in the mid-1990s, but for now, rshey said, "there are fewer students ilable to fill colleges."

The other issue, he said, is the nomy.

"It may be that there are more high ool graduates going on to college, but re are fewer going away to college."

Colleges also are being forced to change d services. University of Akron food vices director Chester Taffi said col-es have to be more competitive in nus and operating hours with what dents can get elsewhere.

omecoming is here

• Finally, Homecoming is here. The rit rally will start up at noon today d go through 1:50 p.m.

The dance kicks off Friday at 7 p.m. in morial Hall and will go until mid-ght.

The Homecoming football game will k off at 1 p.m. with the Zips taking on d-American Conference defending mpion Bowling Green.

Festivities will also be held before the me, with the Outback student area d a Pouch Party for alums back for mecoming.

RIME REPORT

Two men were arrested Sunday on mpus and charged with criminal tres-

Volume 104, Number 24

the buchtelite

Established 1

Serving the University Community for over 104 Years.

Homecoming gives students reason to part

by Chris Freeman
News Editor

It's been five weeks since the Akron football team visited the friendly confines of the Rubber Bowl, and as the Zips return home for the first of a four-game homestand, the fans are ready.

At the Acme-Zip game against Toledo, the Student Alumni Association set up its first tailgate party of the year called the Outback.

At the Outback, students were able to sign up for three big prizes, a $500 tuition scholarship and a pair of $100 cash prizes. All three were given away before the fourth quarter of the game.

Around 800 students signed up for the tuition scholarship, said Alumni Director Carole Lick, and when the name was drawn from the barrel, William Blue was the lucky winner.

"It was a particularly nice situation with him," said Lick. "He's married and has a family and is putting himself through school and this money was like a Godsend."

Lick said the feedback from the first game was good.

"The response was tremendous, particularly given the students were not given much time to learn about it," she said. "The Roo Crew (student section) was very responsive to the team, and the coaches and players expressed their appreciation for the support and noise they made at the game."

The director of alumni relations said things are looking good for the Outback and Pouch Party in its first year of existence.

"We want it to be a tailgate party for the students," she said. "We moved the tent a little closer to the main entrance so it's easier to get to. WKDD will be there, and we'll have some food vendors in the tent with reasonably-priced food.

"I hope that everyone enjoys the opportunity. The weather promises to be excellent and it's a great opportunity to come out and have a good time."

She also said that the party should keep going.

"It's my hope to continue it every year," said Lick. "It's a wonderful thing to provide this kind of support for the students, but to keep it going, we need to get alumni and other people to raise money for the students.

"The money for the tuition scholarship and cash prizes is not University money, but is raised by people like Don Krizo and Don Davidson."

Nine former Zippys will be back on campus, for the Homecoming game including Pete Deming, the first Zippy, Todd Bowers, who finished third in the national mascot competition while he was in a Zippy suit and Jim Otto, who took second in the national competition while he was at Akron.

There will also be an historical display of Zippy from its inception to the present put together by former UA Sports Information Director Ken MacDonald.

Finally, a 6-foot-0 ice sculpture of Zippy will be carved by Dick professor in hospitality man at Akron.

There are a number of scheduled for the Homecomir Party. They are: Accounting Alpha Delta Pi sorority, Gamma Delta sorority, Amba Babcock and Wilcox, Band Black alumni, *Buchtelite* staf Chi Omega alumni, Class reunion, Delta Gamma soror cation alumni, Honors p Kappa Kappa Gamma s Lambda Chi Alpha fraterni Star fraternity, Milestone alumni), Mortor Board, alumni, ODK alumni, Phi De fraternity, Phi Gamma Delt nity, Phi Sigma Kappa fr Residence Halls alumni, Re ulty and staff, Senior Clas Sigma Pi fraternity, Smucke Tau Kappa Epsilon fraternit masters, Varsity A Ass WAUP/WZIP alumni and letic Club members.

Debate opens floor for ideas

photo by Bryan Hulsey

Discussion reveals little

by Chris Freeman
News Editor

It was on, then it was canceled and then it was back on again. And after 1 1/2 hours of talking, the first campus debates were over.

The University Democrats, [...] swers were pulled from the candidates' position papers and answers in the debates, but some spirited exchanges did take place.

"The Democrats entire platform is to discredit the Reagan years," said College Republicans President Mark Whitt.

Later, Brian Fallon, a student in the University Democrats who is running for a State Representative position in his hometown of Medina said, "It seems that George Bush's health-care plan is — don't get sick."

But for the most part, the de-

Fallon gets top marks

by Chris Freeman
News Editor

The first and only campus debate was turned into a possible showcase for future politicians.

Though it nearly did not come off because of differing opinions from the two party-affiliated groups, the College Republicans and Univer- [...] into sound bites.

Both of the presidents schools presented themselv

Mark Whitt, the head of lege Republicans, was Fallo counterpart. He had also don of pre-planning for the deb was able to present his can position with ease and clar

Anthony Fossaceca, the sity Democrats leader, usu the lead-in for Fallon. He ke issues very well, and was give Fallon a lead-in for h bers and one-liners.

Another stellar performa

CHAPTER 11
1990–1999

A 1990 University of Florida poster with the final score of the game against Akron. Courtesy of Julie Gammon.

November 17, 1992

Akron Content to Take 10–10 Tie with YSU

By Danny Dragin

Saturday's Akron-Youngstown State game came down to the wire, as the Zips were able to battle to a 10–10 tie. It was a wild one at the Rubber Bowl, as both teams fought miserable winds and a 28-degree kickoff weather.

With 8:18 remaining in the game, YSU kicker, Jeffrey Wilkins booted a 22-yard field goal to put the Penguins up 10–7. The drive that led to the field goal took 18 plays and totaled 61 yards. The drive took 8:34 off the clock.

When Akron did get the ball back, they were able to move, until an interception thrown by Marcel Weems put the drive to a halt.

"I never said a word to him (Weems), because it was a legitimate, good throw," said Head Coach Gerry Faust.

Akron was able to put on a strong defensive stand and got the ball back at their own 21 yard line with 2:22 remaining in the game.

The Zips were able to move the ball up-field with short plays as the Penguins fell into a prevent like defense. When they got to the Penguins' 21 yard line, things came to a halt.

On first-and-10, Weems spiked the ball to stop the clock.

On second-and-10, Weems threw incomplete to Darrien Gouch.

On third-and-10, Weems again threw incomplete to Gouch.

On fourth-and-10, it was decision time.

Do you go for the field goal and the tie, or do you attempt the first down or the end zone and go for the win?

Faust chose to go for the field goal and expressed no remorse for the decision.

"We didn't have any choice in the end. After all the time-outs we had used, we had to go for the field goal," said Faust. "That's not what we wanted to do."

"I like to win, but I'm not going to take a loss because of stupidity."

The tie is something neither team was looking for.

"I don't feel good about the tie. In close proximity games like this, you like to find out every year who the better team is," said YSU Head Coach Jim Tressel. Faust said some of the players wanted to go for it. "But they understand now," he said.

Prior to sending Alcorn on to the field, YSU called a time out to try and ice him.

"I wasn't concerned about him not making it. He's (Alcorn) got a lot of confidence in himself," Faust said.

Alcorn's making of the field goal did not surprise Tressel in the least.

"Alcorn's great. I asked him during the pre-game if this was his eighth year. I was tired of seeing him kick. He's just a great kicker," said Tressel.

The tie brings the Zips record to 6–3–1.

After thinking about going for the field goal, Faust had this to say: "Any coach in the country would have made the same decision. It's stupid not to make that decision."

November 24, 1992

Zips Defeat Cincinnati to End 7–3–1 Season

By Danny Dragin

The Zips football team finished its season on an up note by defeating the Cincinnati Bearcats in a see-saw battle, 24–22.

The Zips (7–3–1) controlled the clock; 34:38–25:22. They also converted 8-of-16 third downs.

But the most revealing stat that led to the victory was the ground game. The Zips pounded out 258 yards on the ground on 60 attempts.

Junior quarterback Marcel Weems was forced to leave the game at the end of the first quarter. Weems has been the starter the entire season and is recovering from an injury that occurred during the Youngstown State game the week before.

In steps redshirt freshman, Matt Kaulig. Kaulig, having taken only two snaps the entire season, was able to move the Zips up and down the field.

"I thought Matt did an excellent job stepping in," said Head Coach Gerry Faust. "He's looked good in practice. Coach (Greg) Seamon's done an excellent job working with him."

For the game, Kaulig completed 6-of-12 for 91 yards and rushed for 59 yards.

"He was settled down. He had a lot of confidence in himself and just did one heck of a job," Faust said.

Also impressive was the bone-crushing running of Petu Ieli. The sophomore back stomped out 119 yards and punched in two touchdowns.

"Petu just played heads up football. I mean, the kid just played with his heart and did an excellent job. I couldn't ask a full back to do a better job than he did," said Faust.

The Cincinnati game represented a homecoming for Faust. It was there, at Cincinnati Moeller High School, that he began coaching. Now, 12 years later, Faust returned to the town that made him famous, and the people didn't forget.

"They had a thing for me on Friday night out there at Moeller and about 300 or 400 people were there," said Faust.

He did, however, put more attention into the fact that this was the seniors' last college game, even overshadowing that this was his return to Cincinnati.

"I didn't say anything at all to the players. I felt it was the seniors' last game and that was more important," he said.

The 7–3–1 record is the best finish the Zips have had under the tutelage of Faust, whose overall record becomes 47–47–3.

Top: The 1994 team's Darin Ford races down the field with the Ohio defense in hot pursuit. Photo from Tel-Buch, *courtesy of Archival Services, University Libraries, The University of Akron.*

Right: The 1994 team's Deshawn Brown battles for yardage in the Central Michigan game. Photo from Tel-Buch, *courtesy of Archival Services, University Libraries, The University of Akron.*

"We're very proud of what we were able to accomplish this year, because it's great for the University," Faust said.

The Zips finished the season tied for third place in the Mid-American Conference, a far cry from the eighth and ninth place predictions prior to the season.

October 3, 1995

The Zips Concoct Winning Recipe

The Zips Give One Part Effort, and Two Parts Determination in Victory

By Jim Seeger

Head Coach Lee Owens selected a specific recipe to return the football program to respectability and championship success.

Owens is carefully using specific ingredients and techniques like a master chef, who begins with his expertise, then adding the best ingredients, building the gourmet feast one course at a time. Last Saturday evening Owens had a tantalizing bite of the appetizer.

The Zips, at home for the annual Acme-Zip game, gave the 17,246 fans a 16–13 win and real taste of the future.

The Chippewas of Central Michigan started their first offensive possession on their own 25 yard line with three plays and a punt by CMU's Alex Kemp but the Zip's special team was charged with roughing the punter. Once again a mistake would cost the Zips in this 1995 campaign. This penalty resulted in 16 yards and a first down to Central's own 46-yard line. Central Michigan then moved the ball on the Zips defense culminating with a 12-play scoring drive, moving 60 yards with a field goal of 32 yards from place kicker Brad Blasy. This game began with familiar taste.

The Zips' attitude after CMU's field goal differed from previous opponents scoring drives. They did not give up, but rather stayed in the game both mentally and physically. This was mentioned by Chippewa Quarterback Chad Darnell who credited the Zips effort. "The longer they stayed in the game the harder they played. They played 60 minutes of football and we didn't," said Darnell.

UA retaliated late in the first quarter when quarterback Mike Junko completed a 73-yard bomb to Lew Lawhorn. "On the TD to Lew, we had the route, I drew the secondary to the tight end and threw the ball to Lew and he was right there," said Junko.

The second quarter continued with the Zips leading 7–3, not only on the score board but on the field. The UA defensive dropped CMU's tailback for a loss in the backfield and secondary forced Darnell's pass to CMU's split end Bryan Schorman stopping the drive, forcing Blasy to kick a 29-yard field goal. The Zips continued to lead 7–6. The UA defensive line provided indications that the recipe for this team was brewing and beginning to boil. Along with the defense, a big ingredient for the Zips was punter Lloyd Kessler. He pinned the Chippewas deep in their own territory several times helping the Zips win the important field possession battle. "Their punter was a major factor in the game, we had bad field possession all night," said Central Michigan Head Coach Dick Flynn.

The first half scoring concluded with added flavor by Zips' placekicker Josef Jakab. He kicked his first field goal of the season resulting in a career long 47 yarder. That capped 14 play, 50 yard scoring drive. The Zips were still cooking and leading 10–6 going into the locker room at the intermission.

UA took the second half kickoff and stumbled quickly with a holding penalty which resulted three plays and out for the Chippewas. Central Michigan came back offensively with Darnell and tailback Silas Massey combining for a scoring drive. Darnell scored on a quarterback draw, rushing up the middle for 11 yards, ending an 11 play drive for 58 yards. The Zips were back to a familiar position three 13–10. They were in this ball game.

Coach Owens continued to add his ingredients, encouraging the players and emphasizing all the work and sacrifice the players committed from day one. The UA defense realized and gained confidence as the game continued, playing together and keeping Akron in the game. The offense struggled in the third quarter stopping

The 1995 team. Courtesy of The University of Akron Department of Intercollegiate Athletics.

themselves with incomplete passes, penalties and a lateral which fortunately was out of bounds.

The fourth quarter had the ingredients for an entire meal. The Zips special spice was added to the mixture, changing the flavor of the UA season, giving players, and fans a taste of winning. Kessler continued to give the Zips an added defensive weapon driving Chippewas down the field. Trailing in the game but only by the poor field position paid big dividends for UA.

The Zips defense stopped CMU's offense deep in their own end of the field with three plays and out. Chippewa's punter, Alex Kemp standing in his own endzone, kicked the ball to Lawhorn and he returned the football 53 yards for a touchdown. Lawhorn's punt return for a TD completed the cycle this season scoring on a kickoff return, offense and now the punt team. "I give the credit to coach Williams and the other coaches because they set it up," said Lawhorn. "The guys up front did a great job. I just had the wall."

The 1996 team's Willie Spencer pushes toward the end zone while his teammates clear the way in a close loss to nationally-ranked Virginia Tech. Photo by Jeff Harwell, from Tel-Buch, *courtesy of Archival Services, University Libraries, The University of Akron.*

This put the Zips back in the lead with five minutes left in the game. The game was not over because CMU's Jason Husband blocked the extra point attempt giving the Chippewas an opportunity to tie with a late field goal. The Zips lead 16–13.

The defense stepped up three more times in the last five minutes of the game. Zips left cornerback Jonathon Eaton intercepted CMU's Darnell with 2:30 left in the contest. UA's offense tried to run the clock out but stopped themselves with negative yardage and a penalty giving Central one last chance. Again the defense stepped up with efforts from all 11 individuals. Zip's Nate Boyd recovered a fumble by CMU's Adam Simonson after a 22-yard completion from Darnell.

The Zips offense ran the clock down to 25 seconds left but this gave Central Michigan a final opportunity. Darnell completed a pass to wide receiver Grant Elmquist for a 20 yard gain moving the ball up the field. Darnell attempted a pass which Zips linebacker Jason Taylor intercepted for the final ingredient of the contest and the first win for Head Coach Lee Owens at the collegiate level.

Owens was more than happy, indicating the post game fireworks were what he felt after his first win with this Zip team. "I can't wait to tell the players I told you so," said Owens. "It adds credibility to the coaches and the kids get something in return."

November 5, 1996

Akron Wins Third Straight Game

Yasin Reeder's Thrilling 84-yard Touchdown Run Capped the Zips First Victory Ever Over Bowling Green

By Jason Blevins

Saturday night the Zips overcame the loss of their best defensive player to beat Bowling Green for the first time since they entered the Mid-American Conference.

However watching Bowling Green's opening drive, it looked like this game would be a copy of previous years. They drove down the field with relative ease.

With the Falcons inside the Zips 15-yard line, Nate Boyd stepped in front of a Falcon receiver to intercept the ball in the end zone. This stop would prove crucial in the outcome of the game.

The Zips struck first as freshman Greg Gromek threw a fade to wide receiver Devon Scott for a 77-yard touchdown, the longest of the season.

However on the next series, star defensive end Jason Taylor would suffer a sprained right ankle and a first degree sprain of the Medial Collateral Ligament of his right knee. Taylor would be lost for the game.

The Zips did not crumble though as Boyd, Andre McCray, and senior John Harpring would step up and provide big play after big play throughout the game.

Bowling Green did put together their best scoring drive of the season on their next possession. They drove 80 yards on 16 plays taking seven minutes and 38 seconds off the clock. They capped off the drive with a 10 yard touchdown strike from quarterback Mark Molk to flanker Damron Hamilton. This left the score tied at seven at the half.

The big story of the first half was the kicking game. The Zip's Mike Hayes and Jamie Stidham were phenomenal. Hayes punted four times for an average of 47 yards a kick, including punts of 45 and 50 yards into a very stiff wind.

In the third quarter, things looked bad for the Zips as Molk and Hamilton connected again on a 43 yard touchdown pass to make the score 14–7 Falcons.

Late in the third quarter, the Zips began to drive. They went 80 yards in 10 plays behind the legs of Chris Rooney and the right arm of Gromek. Rooney ran four times for 19 yards, and Gromek went 2–3 for 25 yards. The big blow was from senior running back Yasin Reeder who took the ball and ran 23 yards for the tying touchdown.

Reeder would strike again. With the Zips facing third down and eight, he took the hand-off and ran 84 yards for the game-winning touchdown.

"I cut it back," said Reeder. "And I said to myself 'Why are you over here'? And then I ran past the safety."

Gromek knew that he was gone. "When Yasin cut back, I knew that they weren't going to catch them."

Bowling Green Head Coach Gary Blackney summed up the run best, "It was a hole big enough to drive a truck through, and Akron had a jack rabbit running through it."

Head Coach Lee Owens said a big key to this win was the pregame talk given by senior quarterback Mike Junko. "Junko's speech was an A, compared to my C-speech," said a comical Owens. "I should have just shut up and let Junko do the whole thing."

The Zips now stand at 4–6 on the season. Next up the Zips travel to face the Eastern Michigan Eagles in the season finale.

The Zips now look like they are turning the corner to becoming a successful program. There are many ways you can describe this resurgence but Blackney described it best when he said, "they are going this way (finger pointing upwards)."

September 16, 1997

Redhawks Scalp the Zips 49–20

Akron Drops MAC Opener in Record Breaking Day for Miami

By Chris Capozzi

The Zips traveled to Yager Stadium in Oxford, Ohio to battle the Miami Redhawks on this past Saturday and unfortunately, for the Zips, Miami returned to the form that had all the sports writers drooling over them in the pre-season.

Looking to start the mid-American Conference season where they left off last year, the Zips found themselves in a hole from the get go. Coming off an expected loss to national powerhouse Nebraska, the Zips had two weeks to re-group and prepare for the Miami attack.

Akron held the Redhawks scoreless in the first quarter, and were led by the great play of middle linebacker Nate Boyd and the rest of the highly regarded Akron defense. However, the Zips offense couldn't punch the ball into the end zone either, leaving the defensive unit on the field all too often.

The Zips defense gave up some big plays and looked a little beaten up in the second quarter.

Akron gave up 28 points in the quarter and went into the locker room down 28–0. In the first half, the Zips gave up 384 yards in total offense, while only racking up 230 yards of their own for the entire game.

The key to Miami's offense was quarterback Sam Ricketts. Ricketts completed 20 of 30 passes for 296 yards and four touchdowns. The 296 yards was a career high, and four touchdowns gave him sole possession of Miami's career passing touchdown record. As if that was not enough Ricketts also became Miami's career leader in passing yards with 4,129. Miami running back Travis Prentice had his great day overshadowed by Ricketts' record breaking day. Prentice, who with 373 yards in three games is ranked third in the MAC rushing race, had 30 carries for 157 yards and two touchdowns.

When the second half started, the Zips made some necessary adjustments and came out with more intensity, hoping to come back and beat Miami as they did last year. However, on this day they just weren't that lucky.

The Zips' offense had a bit of a spark in them, but not enough to start the fire needed to come back for the 28 points they were down. The third quarter gave the fans a little taste of the Zips they had hoped to see more of this season, when they scored 12 points and held the Redhawks to none. Willie Spencer, the former Zips quarterback turned wide receiver, caught one touchdown pass and, then threw for another.

At the beginning of the fourth quarter the Zips tried to keep up the same intensity that had brought them within 16 points, but the Redhawks destroyed any hope by opening the fourth quarter with two touchdowns to bring the score to 42–12 with seven minutes to play. One of the few Akron fourth quarter highlights occurred when Greg Lomax took one of his nine carries on the day 54 yards for the score.

UA's Jason Taylor tackles a Toledo opponent. Courtesy of The University of Akron Department of Intercollegiate Athletics.

Lomax, the Zips leading rusher, had nine carries for 78 yards and one touchdown. Miami scored again with 1:32 left in the game to bring the final score to 49–20.

The Zips were skinned by the Redhawks in their MAC season opener, giving up 583 yards of total offense and a Miami record 33 first downs for the game, leading to the 49–20 disappointing final score.

The Zips did have some key plays from some of the usual names. Willie Spencer led the Zips' offense with four catches for 45 yards and a touchdown as well as throwing a 34-yard strike to Carl Whitt. The defensive unit was led by middle linebacker Nate Boyd who had 19 tackles and Andre McCray who pitched in 11 tackles.

On Saturday, the Bowling Green Falcons invade the Rubber Bowl for the annual Acme-Zip game, and you can believe that Coach Owens will have the Zips fired up and ready to go. This match up will bring back home Kevin O'Neil who played at Walsh High School and after his third game was the MAC's leading tackler, to face our own Nate Boyd who is well on his way to being the first team All-MAC. The game between BGSU and Akron will have a lot of sparks as both teams look to rebound from last week's losses.

The battle to watch will be between the linebackers as these two are not only two of the best in the MAC but also two of the best in the Northeast part of the country.

October 28, 1999

Zips Sink Navy's Battleship

Akron Battles Back from 23–0 Deficit to Win 35–29. The Zips' Comeback was the Biggest One Ever Carried Out Against the Naval Academy.

By Jason Blevins

Are you starting to believe this team is for real yet? Well, after last Saturday's huge comeback against the Naval Academy, maybe you should.

This is one of the biggest wins in Akron history, and it is certainly the most important win for Head Coach Lee Owens.

The Zips won their sixth game of the season when they rallied from a 23–0 first half deficit to hand the Midshipmen a 35–29 loss.

The comeback was the biggest one ever recorded against Navy. It came during the team's homecoming game with alumni such as Roger Staubach looking on.

Navy came out strong to begin the game as they quickly went up 9–0 in the first three minutes. After an Akron safety, the Midshipmen scored on a 56-yard pass play from Brian Broadwater to Dave Rautenbach.

Navy came right back on their next possession and Broadwater was once again the key as this time he hooked up with Brandon Rampani on a 62-yard scoring strike to put Navy up 16–0.

After Broadwater scored on a one-yard run to make the score 23–0, the Zips finally got on the scoreboard as Lavel Bailey and James "Butchie" Washington hooked up on a 41-yard pass play.

The teams exchanged field goals (Akron's Zac Derr from 45 yards and Navy's Tim Shubzda from 42 yards) and went into halftime with Navy leading 26–10.

The third quarter opened with the two teams exchanging field goals once again. Derr hit another 45-yarder, and Shubzda answered right back with a 29-yarder of his own. However, it was Shubzda's missed 44-yard field goal in the beginning of the fourth quarter that was a big key.

If he would have made it, Navy would have been up 32–13 and the Zips would have been all but dead. Instead, the miss kept the Akron hopes alive, and they started to go to work.

The Zips looked to star running back Brandon Payne to lead the comeback bid, and he did just that. After the Zips marched down to the Navy 6-yard line, Payne took the handoff and busted into the end zone. The Zips went for the two-point conversion and Payne again came up huge as he caught the pass from Washington to make the score 29–21.

After the Zips' defense forced Navy to punt the ball after a three-and-out series, Payne again played hero.

He caught the punt at his own 34-yard line, shook off an angle tackle, spun from left to right and raced down the sidelines to make the touchdown.

However, the Zips were still down two and needed to complete the two-point conversion in order to tie up the game.

Akron turned to Washington to get the job done. He did just that as he scored on a quarterback draw to tie the game at 29.

With Uncle Mo on their side, the Akron defense once again came up big, forcing a three-and-out from Navy, setting up the Zips' game-winning drive which started at their own 23 with just over eight minutes to go.

The key play was a 42-yard scamper by junior tailback Jimmie Gray to Navy's 23-yard line. Gray finished off the Zips' march to victory just moments later when he scored from 11 yards out to put the Zips up 35–29.

Unfortunately, Akron left the door open for Navy when Derr's extra point was blocked.

With just under seven minutes remaining in the game, Navy had their final chance to score. They strung together three first downs, including a huge conversion on third-and-10 when receiver Matt O'Donnell wrestled away a jump ball from Akron corner Dwight Smith for a 22-yard gain and a first down on the Akron 34-yard line.

The Zips then tightened up. After a Navy personal foul moved the ball back to midfield, the Akron secondary stepped up and forced Navy to turn the ball over on downs.

Fullback Tony McCray then ran out the clock and cemented the win for the Zips.

The victory moves Akron to 6–2 overall and 4–1 in the Mid-American Conference. The Zips remain a half of a game behind Eastern Division-leading Marshall with three games left to play.

With the loss, Navy falls to 2–5 on the season. They next travel to face the Notre Dame Fighting Irish in South Bend, Ind.

Next up, the Zips come home to play host to Western Michigan on Saturday at 1:30 P.M.

Akron stars: The Zips had many contributors on Saturday. They included Jimmie Gray, 84 yards running on seven carries; Brandon Payne, two touchdowns; James "Butchie" Washington, 208 yards passing and one touchdown; Lavel Bailey, seven catches for 143 yards and one touchdown; and Jon Eaton, 16 tackles.

This is Akron's first four-game winning streak since 1986.

Brandon Payne was named the MAC Special Teams Player of the Week due to his 66-yard punt return against Navy that ignited the Zips to a 35–29 comeback victory.

Tuesday, November 9, 2004 • A1

theBuchtelite

Independent voice of the University of Akron since 1889

FREE

Volume 122, Issue

lews Briefs

AL PARKERS ARE

ctive Jan. 1, 2005, g fines will be sed. Most violations st $25, up from $10. additional violation st $5 more, to a max- of $35. Parking es insists it is not to se revenue, but to ese without permits king valuable park- aces.

CASES FOR KIDS

dent Social Work e and Golden Key tional Honour are collecting suit- and duffle bags in the at Union and the building, room 411, h November. They to foster children ken times have only a bag to carry their ings.

VRITING KSHOP

orkshop on APA writ- le will be held tomor- ening by SAGE. All ts are welcome. It at 7:15 p.m. in the at Union, room 316.

ING FOR A MATE?

art of the 2nd l Gospel Choir Week, will be a presentation What to find in a part two" tonight ion is free and dona- re welcomed. It at 7 p.m. and is in the Student room 312.

RE FEELING Y

notist Michael C. y will be performing in the Student Ballroom. Hypnosis at 9:00 p.m.

H TO MUSIC

nists Kathleen ns & Juan Menendez rform tomorrow on in the Student next to the Union . Their performance, t to you by ArtsView, from noon to 1 p.m.

OOR FUN EASY

Outdoor Adventure es Center is now open Recreation and ss Center. They offer hest quality in out- uipment for back- g, camping, kayaking noeing. Rental is le for all of the cam- munity. They also

Drinking and riding

UA graduate's drunk bus is a hit among college students

By Mike Rasor
The Buchtelite

An intoxicated woman crouched into a catcher's position at the front of the bus while the driver was speaking with passengers in the back.

Suddenly, a flow of urine began trickling down the bus steps.

"We don't approve of (such behavior)," the business's owner Travis Sholley said, "but we tolerate it a lot more."

Other "tolerable" actions include passengers doing their best Paul Hamm impersonation on the bars that are used to support standing customers.

"People get a little acrobatic on those," Sholley said.

Sholley is owner of Rockin' Cleveland, a limo service that features party buses for shuttling customers from bar to bar in Akron.

"People get the wrong idea from drinking on the bus, but it helps keep people from drinking and driving"

—Rockin' Cleveland owner Travis Sholley

Sholley, a Copley High School graduate, finished his degree in sales management this past summer at the University of Akron. He uses renovated buses for a traditional limousine service, but on the side, his "limos" lead a less conventional lifestyle.

As a way to market his business, Sholley decided to shuttle UA students from campus to the bars in downtown Akron for $3 on Thursday nights.

The owner said the adventures aren't profitable, but also aren't meant to be. Sholley cannot put a price on the amount of people who have been attracted to the limo service by hearing about their bar shuttle service.

"It's gotten a lot of people on the bus," Sholley said. "Word of mouth has been our best marketing

See BUS, Page A2

Zips control own destiny

UA Athletic Department

Kicker Jason Swiger follows through on a field goal that clinched a 31-28 victory for the Zips over Marshall. The game was Akron's first-ever nationally-televised home game. The win allows Akron to control its own destiny in the Mid-American Conference East Division and may set up a rematch with the MAC West leading Northern Illinois Huskies for the conference title. For more on the Zips, see B1

What's to eat around here?

Poll finds Luigi's, Swensons, Panera and Aladdin's are tops

NYC artist depicts Ira

By Bob Barrett
The Buchtelite

When assistant profe of art Matthew Kolodzie introduced artist and jou nalist Steve Mumford to packed auditorium in Fo Hall Nov. 3, he asked ho many people knew some serving in the military i Iraq or Afghanistan.

About half the audien raised their hands.

Mumford had just returned from Iraq a wee and a half before, first to New York, which he described as a crowded c with scenery not too diffe ent from Baghdad.

Arriving the day Saddam's statue toppled, Mumford made four trip Iraq for a total of 10 and one-half months, as an a and war correspondent f Artnet.com. His watercol paintings can be seen on campus through Dec. 3, i the Emily Davis Gallery inside Folk Hall.

"I didn't want received imagery. I wanted to get own impression of what i was like," Mumford said. "Being in a war zone isn' bullets flying. People stil have to live their lives."

He usually sketched o the spot, recording scene from the daily lives of bo the Iraqis and the Ameri soldiers. That wasn't pa

See IRAQ, Pa

Engineers create more efficient SU

By Lisa Kopec
Buchtelite Contributor

Sportsmen traveling t countryside are no longe the only SUV owners. No matter what walk of life, everyone seems to own these powerful, gas-sucki modes of transportation. This is good for the autom tive industry, but it pose challenge for those con- cerned with reducing ene use and emissions.

Selected students from the University of Akron's School of Engineering undertook this challenge Challenge X: Crossover t Sustainable Mobility is a competition series where sponsors asked students re-engineer a General Motors Equinox, a crosso sport utility vehicle.

UA students traveled t Chicago Nov. 4 to compet

CHAPTER 12
2000–2008

The 2004 team's Charlie Frye prepares for the snap in the game against Marshall. Courtesy of The University of Akron Department of Intercollegiate Athletics.

November 27, 2001

Zips Outlast Eastern Michigan in Triple Overtime

Derr Nails Game-Winner for 65–62 Victory

Zac Derr's 35-yard field goal in the third overtime snapped a 62-all tie and gave Akron a 65–62 victory over Eastern Michigan in the highest scoring football game in Mid-American Conference history. The two teams combined for 127 points, topping the old mark of 108 set in 1968 when Ohio beat Cincinnati, 60–48. Western Michigan's 76–27 win over Kent State in 1996 had been the highest combined score (103) in a MAC game.

It was Derr's 37-yard field goal with 0:01 to play in regulation time that sent the game into overtime with the two teams knotted at 52. Derr finished with 17 kicking points (three field goals and eight points), a career high, and became Akron's all-time leading scorer with 266 career points, surpassing kicker Bob Dombroski's (1986–89) total of 253. His eight extra points also are a UA mark.

The Zips closed the season at 4–7 overall, 4–4 in the MAC. Eastern Michigan slipped to 2–9, 1–6 in MAC play.

Protecting a 49–45 lead with just under 2:00 to play, Akron quarterback Charlie Frye was stripped of the ball in Akron territory. Eastern's James Turner returned the fumble to the Akron 12. On fourth down-and-15 at the Akron 17, Eastern Michigan quarterback Kainoa Akina, scrambling under pressure, hit Jamal Stevens for the touchdown with 0:56 left to play. Toller Starnes added the PAT and Eastern led, 52–49. Starting from their own 20, the Zips converted on 4th-and-1 when running back Bob Hendry popped a 12-yard run to the Akron 41. The Zips called a timeout with 0:16 left.

On the ensuing play, Frye, running to his right, threw back across the field and found Nick Sparks for a 39-yard gain to the Eastern 20. After consecutive timeouts by Akron and Eastern, and with 0:06 showing on the clock, Derr came on the field and calmly punched through a 35-yard field goal with one tick left.

On the first possession of overtime, with the ball placed at 25-yard line, Eastern scored on its first play when Akina tossed a dump pass to running back Chris Roberson, who weaved the distance through Akron's defense and scored a touchdown. Starnes' PAT was good. Akron answered with Hendry's seven-yard TD and Derr's all-important PAT.

The Zips took possession to start the second OT. The drive stalled out at the EMU 3 and Derr booted a 20-yard field goal. Eastern drove to the Akron 7, but Akina was sacked for a 9-yard loss on second down. His third-down pass fell incomplete. On fourth down, Starnes converted a 33-yard field goal to extend the game.

The 2000 team challenges Central Florida. Photo by Jeff Harwell, from Tel-Buch, *courtesy of Archival Services, University Libraries, The University of Akron.*

Akron's Jesse Smith intercepted Akina on the first play of the third overtime. At that point, an Akron score would end the game.

After two Hendry runs netted seven yards, Zip Coach Lee Owens sent Derr out to kick the winner. The senior captain responded with a 35-yarder for the win.

Hendry, a sophomore, tied an Akron record with five touchdowns, all rushing, and registered his fourth 100-yard game of the season with 154 yards on 39 carries. Senior wide receiver Jake Schifino caught five passes for 99 yards and finished his career with 131 receptions, second on Akron's all-time list.

Zip redshirt freshman quarterback Charlie Frye connected on 21-of-33 passes for 313 yards, a career high, and two TDs. He became just the fourth Akron passer to go over 2,000 yards through the air in a single season.

Akina tossed an Eastern record six TD passes and finished 27-of-50 for 392 yards and three INTs. EMU receiver Terrance Lloyd caught nine passes for 195 yards. Starnes hit an EMU record eight extra points as well.

Senior linebacker Ed March had 10 total tackles to lead Akron. Senior whip linebacker Eric Culberson had two interceptions, including a 41-yard return for a TD early in the third quarter, which cut into Eastern's 31–21 halftime lead.

The two teams combined for 1,035 yards of total offense, far short of the all-time MAC record set earlier this season when Marshall and Akron combined for 1,249 yards. The Herd won that game 50–33.

The 2001 team. Photo from Tel-Buch, *courtesy of Archival Services, University Libraries, The University of Akron.*

November 12, 2002

Zips' QB Frye Sets Passing Record Despite Loss at Ohio

By Mike Dyer

A week after what may have been the most significant victory in Lee Owens' tenure at Akron, the Zips fell to Ohio University 27–10 last Saturday, ending its three-game winning streak over the Bobcats.

Owens denied speculation of a letdown after defeating Marshall University at the Rubber Bowl on Nov. 2.

"We tried to guard against that all week," said Owens. "We kept trying to turn the page, but there was a lot of people that didn't want to and you lose your focus for getting ready the next week. But yet, I think if you look at how we came out to start the game, it was not as big a factor as you would think."

The Zips (2–8, 1–5 Mid-American Conference) got off to a good start.

Sophomore quarterback Charlie Frye found Morris Ellington (first career touchdown catch) for a six-yard score, and a 19-yard field goal by Billy Sullivan put Akron ahead 10–0 in the first quarter.

However, after three fumbles, an interception and a blocked field goal attempt, the Bobcats battled back with a 21-point third quarter.

Junior running back Bob Hendry rushed for 91 yards and is only 173 shy of reaching the 1,000-yard mark with two games remaining.

"It really started in the first half," said Owens. "We got into the red zone a couple of times and didn't finish. That set the tone for what happened in the second half."

The 2003 team downs the Central Michigan offense. Courtesy of The University of Akron Department of Intercollegiate Athletics.

Frye set the UA single-season passing yards record with his first completion of the day—a 30-yarder to Mike Brake. Frye (2,504 yards) broke Butchie Washington's two-year-old mark (2,319 in 2000).

"So much depends on how your quarterback plays, and Charlie has been so good all year long and all of a sudden, he started to look human out there today," said Owens.

It was also a milestone day for senior running back Brandon Payne, who set the UA single-season record for receptions by a running back with four catches against Ohio. Payne's 37 receptions passed Jack Beidleman's 33 in 1968.

As an extra note, Charlie Frye leads the Most Valuable Player voting race on UA's athletics Web site, gozips.com. Frye received more than 66 percent of the votes as of yesterday morning. Nick Fortener, Matt Cherry and Chase Blackburn each had 11.1 percent.

November 11, 2003

Zips Pound Chippewas

Frye Sets Single-Game Passing Record in 40–28 Win

By Greg Kohntopp

Charlie Frye threw for an Akron single-game record 416 yards and two touchdowns and also had a school-best 460 yards of total offense to lead Akron to a 40–28 win over Central Michigan Saturday at Kelly/Shorts Stadium. The win puts the Zips at 6–5 overall and 4–3 in Mid-American Conference play.

Central Michigan (3–7, 1–6 MAC) took a 14–0 lead in the first quarter as quarterback Derrick Vickers threw touchdown passes to receivers Scott Gibson and Tory Humphrey.

A 38-yard field goal by kicker Jason Swiger cut the lead to 14–3 in the second quarter.

The Chippewas pushed the lead to 21–3 on a one-yard touchdown run by Terrence Jackson.

The Zips answered the Chippewa's touchdown by scoring three of their own in a nine-minute span in the second quarter. Frye hit receiver Nick Sparks for a 59-yard touchdown and running back Bobby Hendry scored on touchdown runs of one and seven yards to give the Zips a 24–21 lead at the break.

The Zips extended their lead to 30–21 in the third quarter when Frye connected with Matt Cherry for a six-yard touchdown.

The Chippewas cut the score to 30–28 in the third quarter when Vickers connected with Steve Messam on a 13-yard pass, but that's as close as they would get.

Swiger kicked another field goal to make the score 33–28, and Hendry scored his third touchdown of the game with a three-yard run to cap off the scoring.

Akron finished the game with 607 total yards, the most ever for the team in a MAC game. Hendry led the ground attack by finishing the game with 132 yards on 33 carries. He also moved into sixth place on the Zips all-time scoring list.

Frye's 416 passing yards and 460 total yards earned him MAC East Player of the Week. Sparks and Cherry both went over the 100-yard mark with Sparks hauling in eight balls for 137 yards and Cherry had eight for 115 yards.

Jerry Seymour led the Chippewa attack with 105 yards on 19 carries while Jackson had 18 carries and 92 yards.

Frye set a number of offensive records on the day, becoming the ninth quarterback in MAC history to amass 3,000 yards in a season and the eighth QB in MAC history with 8,000 career yards. He has 8,149 career passing yards and 3,272 on the year. It was also his 11th career 300-yard game.

His .794 pass percentage (27-of-34) in the game was the school's single-game mark as well, passing the .789 (15-of-19) by Mike Johnson against New Mexico State on Nov. 5, 1988.

In addition, Frye's 263 passing yards in the first half set the school's record for passing yards in a half. The junior signal caller passed the mark of 254 he set against Miami (Ohio) on Oct. 31, 2001.

November 9, 2004

Zips Tame Herd in Stunning Victory

By Andrew Adam

Charlie Frye and the Zips gave the nation something to talk about Monday morning in their first ESPN broadcast since 1986.

In arguably the most important game of his college career, Frye helped orchestrate one of the greatest comebacks in Akron football history, as the Zips slipped by Marshall 31–28.

"Their hard work and investment is paying off," Akron head coach J.D. Brookhart said. "They put their heart and soul into this game."

Down 28–7 late in the third quarter, most of the 29,621 Zips fans began to leave the Rubber Bowl, believing the game and a Mid-American Conference championship were lost. The 3,000 faithful that stuck around until the end witnessed a performance worth re-telling for years to come.

With 4:30 left in the third, Frye and the Zips began an unimaginable comeback. Frye started the drive by hitting his favorite target, wide receiver Domenik Hixon, for 23 yards. On the next play, he sacrificed his body to rush for a few yards, taking a late hit for a penalty which sent him flying out of bounds. The shot did not phase the senior as he walked back to the huddle limping with a swagger.

Three plays later, on a critical 4th and 3, Frye found Hixon again. A few nice moves by the Zip wide receiver and he was in for his fourth receiving touchdown of the year.

It cut the lead to 28–14, but that was just the beginning.

Later in the fourth quarter, Marshall running back Earl Charles fumbled inside the Zips' one-yard line, with Akron recovering the loose ball. Frye found himself on the twenty yard line with only 4:40 to go in the game.

He easily drove the team down the field. Taking his team down to Marshall's six-yard line, Frye used his cerebral vision to find receiver Jason Montgomery wide open in the end zone to bring the Zips within a score at 28–21.

This left only a little more than two minutes on the game clock. It was time for Akron kicker Jason Swiger to shine. Swiger perfectly placed an onside kick into the waiting hands of diving Akron's Reggie Corner, bringing the Zip offense back to the field.

Then it was back to the Frye show. The Zips had to go to the no-huddle offense, which Frye had no problem handling.

"I feel comfortable in that situation (two-minute drill)," he said. "I don't know if that is normal or not … it should be urgent, but it is more like a calm feeling for me."

Frye showed his cool as he connected on a quick pass to begin the drive. Then the true drama commenced. Unable to earn a first down, the Zips were faced with a 4th and 3. Frye had one last chance to continue the drive or the game would be over.

Sure enough, he connected with Hixon, who finished the game with 13 catches for 192 yards, only nine yards short of the Zips' all-time single-game record.

The reception gave the Zips a first down inside the 20-yard line.

Marshall's defense then stepped it up again, forcing Frye to throw three straight incompletions and set up 4th and 10 with less than a minute to go.

Once again, it was do or die.

Frye called hike, dropped back and went to his left, but no one was open. Marshall linemen bore down on him, but Frye evaded their grasp as he rolled back right looking for an open receiver. With a defender closing in from behind, Frye threw a rainbow pass to the back of the end zone to the waiting arms of Montgomery, who not only brought down the catch but managed to keep one foot in-bounds before being pushed out.

Touchdown.

The game was dead-locked at 28–28, as the remaining fans made more noise than the entire crowd did previously during the game.

With only 45 seconds to go, the Zips would have been content to go into overtime after trailing by 21 points not long ago.

Marshall tried to avoid that, attempting to drive against a rejuvenated Zips defense. Akron would have none of it and forced the Thundering Herd to punt with only 12 seconds to go. Their punter, Ian O'Conner, fumbled the snap, and the Zips recovered on the 26-yard line with only six seconds left.

This set the stage for Swiger to finish what Frye, Hixon, and Montgomery had started.

Calm and collected, he split the uprights as the final seconds ticked away.

"The kicks I try in practice seem harder," Swiger said. "The guys all stand around me and shout in my ears. It's so loud I can't hear anything. That's a lot of pressure. The onside kick was the miracle."

Game over.

One of the greatest comebacks in Akron football history complete. Fans charged the field to celebrate with their team. A dejected Marshall team slowly staggered off the field in shock and disappointment.

"I have been on the flipside of a couple of games like this," Frye said. "A couple years ago, we got beat by Miami on a Hail Mary. Once Swiger went out there, I knew he was going to make it. This is the greatest I have ever felt after a win."

Even coach Brookhart could not believe it.

"You guys are going to have to tell me what happened, because I have no idea," Brookhart said upon entering the press conference.

It was a must-win game, and the Zips won.

The win gave the Zips (5–4, 5–1 MAC) the important tie-breaker against Marshall (5–4, 5–1 MAC), in case both teams finish the season with the same conference record.

After Friday night's performance, Frye will still not win the Heisman. But after Friday night's performance, he and his team can still win the prize they all desire most—a MAC championship.

The Zips control their own destiny for the rest of the season. This Saturday, they will take on Ohio (4–6, 2–5 MAC) in Athens, Ohio. The Bobcats have struggled this season, and should be a much easier opponent than Marshall.

The game will kickoff Saturday at 3 P.M.

December 6, 2005

Football Team Rocks in Detroit

By Adam Ferrise

Detroit: Historic.

That's the best way to describe Akron's 31–30 win over Northern Illinois to clinch the Mid American Conference championship Thursday in Detroit. Not only was it the school's first ever MAC title, but the win will send the Zips to their first division I–A bowl game since they joined the top collegiate division in 1986.

The game was decided on a 36 yard touchdown pass from junior Luke Getsy to senior Domenik Hixon that tied the game at 30. Jason Swiger's extra point gave Akron a 1-point lead with only 10 seconds left.

"I couldn't be more proud of this team," an emotional Brookhart said after the game. "What they've gone through and what they've committed to—its been a heck of a ride."

The Zips jumped out to a commanding 10–0 first quarter lead. Jason Swiger nailed the longest field goal in MAC championship game history with a 46 yard field goal on the Zips first possession. The Huskies tried to answer with a 49-yard field goal attempt of their own but senior defensive tackle Kiki Gonzalez blocked it. That set up Akron's first touchdown—a 3 yard run by freshman Dennis Kennedy.

The Zips saw their momentum vanish in the second quarter when Garrett Wolfe got his feet moving. The nation's career leader in rushing yards per game was held to a season low, 52 rushing yards, in NIU's 48–42 loss to Akron on Sept. 24th. He made up for that Thursday by running for 270 yards.

Wolfe put Northern Illinois on the board with a 1-yard touchdown run with 11:24 remaining in the half. On the next offensive possession by the Huskies, Wolfe chewed up 42 yards and set up a field goal to tie the score at 10.

The third quarter was no different than the second for the Zips. The Zips couldn't find a rhythm on offense and couldn't stop Wolfe on defense. The junior back accounted for all but two yards on an 81 yard drive that featured a 62-yard dash and an 11-yard touchdown run from Wolfe. After the Huskies recovered a Jason Montgomery fumble, Northern Illinois pulled ahead 24–10 with a 19 yard touchdown pass from freshman quarterback Dan Nicholson to First-Team All MAC selection Sam Hurd.

Akron running back Brett Biggs returned the score with a 3-yard touchdown run.

The 2005 team hoists the Mid-American Conference championship trophy. Courtesy of The University of Akron Department of Intercollegiate Athletics.

Northern Illinois responded with a 52-yard field goal by kicker Chris Nendick. The field goal replaced Swiger's 2-hour old record for longest in a MAC championship game. It gave the Huskies a 10-point lead with 10:49 remaining in the game.

With their backs against the wall, Getsy made the essential plays. On the next drive, Getsy completed four passes for 62 yards. He narrowed NIU's lead to three after scampering for a 7-yard touchdown off a quarterback draw on third and goal.

On the next drive, the Huskies widened their lead to six with another Nendick field goal.

The Zips seemingly had one drive to take the lead. Getsy drove the Zips inside the Huskies 35-yard line. A high pass slipped through Montgomery's hands and NIU linebacker Phil Brown intercepted it with 2:10 remaining in the game.

Using timeouts and defensive stops, the Zips regained the ball with 1:41 left. So the Zips had 81 yards to drive, and needed to do it through the air because the clock

The 2008 team with the Wagon Wheel after their victory over Kent State. Courtesy of The University of Akron Department of Intercollegiate Athletics.

was running low. And they had to do it without Hixon, who was suffering from severe stomach cramps.

On the sidelines, an ailing Hixon pleaded with coaches to return. And he did. With 18 seconds left, Hixon returned on the field, possibly as a decoy. Hixon ran a route to the center of the end zone and was wide open. He made a sliding catch that caused an eruption in the Zips student section.

"We just kept saying to each other 'We got to keep believing,'" said Getsy, who threw for a career high 413 yards on 30 of 50 passing. "We could have went down and lost the game, but we kept believing."

For Brookhart, it was an accumulation of everything he and his staff had been preaching the entire year.

"We have been talking all year long about going three more feet in everything we do," he said. "All these guys did was just keep plugging away and keep fighting and it paid off. We did our job."

Wolfe totaled 270 yards on the ground and broke the NCAA record for rushing yards in a conference championship game. He had nothing but high praise for the Zips."

"The University of Akron did an unbelievable job playing football today," Wolfe said. "They played hard throughout the entire game and I never felt any fatigue in their defense. It's obvious that those guys work very hard."

Domenik Hixon moved into third on the all-time UA reception list, broke his own UA record for receptions in a single season and shattered the 26-year old record for the most all-purpose yards in a single season.

After the victory, the Zips were extended a bid to Akron to the Motor City Bowl on Dec. 26. Like the MAC Championship, the game will be played at Ford Field in Detroit. It will be the Zips' first appearance in a Division 1–A bowl game.

October 7, 2008

Zips Prove Dominant Over Flashes

The Zips Come Out Victorious Against the Flashes after Two Overtimes

By Vincent Dorsey

KENT—It wasn't pretty. It took two overtimes. But, the Wagon Wheel again rests in the lobby of the football office in Stile Field House, after the University of Akron defeated Kent State 30–27 Saturday at Dix Stadium.

The Zips' chances of retaining the coveted rivalry trophy seemed dim for most of the game, as UA spent the second half battling back from a 21–10 halftime deficit.

Down 21–17 with less than five minutes in the game, the Zips (3–3, 1–1 MAC) were forced to punt the ball back to the Golden Flashes (1–5, 0–2 MAC).

The punt, however, would turn the game into one of the most memorable of the 51 meetings between the two neighborhood schools.

KSU's Phil Garner muffed the John Stec punt, and UA's Tyler Campbell recovered the ball at KSU's 42-yard line.

"I think it was a huge play in the game, without question," UA head coach J.D. Brookhart said. "It gave us a short field, and in our minds, a little momentum because that was about after our fourth (consecutive) three-and-out."

The Zips drove to the Golden Flashes' 24-yard line before facing fourth-and-11 with about a minute-and-a-half to go in the game. Junior quarterback Chris Jacquemain threw a pass to Deryn Bowser in the end zone. The pass was ruled incomplete.

As the Golden Flashes lined up for the start of their next offensive possession, Brookhart called a timeout, hoping the replay official would ask for the game-changing play to be reviewed during the break in play.

He did, and the play was ruled a completed pass. The Zips were suddenly ahead, 24–21.

UA's defense looked to the shift in momentum to seal the victory on KSU's ensuing possession, after forcing the Golden Flashes into fourth-and-nine from their own 38-yard line.

KSU senior quarterback Julian Edelman had other ideas.

Edelman, who Brookhart referred to as Houdini earlier in the week, evaded several Zips' defenders while scrambling out of the pocket and rushed for 34 yards to UA's 28-yard line. After moving the ball to the 15-yard line, Nate Reed kicked a 32-yard field goal to tie the game at 24 at the end of regulation.

The teams traded field goals in the first overtime period. Reed first converted a 34-yard field goal that was tipped by the Zips' defensive front. UA's Igor Iveljic countered by converting a 32-yard attempt.

The Zips moved the ball to the Golden Flashes' 8-yard line, before having to settle for a 25-yard Iveljic field goal to begin the second overtime.

KSU appeared to be on the verge of sending the game into a third overtime after Jacquise Terry rushed for 16 yards on a third-and-19 to position Reed for a 23-yard field goal.

Reed's attempt, however, sailed wide right, giving the Zips the win in the storied series' first overtime contest.

UA was outgained 413–301 and managed 10 less first downs (15) than KSU in the win.

Both head coaches alluded to the statistical discrepancies after the game.

"I feel very fortunate to have won that football game," Brookhart said. "We put ourselves in a hole and we had to fight our way out. I give our kids credit for fighting their way out. I didn't think we played great and we were able to win the game."

Fifth-year KSU head coach Doug Martin said costly mistakes in pivotal situations hurt his team.

"We just made some mistakes down the line that cost us the game with the fumble on the punt return and the couple of missed field goals," Martin said. "Obviously, statistically, we dominated this football game in every phase."

Jacquemain threw for 243 yards and two touchdowns, but was intercepted three times by sophomore Brian Lainhart.

Edelman threw for 157 yards and two touchdowns and gained 113 yards rushing.

Bowser described what the win means for the entire team after participating in the rivalry for the first time.

"That felt great," the junior wide receiver said. "We preached on that all week. We did not want those players to come across the field and take the Wagon Wheel from us, and have to take that short, but long, bus ride back to campus."

EXTRA POINT

Akron's First I-A Bowl: The 2005 Motor City Bowl

After winning its first Mid-American Conference Championship, a dramatic 31-30 win over Northern Illinois on Dec. 1, 2005, The University of Akron earned a berth to its first bowl as an NCAA Division I-A member.

The Zips, who won that MAC title game at Detroit's Ford Field, returned to the venue 25 days later (Dec. 26) for the Motor City Bowl to face the Memphis Tigers, a team that featured one of the nation's top running backs—DeAngelo Williams.

Akron with record-setting quarterback Luke Getsy and record-setting receiver Domenik Hixon, got on the board early, but trailed 20-3 late in the third quarter. The Zips would score 28 points over the final 15 minutes, including two TDs in the last 1:46, but it was not enough in the 38-31 setback.

Getsy set a Motor City Bowl record with 455 passing yards and Jabari Arthur set a bowl record with eight catches for 180 yards.

Courtesy of The University of Akron Department of Intercollegiate Athletics

The 2005 team battles against the Memphis Tigers in the Motor City Bowl. Photo from Tel-Buch, *courtesy of Archival Services, University Libraries, The University of Akron.*

TIME-OUT

The Playing Fields

Buchtel Field

Located on block south of campus as the corner of Wheeler and Kling streets, The University of Akron's Buchtel Field is certainly at the "grass roots" of the Zip athletic program. The land itself was purchased in 1891 for approximately $8,700.

The official opening of the athletic facility occurred Oct. 15, 1892, as the Buchtel College football team hosted Case. Unfortunately, Case spoiled Buchtel's first home contest, 14-9.

Grandstands have gone up and down in the 118-year history of Buchtel Field. Approximately $3,700 was spent preparing the grounds and erecting grandstands for 300 spectators. The grounds included a running track, tennis courts, and fencing to enclose the entire area.

In 1904, a fire destroyed the grandstands and part of the fence at Buchtel Field. Grandstand facilities became a reality in 1923, when seating for 5,500 spectators was erected. Room for an additional 1,500 bleacher seats was also made available. In 1940, the UA football team moved to Akron Municipal Stadium, better known as the Rubber Bowl. After a brief return to Buchtel Field in 1942 due to wartime conditions, the demise of Buchtel Field as a playing facility for the football team became official in 1948.

Since 1980, Buchtel Field has been home to the Zip softball team and was the site of the 1986 NCAA Division II Softball Championship—the first and only NCAA title ever contested at Akron.

The Rubber Bowl

Opened in 1940, The University of Akron's Rubber Bowl ties for largest football stadium in the Mid-American Conference, and is the second largest collegiate stadium in the state of Ohio. With current capacity at 31,000, the Bowl is runner-up to Ohio State's Ohio Stadium which packs in 101,568.

As far as MAC stadiums go, the Rubber Bowl is tied with UB Stadium (Buffalo) as the largest in terms of seating capacity.

The Zips' horseshoe-shaped home has been a gathering spot for Northeast Ohio football fans and event goers for 65 years. In 1999, UA football fan No. 3,000,000 passed through the Rubber Bowl turnstiles, marking six decades of Zips gridiron action at The Bowl.

The site of 325 UA football contests, 19 preseason Cleveland Browns' games, a regular-season NFL game in 1952, over 1,500 high school games (including dozens of OHSAA

Top: Buchtel College Athletic Field. Photo from Tel-Buch, *courtesy of Archival Services, University Libraries, The University of Akron.*

Left: Inside the Rubber Bowl. Courtesy of Archival Services, University Libraries, The University of Akron.

Bottom: The Rubber Bowl. Courtesy of Archival Services, University Libraries, The University of Akron.

playoff games), as well as many soccer matches and scores of concerts and shows, the Rubber Bowl has stood the test of time.

In 1940, the UA football team abandoned well-worn Buchtel Field to play at the municipally owned Rubber Bowl.

The Bowl began to develop under the plans of B.E. (Shorty) Fulton in 1933. With the help of the Civil Works Authority, Fulton had 180,000 cubic yards of dirt carved out of the side of the hill neighboring Akron Municipal Airport. Fulton, the airport manager, turned the site into a recreation area.

Then in 1939, civic-minded citizens, headed by C.W. Seiberling and James Schlemmer, sports editor of the *Akron Beacon Journal*, raised $30,000 to help construct the stadium on the site. The amount was raised by subscribing $1 from 30,000 Akronites. A federal grant of $516,000 was obtained and construction began. The stadium was dedicated before 37,000 people on August 10, 1940.

Akron opened its playing history in the Rubber Bowl on Oct. 5, 1940, against Western Reserve, before 17,472 spectators. Although the Zips lost 6-0, the Rubber Bowl has since been an excellent home field, as evidenced by UA's overall mark of 191-124-10 (60 percent).

In June 1971, the University accepted the title to the Rubber Bowl, paying $1 for the facility, from the City of Akron and began a program of refurbishing the stadium. University trustees authorized $175,000 for improvements. First priority went to a lighting system, which increased illumination of the field by more than five times.

The most striking improvement took place in the summer of 1973. Spearheaded by a gift of $200,000 from Elza E. Hopkins and Clarkins Stores, and a community-wide fund-raising drive directed by the Touchdown Club that provided more than $160,000, the University was able to install an all-weather artificial surface. Installation of AstroTurf got UA and area high school football teams "out of the mud."

That same year, the Cleveland Browns played their 19th (and last) preseason football game at The Bowl. The New York Giants defeated the Browns, 21-10, in front of 30,751 spectators. The Cleveland franchise had a 14-5 mark at The Bowl and attracted more than one-half million fans.

In 1983, after 10 years, a new carpet was installed at a cost of more than $500,000. The funds to pay for the repairs and installation came from a UA bond issue.

In 1991, more than $100,000 was contributed by the Coca Cola Bottling Company of Ohio, Summa Health Systems, National City Bank of Ohio and the Varsity (A) Association to purchase a new scoreboard.

Prior to the start of the '94 season, the University Board of Trustees authorized funds of about $750,000 to fix the facilities' drainage system and apply new artificial turf to the floor of the Zips' football home. The stadium also got a complete paint job and the seats were refurbished.

A new AstroPlay surface was installed prior to the 2003 season, giving the Zips a state-of-the-art field.

The 325th and final game in the Rubber Bowl was played on November 13, 2008, against the Buffalo Bulls, before 18,516 spectators. After four overtimes, Akron lost the game 40-43.

InfoCision Stadium-Summa Field. Rendering by HNTB Architecture, Inc., courtesy of The University of Akron Department of Intercollegiate Athletics.

InfoCision Stadium-Summa Field

Construction on the state-of-the-art Multi-Complex Facility began in February 2008 and has remained on schedule. The first game at InfoCision Stadium-Summa Field is September 12, 2009 versus Morgan State University.

The cost for just the Football Stadium Complex, including the Endzone Facility, was $61.6 million.

InfoCision Stadium's capacity is 30,000 (this includes all seats in stadium, as well as projected standing room only in the endzone berm and concourse areas).

Currently, there are approximately 10,000 on-campus parking spaces within walking distance of the stadium.

Summa Field's playing surface is synthetic (similar to Rubber Bowl, Stile Field House and Schrank Field).

Some of the amenities include: 522 club seats (individual, partially-covered chairback seats); 152 loge seats (open-air, but covered—38 boxes with four seats per box); a total of 17 suites (16 private suites with 16 seats per suite and one 52-seat "Presidential Suite" for the University); a state-of-the-art video board with scoreboard and dynamic sound system; 7 press tower levels: (including levels 2-4 with up to 80,000 square feet of academic space to be used six days a week by the University and athletics).

An on-campus facility will enhance the collegiate experience as well as aid in the recruitment and retention of students. By making it easier to attend football games, Akron will experience a new level of excitement, spirit and pride for the University and football program. In turn, there will additionally be a higher likelihood of alumni involvement.
Courtesy of The University of Akron Department of Intercollegiate Athletics

APPENDIX

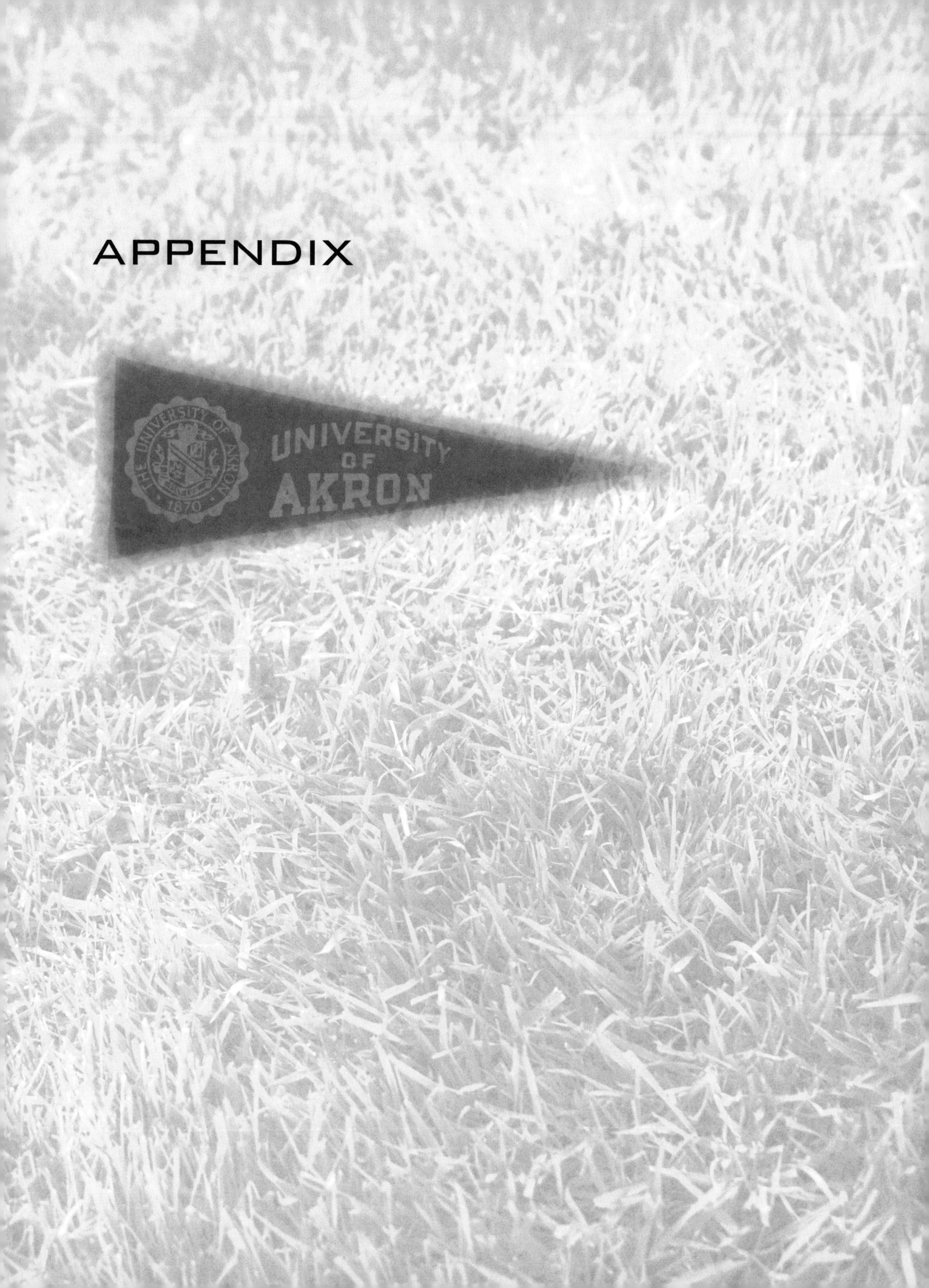

Season Records

1891: 1-3
1892: 3-4
1893: 5-2
1894: 1-0
1895: 3-2
1896: 0-1
1897-98: did not compete
1899: 2-1
1900: 2-3-1
1901: did not compete
1902: 2-5
1903: 0-2
1904-7: did not compete
1908: 3-4
1909: 4-4
1910: 7-2
1911: 3-4-1
1912: 5-2-1
1913: 3-4
1914: 4-4-1
1915: 1-7-1
1916: 2-7
1917: 5-3
1918: 2-2-1
1919: 6-1-1
1920: 4-4
1921: 5-3
1922: 5-3
1923: 4-3-1
1924: 5-3
1925: 1-7
1926: 5-2-2
1927: 5-3
1928: 5-3
1929: 9-1
1930: 7-1
1931: 1-7
1932: 2-4-3
1933: 5-3-1
1934: 3-4-1
1935: 6-3
1936: 6-2-1
1937: 7-2
1938: 6-3
1939: 5-4
1940: 2-5-2
1941: 5-3-1
1942: 0-7-2
1943-45: did not compete
1946: 5-4
1947: 2-6
1948: 2-6
1949: 2-6-1
1950: 2-7
1951: 1-8
1952: 2-6-1
1953: 6-3
1954: 3-5
1955: 6-2
1956: 3-5-1
1957: 7-1-1
1958: 6-2-1
1959: 4-5
1960: 1-8
1961: 6-2
1962: 7-2
1963: 6-3
1964: 6-3
1965: 5-3-1
1966: 6-3
1967: 4-4-1
1968: 7-3-1
1969: 9-1
1970: 7-3
1971: 8-2
1972: 3-4-2
1973: 6-5
1974: 5-5
1975: 7-4
1976: 10-3
1977: 6-4-1
1978: 6-5
1979: 6-5
1980: 3-7-1
1981: 5-5
1982: 6-5
1983: 8-3
1984: 4-7
1985: 8-4
1986: 7-4
1987: 4-7
1988: 5-6
1989: 6-4-1
1990: 3-7-1
1991: 5-6
1992: 7-3-1
1993: 5-6
1994: 1-10
1995: 2-9
1996: 4-7
1997: 2-9
1998: 4-7
1999: 7-4
2000: 6-5
2001: 4-7
2002: 4-8
2003: 7-5
2004: 6-5
2005: 7-6
2006: 5-7
2007: 4-8
2008: 5-7

All-Time Head Coach Records

Year(s)	Coach (Alma Mater)	Yrs	G	W	L	T	Pct.
1891	No coach	1	4	1	3	0	.250
1892	Frank Cook	1	7	3	4	0	.429
1893–94	John W. Heisman (Pennsylvania)	2	8	6	2	0	.750
1895	No coach	1	5	3	2	0	.600
1896	Harry Wilson	1	1	0	1	0	.000
1897–98	Did not compete						
1899	Archie Eves (Buchtel)	1	3	2	1	0	.667
1900	No coach	1	6	2	3	1	.417
1901	Did not compete						
1902	Forest Firestone (Michigan)	1	7	2	5	0	.286
1903	Rev. Alfred W. Place (Chicago)	1	2	0	2	0	.000
1904–07	Did not compete						
1908	Dr. Dwight Bradley (Pennsylvania)	1	7	3	4	0	.429
1909	Clarence Weed (Olivet)	1	8	4	4	0	.500
1910–14	Frank Haggerty (Colby)	5	41	22	16	3	.573
1915–23	Fred S. Sefton (Colgate)	9	71	34	33	4	.507
1924–25	James W. Coleman (Arkansas)	2	16	6	10	0	.375
1926	George Babcock	1	9	5	2	2	.667
1927–35	Howard 'Red' Blair (Ohio State)	9	77	42	30	5	.578
1936–38	James W. Aiken (Wash. & Jeff.)	3	27	19	7	1	.727
1939–40	Thomas W. Dowler (Colgate)	2	18	7	9	2	.444
1941–42	Otis W. Douglas (Wm. & Mary)	2	18	5	10	3	.361
1943–45	Did not compete						
1946–47	Paul Baldacci (William & Mary)	2	17	7	10	0	.412
1948–51	William 'Bud' Houghton (Ohio Wesleyan)	4	35	7	27	1	.214
1952–53	Kenneth 'Red' Cochrane (Akron)	2	18	8	9	1	.472
1954–60	Joseph H. McMullen (Brown)	7	61	30	28	3	.516
1961–72	Gordon K. Larson (Kent)	12	112	74	33	5	.683
1973–85	Jim Dennison (Wooster)	13	144	80	62	2	.562
1986–94	Gerry Faust (Dayton)	9	99	43	53	3	.449
1995–03	Lee Owens (Bluffton)	9	101	40	61	0	.396
2004–PR.	J.D. Brookhart (Colorado State)	5	60	27	33	0	.450
Totals		**108**	**982**	**482**	**464**	**36**	**.509**